CREATIVE
crochet

A LEISURE ARTS PUBLICATION
PRESENTED BY OXMOOR HOUSE

EDITORIAL STAFF

Vice President and Editor-in-Chief:
    Anne Van Wagner Childs
Executive Director: Sandra Graham Case
Executive Editor: Susan Frantz Wiles
Publications Director: Carla Bentley
Creative Art Director: Gloria Bearden
Production Art Director: Melinda Stout

PRODUCTION
Managing Editor: Susan White Sullivan
Senior Technical Editor: Cathy Hardy
Instructional Editors: Sarah J. Green and Teri Sargent

EDITORIAL
Associate Editor: Linda L. Trimble
Senior Editorial Writer: Tammi Williamson Bradley
Editorial Associates: Terri Leming Davidson,
    Robyn Sheffield-Edwards, and Darla Burdette Kelsay
Copy Editor: Laura Lee Weland

ART
Book/Magazine Art Director: Diane M. Hugo
Senior Production Artist: M. Katherine Yancey
Photography Stylists: Sondra Daniel, Karen Hall,
    Aurora Huston, Laura McCabe, Christina Tiano Myers,
    and Zaneta Senger

BUSINESS STAFF

Publisher: Bruce Akin
Vice President, Finance: Tom Siebenmorgen
Vice President, Retail Sales: Thomas L. Carlisle
Retail Sales Director: Richard Tignor
Vice President, Retail Marketing: Pam Stebbins
Retail Customer Services Director: Margaret Sweetin
Marketing Manager: Russ Barnett
Distribution Director: Ed M. Strackbein
Executive Director of Marketing and Circulation:
    Guy A. Crossley
Circulation Manager: Byron L. Taylor
Print Production Manager: Laura Lockhart
Print Production Coordinator: Nancy Reddick Baker

CROCHET COLLECTION SERIES

Library of Congress Catalog Number: 95-81458
Hardcover ISBN 0-942237-62-5
Softcover ISBN 0-942237-63-3

CREATIVE crochet

It's never been more fun or easy to express yourself in crochet, whether you're just starting your first project or adding to your handcrafted collection. You'll find that our clever new designs, updated classics, and fresh approaches to this relaxing hobby will help you get the most out of your leisure time. In Creative Crochet, we've brought together projects to please everyone, from tasteful decorator pieces to jazzy wardrobe accessories!

Designed with you in mind, our rich selection of snuggly afghans will have you covered in irresistible patterns, fabulous colors, and inviting comfort! When company comes a-calling, our home accents will extend an unspoken welcome from the moment guests cross the threshold. We've included an assortment of day-brightening gifts that will take the guesswork out of finding the perfect present — they're all great choices! And you won't need a special occasion to stitch our "bee-utiful" wall decoration or comical clown. You'll want to make them just for fun. Check out our fashion corner and you'll discover wearables for Mom and the kids, and there's a sweet collection to shower a baby with love. We also have a charming selection of designs that will keep you hooked on holidays from Valentine's Day through Christmas.

With the help of our clear-and-easy instructions, practical diagrams, and valuable stitching tips, you can relax and enjoy hour after hour creating these great projects. We even marked the "quick" projects to help you get the most out of your stitching time and to guide beginners toward their first successes. With this fabulous crochet collection and your boundless imagination, you'll have a wonderful time letting your creativity shine!

Anne Childs

LEISURE ARTS, INC.
LITTLE ROCK, ARKANSAS

table of contents

wrapped up in afghans.....6

HEARTS AND FLOWERS...6
GOLDEN TREASURE...10
REVERSIBLE WRAP...12
GARDEN PLOT QUILT...14
CROSSED TREBLES...16
GRANNY CIRCLES...18
HANDSOME RIPPLES...20
BILLOWY BROOMSTICK LACE...22
DELIGHTFUL MILE-A-MINUTE...24

all through the house 26

IN THE LIVING ROOM...26
    Entry Rug...28
    Mantel Skirt...29
FOR THE DINING ROOM...30
    Starflower Tablecloth...30
FOR THE BEDROOM...34
    Victorian Lace Afghan...36
    Sheet and Pillowcase Edging...37
IN THE KITCHEN...38
    Square in a Square Pot Holder...40
    Pinwheel Block Pot Holder...40
    Towel Topper...41
    Dishcloths...42

gifts for all....................44

BASKET FRILLS...44
COZY LAP ROBE...46
RUFFLED PEACOCK SHAWL...48
PRETTY BOOKMARKS...50
ROMANTIC DOILY...52
FRIENDSHIP CUP...54
ROSY COASTER...55
SOFT AND ROOMY TOTE...56

just for fun 58

COLORFUL CLOWN...58
STADIUM CUSHION...61
VICTORIAN CHARMERS...62
BANDANNA AFGHAN...65
BLOOMER MAGNETS...68
SUMMER-FRESH BROOM...70
RAINBOW RIVERS RUG...72

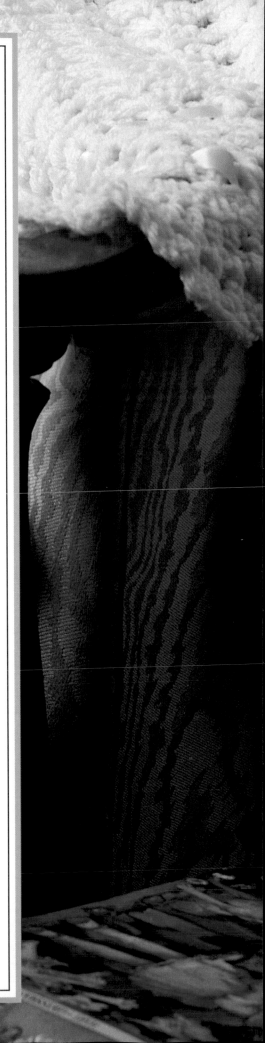

rock-a-bye collection 74

GRANNY SQUARE LAYETTE 74
   Afghan / Bonnet 76
   Sacque 86
   Booties 87
THUMBLESS MITTENS 77
CUDDLY WRAPS 78
   Solid Afghan / Striped Afghan 78
RECEIVING BLANKET EDGING 80
CRIB CATERPILLAR 81
GUMDROP BOTTLE COVER 82
ROCK-A-BYE RIPPLES 84

fashion corner 88

YO-YO CARDIGAN 88
HAIR DRESSINGS 90
   Hair Bow 90
   Ponytail Band 92
KIDS' PERKY PULLOVERS 92
   Striped Pullover/Ladybug Pullover 92
JAUNTY BERET AND SCARF 96
"COOL" VEST SET 98
   Vest 98
   Handbag 101
   Belt 102
PUPPET MITTENS 102
   Dog 102
   Girl 104

hooked on holidays 106

VALENTINE'S DAY 106
   Sweetheart Bears 106
ST. PATRICK'S DAY 109
   Shamrock Table Runner and Coaster 109
EASTER 112
   Daffodil Doily 114
   Rag Basket 115
HALLOWEEN 116
   Pumpkin Jar / Bewitching Kitties Cover-up 118
CHRISTMAS 120
   Soft Santa 120
   Tiny Snowflakes 123
   Holiday Lights 125

GENERAL INSTRUCTIONS 130
CREDITS 144

wrapped up in afghans

When you're wrapped in the warmth and security of a snuggly afghan, the cares of the day seem to melt away. Even the time spent creating one of these cozy cover-ups is a pleasurable interlude for crochet lovers. In this clever and varied collection of hand-stitched afghans, we offer an abundance of projects to tickle your creative fancy, like a pretty garden-patch quilt and a classic mile-a-minute. From familiar favorites to fresh new looks, these choice afghans have you covered!

HEARTS AND FLOWERS

This pretty cover-up will be a treasured addition to a quiet corner. The inviting throw features hearts and flowers blooming on vines of green cross stitches. The hearts are crocheted as you go, and the flowers and vines are embroidered before the panels are joined.

Finished Size: Approximately 43" x 71"

MATERIALS
  Worsted Weight Yarn, approximately:
    MC (Off-White) - 58 ounces, (1,650 grams, 3,810 yards)
    Color A (Blue) - 2½ ounces, (70 grams, 165 yards)
    Color B (Green) - 2½ ounces, (70 grams, 165 yards)
    Color C (Rose) - 2 ounces, (60 grams, 130 yards)
  Crochet hooks, sizes I (5.50 mm) **and** J (6.00 mm) **or** sizes needed for gauge
  Yarn needle

GAUGE: With larger size hook, 13 sc and 14 rows = 4"
          With smaller size hook, 14 dc = 4"

PANEL (Make 3)
With larger size hook and MC, ch 32 **loosely**.
Row 1 (Right side)**:** Sc in second ch from hook and in each ch across: 31 sc.

Note: Loop a short piece of yarn around any stitch to mark last row as **right** side and bottom.
Rows 2-8: Ch 1, turn; sc in each sc across.
Note: When changing colors *(Fig. 22a, page 138)*, keep unused color on **wrong** side of work; do **not** cut yarn until color is no longer needed. Use a separate skein or ball for each color change.
Row 9: Ch 1, turn; sc in first 15 sc changing to Color A in last sc worked, sc in next sc changing to MC, sc in each sc across.
Rows 10-22: Follow Chart A, page 8.
Row 23: Ch 1, turn; sc in first 10 sc changing to Color A, cut MC; sc in next 3 sc changing to MC, cut Color A; sc in next 5 sc changing to Color A, cut MC; sc in next 3 sc changing to MC, cut Color A; sc in each sc across.
Rows 24-78: Ch 1, turn; sc in each sc across.
Rows 79-233: Repeat Rows 9-78 twice, then repeat Rows 9-23 once **more**.
Rows 234-241: Ch 1, turn; sc in each sc across.
Finish off.

PANEL EDGINGS

CENTER LEFT SIDE

Row 1: Hold any Panel with **right** side facing and bottom toward your **left**; using smaller size hook and working in end of rows, join MC with slip st in first row; ch 4 **(counts as first dc plus ch 1, now and throughout)**, skip next row, dc in next row, ★ ch 1, skip next row, dc in next row; repeat from ★ across: 121 dc.

Row 2: Ch 3 **(counts as first dc, now and throughout)**, turn; dc in next ch-1 sp and in each dc and each ch-1 sp across: 241 dc.

Row 3: Ch 3, turn; dc in next dc and in each dc across.

Row 4: Ch 1, turn; sc in each dc across: 241 sc.

Row 5: Ch 3, turn; dc in next sc and in each sc across: 241 dc.

Row 6: Ch 3, turn; dc in next dc and in each dc across.

Row 7: Ch 4, turn; skip next dc, dc in next dc, ★ ch 1, skip next dc, dc in next dc; repeat from ★ across; finish off: 121 dc.

CENTER RIGHT SIDE

Row 1: Hold center Panel with **right** side facing and bottom edge toward your **right**; using smaller size hook and working in end of rows, join MC with slip st in first row; ch 4, skip next row, dc in next row, ★ ch 1, skip next row, dc in next row; repeat from ★ across: 121 dc.

Rows 2-7: Work same as Center Left Side.

LEFT PANEL

On next Panel, work same as Center Left Side, Rows 1-6; finish off.

RIGHT PANEL

On remaining Panel, work same as Center Right Side, Rows 1-6; finish off.

FINISHING

With Color B, add cross stitch design to each Panel between hearts following Chart B, and each Panel Edging across center sc row following Chart C *(Fig. 33, page 142)*.

With Color B, add Satin St leaves to each Panel Edging following Chart C *(Fig. 29b, page 141)*.

With Color C, add Satin St flowers to each Panel following Chart B and add Satin St buds to each Panel Edging following Chart C.

With Color C, add French Knot flower centers to each Panel *(Fig. 32, page 142)*.

With **wrong** sides together and MC, and working through **both** loops, whipstitch Panels together *(Fig. 25a, page 140)*.

BORDER

Rnd 1: With **right** side facing and using smaller size hook, join MC with slip st in end of first row of top right corner; ch 3, dc in same row, ch 1, (dc in end of next row, ch 1) 5 times, † [dc in first st, (ch 1, skip next st, dc in next st) 15 times, ch 1, (dc in end of next row, ch 1) 7 times] twice, dc in first st, (ch 1, skip next st, dc in next st) 15 times, ch 1, (dc in end of next row, ch 1) 5 times, (2 dc, ch 2, 2 dc) in end of last row; working across side, (ch 1, skip next dc, dc in next dc) across to last 2 dc, ch 1, skip last 2 dc †; working across bottom edge, (2 dc, ch 2, 2 dc) in first row, ch 1, (dc in end of next row, ch 1) 5 times, working in free loops of beginning ch *(Fig. 21b, page 138)*, repeat from † to † once, 2 dc in end of same row as joining, ch 2; join with slip st to first dc.

Rnd 2: Ch 1, sc in first 2 dc, 2 sc in each ch-1 sp across to within 2 dc of corner ch-2 sp, sc in next 2 dc, (2 sc, ch 1, 2 sc) in next ch-2 sp, ★ sc in next 2 dc, 2 sc in each ch-1 sp across to within 2 dc of corner ch-2 sp, sc in next 2 dc, (2 sc, ch 1, 2 sc) in next ch-2 sp; repeat from ★ around; join with slip st to first sc, finish off.

Add fringe using 4 strands of MC, each 13" long *(Figs. 26a & b, page 140)*; spacing evenly, attach across each end of afghan.

CHART A

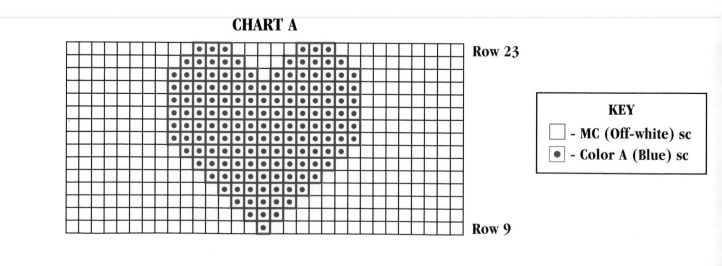

Row 23

Row 9

CHART B

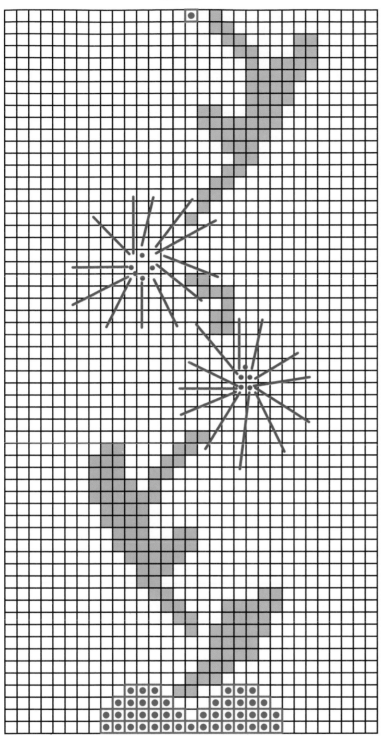

CHART C

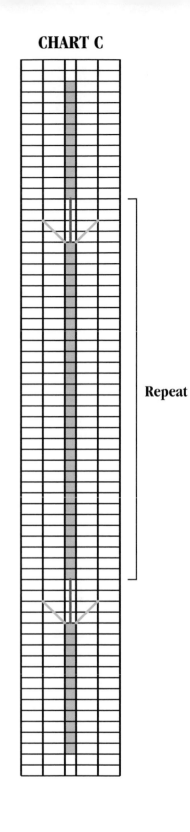

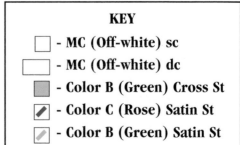

Repeat

KEY

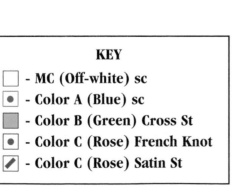

- ☐ - MC (Off-white) sc
- ⊡ - Color A (Blue) sc
- ▨ - Color B (Green) Cross St
- ⊙ - Color C (Rose) French Knot
- ▱ - Color C (Rose) Satin St

KEY

- ☐ - MC (Off-white) sc
- ☐ - MC (Off-white) dc
- ▨ - Color B (Green) Cross St
- ▱ - Color C (Rose) Satin St
- ▱ - Color B (Green) Satin St

9

GOLDEN TREASURE

Earthy shades of gold and brown come together to create this richly textured afghan. Stitched with worsted weight yarn using cross and V-stitches, it's an exciting project for the advanced crocheter. Helpful stitch diagrams make this natural beauty a pleasure.

Finished Size: Approximately 48" x 64"

MATERIALS

Worsted Weight Yarn, approximately:
Color A (Brown) - 13 ounces, (370 grams, 855 yards)
Color B (Dark Gold) - 13 ounces, (370 grams, 855 yards)
Color C (Gold) - 15 ounces, (430 grams, 985 yards)
Color D (Light Gold) - 13 ounces, (370 grams, 855 yards)
Crochet hook, sizes N (9.00 mm) **and** P (10.00 mm) **or** sizes needed for gauge

GAUGE: With larger size hook, 4 Cross Sts = 4"

PATTERN STITCHES

V-ST
(Dc, ch 1, dc) in sp indicated.

FOUNDATION CROSS ST
Work Long sc *(Fig. 5, page 133)* in sp on left side of next dc on Row 1 *(Fig. 1a)*, working **around** Long sc just worked, work Long sc in sp before same dc *(Fig. 1b)*.

Fig. 1a   **Fig. 1b**

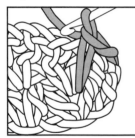 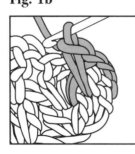

CROSS ST
Working **around** previous row, work Long sc on left side of next Cross St on row below, inserting hook between rows (colors) *(Fig. 2a)*, working **around** Long sc just worked, work Long sc on right side of same Cross St *(Fig. 2b)*.

Fig. 2a   **Fig. 2b**

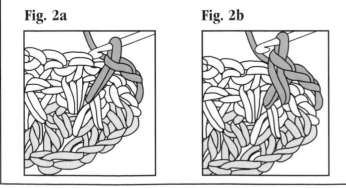

COLOR SEQUENCE
★ 2 Rows each Color A *(Fig. 22a, page 138)*, Color B, Color C, Color D; repeat from ★ throughout.

BODY

With larger size hook and Color A, ch 95 **loosely**.
Row 1 (Right side): 2 Dc in third ch from hook, (skip next ch, 2 dc in next ch) across to last 2 chs, skip next ch, sc in last ch: 46 dc groups.
Note: Loop a short piece of yarn around any stitch to mark last row as **right** side.
Row 2: Ch 2, turn; working in sp **between** dc, (sc, ch 1, dc) in center of first dc group, work V-St in center of next dc group and in center of each dc group across, sc in top of turning ch changing to Color B.
Row 3: Ch 2, turn; working **around** previous row, work Foundation Cross St, (skip next dc on Row 1, work Foundation Cross St) across to last dc, skip last dc, sc in top of turning ch on previous row: 46 Cross Sts.
Row 4: Ch 2, turn; working **around** previous row, (sc, ch 1, dc) in first ch-1 sp on row below *(Fig. 3)*, work V-St in next V-St (ch-1 sp) on row below and in each V-St across, sc in top of turning ch on previous row changing to next color.

Fig. 3

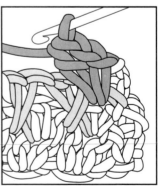

Row 5: Ch 2, turn; work Cross St, (skip next V-St on previous row, work Cross St) across, sc in top of turning ch on previous row.
Repeat Rows 4 and 5 until afghan measures approximately 61½", ending by working Row 4 with Color C.
With Color D, repeat Row 5 changing to Color C in last sc; do **not** finish off.

EDGING

Rnd 1: Ch 1, 3 sc in same st, sc evenly across end of rows to next corner, 3 sc in corner; working in ch-1 sps and free loops of beginning ch *(Fig. 21b, page 138)*, sc evenly across to next corner, 3 sc in corner; sc evenly across end of rows, 3 sc in next corner, (working **around** last row, sc in ch-1 sp on row below, sc in next dc on previous row) across to next corner; join with slip st to first sc.

Rnds 2 and 3: Ch 1, turn; sc in each sc around working 3 sc in each corner sc; join with slip st to first sc.

Rnd 4: Change to smaller size hook, ch 1, do **not** turn; working from **left** to **right**, work reverse sc in each sc around *(Figs. 18a-d, page 136)* working 2 reverse sc in each corner sc; join with slip st to first st, finish off.

11

Quick REVERSIBLE WRAP

At home on the range or right in your living room, this handsome tri-color afghan will surely comfort a weary cowpoke. The reversible pattern is worked in front post double crochets and V-stitch clusters using a large hook with two strands of worsted weight yarn. You can rustle one up before the cows come home!

Finished Size: Approximately 49" x 70"

MATERIALS

Worsted Weight Yarn, approximately:

MC (Tan) - 40 ounces, (1,140 grams, 2,515 yards)

Color A (Brown) - 11 ounces, (310 grams, 690 yards)

Color B (Red) - 10 ounces, (280 grams, 630 yards)

Crochet hook, size P (10.00 mm) **or** size needed for gauge

Note: Entire afghan is worked holding 2 strands of yarn together.

GAUGE: 8 dc and 4 rows = 4"

PATTERN STITCHES

FRONT POST DOUBLE CROCHET (abbreviated FPdc)

YO, insert hook from **front** to **back** around post of dc indicated *(Figs. 15 & 16, page 136)*, YO and pull up a loop, (YO and draw through 2 loops on hook) twice.

V-ST CLUSTER

Work FPdc around next dc, ★ YO, insert hook in **same** dc, YO and pull up a loop, YO and draw through 2 loops on hook; repeat from ★ once **more**, YO and draw through all 3 loops on hook *(Fig. 1a)*, work FPdc around same dc as first FPdc *(Fig. 1b)*.

Fig. 1a　　　　**Fig. 1b**

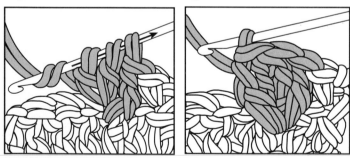

BODY

With MC, ch 95 **loosely**.

Row 1: Dc in fourth ch from hook **(3 skipped chs count as first dc)** and in each ch across changing to Color A in last dc *(Fig. 22a, page 138)*: 93 dc.

Row 2: Ch 1, turn; sc in first dc, (skip next dc, work V-St Cluster, skip next dc, sc in next dc) across changing to MC in last sc: 23 V-St Clusters.

Row 3: Ch 3 **(counts as first dc, now and throughout)**, turn; dc in next st and in each st across changing to Color B in last dc: 93 dc.

Row 4: Repeat Row 2.

Row 5: Ch 3, turn; dc in next st and in each st across changing to Color A in last dc.

Row 6: Repeat Row 2.

Rows 7-9: Ch 3, turn; dc in next st and in each st across changing to Color B in last dc on Row 9.

Row 10: Repeat Row 2.

Rows 11-13: Ch 3, turn; dc in next st and in each st across changing to Color A in last dc on Row 13.

Rows 14-90: Repeat Rows 2-13, 6 times, then repeat Rows 2-6 once **more**.

Row 91: Ch 3, turn; dc in next st and in each st across; do **not** finish off.

EDGING

Rnd 1: Ch 1, do **not** turn; sc evenly around, working 3 sc in each corner (total sc must be a multiple of 2); join with slip st to first sc.

Rnd 2: Turn; (ch 3, slip st in next sc, ch 1, slip st in next sc) around working last slip st in first st; finish off.

13

GARDEN PLOT QUILT

Pick this pretty afghan to bring nature's splendor indoors! Featuring an intricate arrangement of motifs in shades of rose and teal, the springtime throw is made up of blocks that are whipstitched together. A color placement diagram makes assembly a breeze.

Finished Size: Approximately 54" x 67"

MATERIALS

Worsted Weight Yarn, approximately:
  Color A (Light Rose) - 3 ounces, (90 grams, 225 yards)
  Color B (Rose) - 12 ounces, (340 grams, 890 yards)
  Color C (Dark Rose) - 15 ounces, (430 grams, 1,115 yards)
  Color D (Teal) - 9 ounces, (260 grams, 670 yards)
  Color E (Light Teal) - 11 ounces, (310 grams, 815 yards)
  Color F (Dark Teal) - 5 ounces, (140 grams, 370 yards)
Crochet hook, size J (6.00 mm) **or** size needed for gauge
Yarn needle

GAUGE: One Motif = 6¹/₂"

PATTERN STITCHES

CLUSTER

★ YO twice, insert hook in st indicated, YO and pull up a loop, (YO and draw through 2 loops on hook) twice; repeat from ★ 5 times **more**, YO and draw through all 7 loops on hook *(Figs. 9a & b, page 134)*.

SC DECREASE (uses next 4 sc)

Pull up a loop in next 4 sc, YO and draw through all 5 loops on hook **(counts as one sc)**.

DC DECREASE (uses next 5 sts)

★ YO, insert hook in **next** st, YO and pull up a loop, YO and draw through 2 loops on hook; repeat from ★ 4 times **more**, YO and draw through all 6 loops on hook **(counts as one dc)**.

MOTIF (Make 80)

FLOWER SECTION

With Color A, ch 4; join with slip st to form a ring.

Rnd 1 (Right side)**:** Ch 1, 8 sc in ring; join with slip st to first sc, finish off.

Note: Loop a short piece of yarn around any stitch to mark last round as **right** side.

Rnd 2: With **right** side facing, join Color B with slip st in any sc; ch 3 **(counts as first dc, now and throughout)**, 2 dc in same st, ch 2, work Cluster in next sc, ch 2, ★ 3 dc in next sc, ch 2, work Cluster in next sc, ch 2; repeat from ★ around; join with slip st to first dc, finish off: 4 Clusters.

Rnd 3: With **right** side facing, join Color C with slip st in same st as joining; ch 1, sc in each dc and in each ch around working 3 sc in top of each Cluster; join with slip st to first sc, finish off: 40 sc.

FIRST STRIPED SECTION

Row 1: With **right** side facing, join Color D with slip st in center sc of any corner of Flower Section; ch 1, sc in same st and in next 10 sc changing to Color E in last sc worked *(Fig. 22a, page 138)*, leave remaining sts unworked: 11 sc.

Row 2: Ch 1, turn; sc in first sc, (tr in next sc, sc in next sc pushing tr to right side) across changing to Color F in last sc worked.

Row 3: Ch 1, turn; sc in first sc, (ch 1, skip next tr, sc in next sc) across; finish off: 5 ch-1 sps.

Row 4: With **right** side facing, join Color D with slip st in first sc; ch 1, sc in same st and in each ch-1 sp and each sc across changing to Color E in last sc worked: 11 sc.

Rows 5-10: Repeat Rows 2-4, twice; do **not** change colors at end of Row 10, finish off.

SECOND STRIPED SECTION

Row 1: With **right** side facing, join Color D with slip st in same corner sc as last sc worked into on Row 1 of First Striped Section; ch 1, sc in same st and in next 10 sc changing to Color E in last sc worked, leave remaining sts unworked: 11 sc.

Rows 2-10: Work same as First Striped Section.

PETAL

Row 1: With **right** side facing and working in end of rows, join Color C with slip st in last row of First Striped Section; ch 1, work 10 sc evenly spaced across each Striped Section: 20 sc.

Row 2: Ch 1, turn; sc in first 8 sc, work sc decrease, sc in last 8 sc changing to Color B in last sc worked: 17 sc.

Row 3: Ch 3, turn; dc in next 5 sc, work dc decrease, dc in last 6 sc: 13 dc.

Row 4: Ch 3, turn; dc in next 3 dc, work dc decrease, dc in last 4 dc changing to Color A in last dc worked: 9 dc.

Row 5: Ch 4, turn; tr in next dc, skip next 2 dc, work Cluster in next dc, skip next 2 dc, tr in last 2 dc: 5 sts.

Row 6: Ch 1, turn; pull up a loop in first tr, skip next tr, pull up a loop in next Cluster, skip next tr, pull up a loop in top of beginning ch-4, YO and draw through all 4 loops on hook; finish off.

BORDER

With **right** side facing, join Color C with slip st in corner sc of Flower Section; ch 1, 3 sc in same st, work 20 sc evenly spaced across each side working 3 sc in each corner; join with slip st to first sc, finish off: 92 sc.

ASSEMBLY

With **wrong** sides together and Color C, and working through **inside** loops only, whipstitch 4 Motifs together to form a Block following Diagram, page 16 *(Fig. 25b, page 140)*. Whipstitch Blocks together forming 4 vertical strips of 5 Blocks each following Placement Diagram; then whipstitch strips together.

EDGING

Rnd 1: With **right** side facing, join Color C with slip st in any sc; ch 1, sc in same st and each sc around working 3 sc in each corner sc; join with slip st to first sc.

Rnd 2: Ch 3, dc in next sc and in each sc around working 5 dc in each corner sc; join with slip st to first dc, finish off.

Rnd 3: With **right** side facing, join Color B with slip st in any dc; ch 1, working from **left** to **right**, work reverse sc in each st around *(Figs. 18a-d, page 136)*; join with slip st to first st, finish off.

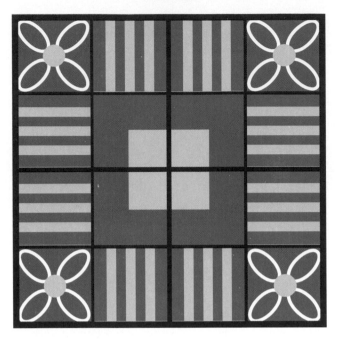

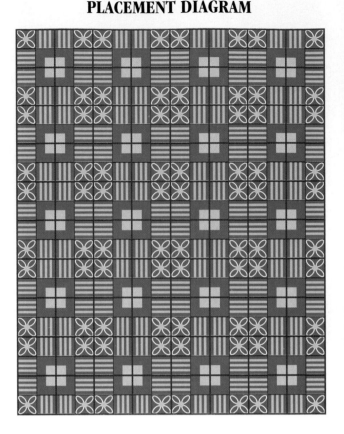

CROSSED TREBLES

*W*orked in ivory worsted weight yarn, this afghan blends with almost any decor. The distinctive afghan features rows of clusters and treble crochet cross stitches, and an abundant fringe offers a lavish finish.

Finished Size: Approximately 51" x 68"

MATERIALS

Worsted Weight Yarn, approximately:
54 ounces, (1,530 grams, 3,550 yards)
Crochet hook, size I (5.50 mm) **or** size needed for gauge

GAUGE: 7 Cross Sts and Rows 1-8 = 4"

Note: Each row is worked across length of afghan.

PATTERN STITCHES

CROSS ST

Skip next st, tr in next st, working **around** tr just made, tr in skipped st *(Figs. 14a & b, page 135)*.

CLUSTER

★ YO, insert hook in st indicated, YO and pull up a loop, YO and draw through 2 loops on hook; repeat from ★ 4 times **more**, YO and draw through all 6 loops on hook *(Figs. 9a & b, page 134)*. Push Cluster to **right** side.

BODY

Ch 237 **loosely**.

Row 1: Sc in second ch from hook and in each ch across: 236 sc.

Row 2 (Right side)**:** Ch 4 **(counts as first tr, now and throughout)**, turn; work Cross Sts across to last sc, tr in last sc: 117 Cross Sts.

Row 3: Ch 1, turn; sc in first tr, ch 1, ★ skip next Cross St, sc in sp **before** next Cross St, ch 1; repeat from ★ across to last Cross St, skip last Cross St, sc in sp **before** last tr, sc in last tr: 236 sts.

Row 4: Ch 4, turn; work Cross Sts across to last sc working in sc and in chs, tr in last sc: 117 Cross Sts.

Rows 5-17: Repeat Rows 3 and 4, 6 times, then repeat Row 3 once **more**.

Rows 18-20: Ch 1, turn; sc in each st across: 236 sc.

Row 21: Ch 1, turn; sc in first 4 sc, work Cluster in next sc, (sc in next 5 sc, work Cluster in next sc) across to last 3 sc, sc in last 3 sc: 39 Clusters.

Row 22: Ch 3 **(counts as first dc, now and throughout)**, turn; dc in next sc and in each st across: 236 dc.

Row 23: Ch 1, turn; sc in first 7 dc, work Cluster in next dc, (sc in next 5 dc, work Cluster in next dc) across to last 6 dc, sc in last 6 dc: 38 Clusters.

Row 24: Ch 3, turn; dc in next sc and in each st across.

Row 25: Ch 1, turn; sc in each dc across.

Rows 26-113: Repeat Rows 2-25, 3 times, then repeat Rows 2-17 once **more**.
Finish off.

Add fringe using 6 strands, each 15" long **(Figs. 26a & b, page 140)**; spacing evenly, attach across ends of rows on each end of afghan.

Quick GRANNY CIRCLES

This fanciful afghan is an old-fashioned beauty in classic blue and white. Worked with worsted weight yarn, the circles are joined as you go, then the fill-in motifs are added. A sweet picot edging completes this lovely quilt-look wrap.

Finished Size: Approximately 48" x 67"

MATERIALS

Worsted Weight Yarn, approximately:

Color A (Light Blue) - 8 ounces, (230 grams, 560 yards)

Color B (Blue) - 9 ounces, (260 grams, 635 yards)

Color C (Dark Blue) - 11 ounces, (310 grams, 775 yards)

Color D (White) - 12 ounces, (340 grams, 845 yards)

Crochet hook, size K (6.50 mm) **or** size needed for gauge

GAUGE: One Circle = 6¹/₂"

FIRST STRIP
FIRST CIRCLE

With Color A, ch 4; join with slip st to form a ring.

Rnd 1 (Right side): Ch 3 **(counts as first dc, now and throughout)**, 11 dc in ring; join with slip st to first dc: 12 dc.
Note: Loop a short piece of yarn around any stitch to mark last round as **right** side.

Rnd 2: Ch 3, dc in same st, ch 1, (2 dc in next dc, ch 1) around; join with slip st to first dc, finish off: 24 dc.

Rnd 3: With **right** side facing, join Color B with slip st in any ch-1 sp; ch 3, 2 dc in same sp, ch 1, (3 dc in next ch-1 sp, ch 1) around; join with slip st to first dc, finish off: 36 dc.

Rnd 4: With **right** side facing, join Color C with slip st in center dc of any 3-dc group; ch 3, 4 dc in same st, sc in next ch-1 sp, skip next dc, (5 dc in next dc, sc in next ch-1 sp, skip next dc) around; join with slip st to first dc, finish off: 60 dc.

Rnd 5: With **right** side facing, join Color D with slip st in any sc; ch 1, sc in same st, ch 3, skip next 2 dc, sc in next dc, ch 3, (skip next 2 dc, sc in next sc, ch 3, skip next 2 dc, sc in next dc, ch 3) around; join with slip st to first sc, finish off: 24 ch-3 sps.

ADDITIONAL CIRCLES

Work same as First Circle through Rnd 4.

Rnd 5 (One-sided joining): With **right** side facing, join Color D with slip st in any sc; ch 1, sc in same st, (ch 3, skip next 2 dc, sc in next st) 20 times, ch 1, holding **previous Circle** with **right** side facing, slip st in corresponding ch-3 sp, ch 1, ★ skip next 2 dc on **new Circle**, sc in next st, ch 1, slip st in next ch-3 sp on **previous Circle**, ch 1; repeat from ★ 2 times **more**, skip last 2 dc on **new Circle**; join with slip st to first sc, finish off.

To complete First Strip, work and join 8 **more** Circles in the same manner, skipping 8 ch-3 sps on previous Circle when joining.

REMAINING 6 STRIPS
FIRST CIRCLE

Work same as First Circle of First Strip through Rnd 4.

Rnd 5 (One-sided joining): Work same as First Strip, skipping 2 ch-3 sps on First Circle of previous Strip when joining.

ADDITIONAL CIRCLES

Work same as First Circle of First Strip through Rnd 4.

Rnd 5 (Two-sided joining): With **right** side facing, join Color D with slip st in any sc; ch 1, sc in same st, (ch 3, skip next 2 dc, sc in next st) 14 times, ch 1, with **right** side facing, skip 2 ch-3 sps on next Circle of **previous Strip**, † slip st in next ch-3 sp, ch 1, (skip next 2 dc on **new Circle**, sc in next st, ch 1, slip st in next ch-3 sp on **previous Circle**, ch 1) 3 times, skip next 2 dc on **new Circle** †, sc in next sc, (ch 3, skip next 2 dc, sc in next st) twice, ch 1, skip 2 ch-3 sps on **previous Circle** of same Strip, repeat from † to † once; join with slip st to first sc, finish off.

To complete Strip, work and join 8 **more** Circles in the same manner.

FILL-IN MOTIF

With Color D, ch 4; join with slip st to form a ring.

Rnd 1 (Right side): Ch 3, 2 dc in ring, ch 1, (3 dc in ring, ch 1) 3 times; join with slip st to first dc: 12 dc.
Note: Mark last round as **right** side.

Rnd 2: Ch 1, sc in same st, ch 1, with **right** side facing and working in intersection of 4 Circles, slip st in unworked ch-3 sp to **left** of any joining, ★ † ch 1, sc in next dc on **Motif**, ch 1, slip st in next unworked ch-3 sp on **Circle**, ch 1, sc in next dc on **Motif**, ch 2, slip st in sp to **right** of next joining on **Circle**, ch 2, sc in next ch-1 sp on **Motif**, ch 2, slip st in sp to **left** of same joining on next **Circle**, ch 2 †, sc in next dc on **Motif**, ch 1, slip st in next unworked ch-3 sp on **Circle**; repeat from ★ 2 times **more**, then repeat from † to † once; join with slip st to first sc, finish off.

Repeat for remaining 53 Fill-in Motifs.

EDGING

Rnd 1: With **right** side facing, join Color B with slip st in sc to **left** of any joining; ch 1, sc in same st, ch 1, (3 dc, ch 1, 3 dc) in next sc **(Shell made)**, ch 1, ★ sc in next sc, ch 1, (work Shell in next sc, ch 1, sc in next sc, ch 1) across to next Circle; repeat from ★ around; join with slip st to first sc, finish off.

Rnd 2: With **right** side facing, join Color D with slip st in first Shell (ch-1 sp); ch 1, in same sp work (sc, ch 3, slip st in third ch from hook, sc), ch 3, sc in next sc, ch 3, ★ (sc, ch 3, slip st in third ch from hook, sc) in next Shell, [ch 3, sc in next sc, ch 3, (sc, ch 3, slip st in third ch from hook, sc) in next Shell] across to next Circle, ch 1, skip next 2 sc; repeat from ★ around; join with slip st to first sc, finish off.

HANDSOME RIPPLES

Crafted with worsted weight yarn, this bold afghan invites compliments on your good taste. Front post double crochets enhance the cover's familiar ripple pattern, and generous tassels at both ends provide a handsome finish.

Finished Size: Approximately 50" x 65"

MATERIALS

Worsted Weight Yarn, approximately:

MC (Beige) - 29 ounces, (820 grams, 1,825 yards)

Color A (Maroon) - 10 ounces, (280 grams, 630 yards)

Color B (Blue) - 6 ounces, (170 grams, 375 yards)

Crochet hook, size K (6.50 mm) **or** size needed for gauge

GAUGE: In pattern, 1 repeat = 5¹/₂" and 12 rows = 7"

> **Gauge Swatch:** (11" x 7")
> With MC, ch 42 **loosely**.
> **Rows 1-12:** Work same as Body.
> Finish off.

PATTERN STITCHES

DC DECREASE (uses next 2 sts)

★ YO, insert hook in **next** st, YO and pull up a loop, YO and draw through 2 loops on hook; repeat from ★ once **more**, YO and draw through all 3 loops on hook (**counts as one dc**).

SC DECREASE

Pull up a loop in next 2 sts, YO and draw through all 3 loops on hook (**counts as one sc**).

FRONT POST DOUBLE CROCHET (*abbreviated FPdc*)

YO, insert hook from **front** to **back** around post of dc indicated (**Figs. 15 & 16, page 136**), YO and pull up a loop, (YO and draw through 2 loops on hook) twice. Skip dc behind FPdc.

BODY

With MC, ch 196 **loosely**.

Row 1: Dc in third ch from hook and in next 7 chs, (dc, ch 3, dc) in next ch, dc in next 7 chs, dc decrease, ★ skip next 3 chs, dc decrease, dc in next 7 chs, (dc, ch 3, dc) in next ch, dc in next 7 chs, dc decrease; repeat from ★ across: 162 dc.

Row 2 (Right side)**:** Ch 2, turn; dc in next 8 dc, (dc, ch 3, dc) in next ch-3 sp, dc in next 7 dc, ★ dc decrease twice, dc in next 7 dc, (dc, ch 3, dc) in next ch-3 sp, dc in next 7 dc; repeat from ★ across to last 2 dc, dc decrease.

Note: Loop a short piece of yarn around any stitch to mark last row as **right** side.

Rows 3 and 4: Repeat Row 2 changing to Color A in last decrease on Row 4 (**Fig. 22a, page 138**).

Row 5: Repeat Row 2, changing to Color B in last decrease.

Row 6: Ch 1, turn; pull up a loop in first 2 sts, YO and draw through all 3 loops on hook, ★ † work FPdc around next dc, (sc in next dc, work FPdc around next dc) 3 times, (sc, ch 3, sc) in next ch-3 sp, work FPdc around next dc, (sc in next dc, work FPdc around next dc) 3 times †, work sc decrease twice; repeat from ★ 7 times **more**, then repeat from † to † once, work sc decrease changing to Color A.

Row 7: Ch 2, turn; working in Front Loops Only (**Fig. 20, page 138**), dc in next 8 sts, skip next ch, (dc, ch 3, dc) in next ch, skip next ch, dc in next 7 sts, ★ dc decrease twice, dc in next 7 sts, skip next ch, (dc, ch 3, dc) in next ch, skip next ch, dc in next 7 sts; repeat from ★ across to last 2 sts, dc decrease.

Row 8: Ch 2, turn; working in both loops, dc in next 8 dc, (dc, ch 3, dc) in next ch-3 sp, dc in next 7 dc, ★ dc decrease twice, dc in next 7 dc, (dc, ch 3, dc) in next ch-3 sp, dc in next 7 dc; repeat from ★ across to last 2 dc, dc decrease changing to MC.

Rows 9-16: Repeat Row 2, 8 times changing to Color A in last decrease on Row 16.

Rows 17-108: Repeat Rows 5-16, 7 times, then repeat Rows 5-12 once **more**.

Finish off.

Using MC, add 5" long tassels (**Figs. 27a & b, page 141**), across each end of afghan.

BILLOWY BROOMSTICK LACE

A summons to softness, this intricate afghan is stitched with downy brushed acrylic yarn. Its billowing waves alternate with rows created using a broomstick lace pin. You're sure to enjoy many sweet moments with this lavish wrap.

Finished Size: Approximately 50" x 71"

MATERIALS

Worsted Weight Brushed Acrylic Yarn, approximately:
39 ounces, (1,110 grams, 3,010 yards)
Crochet hook, size J (6.00 mm) **or** size needed for gauge
Broomstick Lace Pin, size 50 (25.00 mm)

GAUGE: In pattern, 1 repeat (17 sts) = 5"
and Rows 1-8 = 4"

Gauge Swatch: (10" x 7")
Ch 35 **loosely**.
Rows 1-13: Work same as Body.
Finish off.

PATTERN STITCHES

DECREASE (uses next 2 sts)
★ YO, insert hook in **next** st, YO and pull up a loop, YO and draw through 2 loops on hook; repeat from ★ once **more**, YO and draw through all 3 loops on hook (**counts as one dc**).

PUFF ST
(YO, insert hook in st indicated, YO and pull up a loop even with loop on hook) 4 times (***Fig. 12, page 135***), YO and draw through all 9 loops on hook.

BODY

Ch 171 **loosely**.

Row 1: Dc in third ch from hook, decrease twice, ch 1, (work Puff St in next ch, ch 1) 5 times, ★ decrease 6 times, ch 1, (work Puff St in next ch, ch 1) 5 times; repeat from ★ across to last 6 chs, decrease 3 times: 50 Puff Sts.

Row 2 (Right side)**:** Ch 1, turn; sc in each st and in each ch-1 sp across to beginning ch-2, leave ch unworked: 170 sc.

Row 3: Ch 2, turn; dc in next sc, decrease twice, ch 1, (work Puff St in next sc, ch 1) 5 times, ★ decrease 6 times, ch 1, (work Puff St in next sc, ch 1) 5 times; repeat from ★ across to last 6 sc, decrease 3 times.

Row 4: Ch 1, turn; sc in each st and in each ch-1 sp across to beginning ch-2, leave ch unworked.

Rows 5-8: Repeat Rows 3 and 4 twice.

Row 9 (Broomstick lace)**:** Do **not** turn; slip loop from hook onto pin (***Fig. 1***), working from **left** to **right**, skip first sc, ★ insert hook in next st, YO and pull up a loop, slip loop onto pin; repeat from ★ across: 170 loops.

Fig. 1

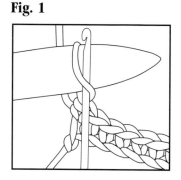

Row 10: Do **not** turn; insert hook from **left** to **right** through first 3 loops on pin (***Fig. 2a***) and slip these 3 loops off, being careful not to tighten first loop, YO and draw through all 3 loops on hook, ch 1 (***Fig. 2b***), 3 sc in center of same 3 loops (***Fig. 2c***), ★ insert hook from **left** to **right** through next 4 loops, slip these 4 loops off, YO and draw through all 4 loops on hook, 4 sc in center of same 4 loops; repeat from ★ across to last 3 loops, insert hook from **left** to **right** through last 3 loops, slip these 3 loops off, YO and draw through all 3 loops on hook, 3 sc in center of same 3 loops: 170 sc.

Fig. 2a

Fig. 2b

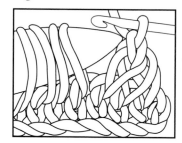

Fig. 2c

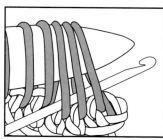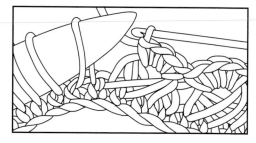

Row 11: Ch 1, turn; sc in each sc across.

Rows 12-20: Repeat Rows 9-11, 3 times.

Rows 21-28: Repeat Rows 3 and 4, 4 times.

Rows 29-148: Repeat Rows 9-28, 6 times.

Finish off.

DELIGHTFUL MILE-A-MINUTE

Worked in strips that are easy to join, the familiar mile-a-minute afghan is a favorite among stitchers. This garden-fresh delight is crafted using a natural combination of green and cream worsted weight yarns. It's ideal for a cool spring morning among the flowers!

Finished Size: Approximately 50" x 66"

MATERIALS

Worsted Weight Yarn, approximately:
    Color A (Light Green) - 28 ounces,
      (800 grams, 1,970 yards)
    Color B (Green) - 16 ounces, (450 grams, 1,125 yards)
    Color C (Cream) - 13 ounces, (370 grams, 915 yards)
Crochet hook, size H (5.00 mm) **or** size needed for gauge
Yarn needle

GAUGE: 8 rows on Center = 4"
         One Strip = 2³/4" wide

STRIP (Make 18)

CENTER

With Color A, ch 7 **loosely**.

Note: To work **V-St**, (Dc, ch 1, dc) in st or sp indicated.

Row 1 (Right side): Work V-St in in fourth ch from hook, skip next ch, work V-St in next ch, dc in last ch.

Note: Loop a short piece of yarn around any stitch to mark last row as **right** side and bottom edge.

Rows 2-127: Ch 3, turn; work V-St in next 2 V-Sts (ch-1 sp), dc in top of beginning ch.
Finish off.

EDGING

Rnd 1: With **right** side facing and working in end of rows, join Color B with slip st in first row; ch 3, 2 dc in same row, (sc in next row, 3 dc in next row) across; work 9 tr in sp **between** next 2 V-Sts; 3 dc in end of first row, (sc in next row, 3 dc in next row) across; working over beginning ch, work 9 tr in sp **between** next 2 V-Sts; join with slip st to top of beginning ch-3, finish off: 528 sts.

Rnd 2: With **right** side facing and working in Back Loops Only *(Fig. 20, page 138)*, join Color C with slip st in same st as joining; ch 1, sc in same st, † working in **front** of next 3-dc group, work tr around dc **below** same 3-dc group *(Fig. 1)*, (skip dc behind tr, sc in next 3 sts on Rnd 1, work tr around dc **below** next 3-dc group) 63 times, skip dc behind tr, (sc in next st, 2 sc in next st) 5 times †, sc in next dc, repeat from † to † once; join with slip st to first sc, finish off.

Fig. 1

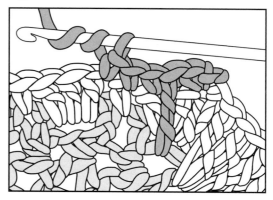

ASSEMBLY

With **wrong** sides together and Color C, and working through **inside** loops only, whipstitch Strips together, placing bottom edges at the same end and matching sts. Always working from the same direction, begin in the first tr and end in the last tr on **each** side *(Fig. 25b, page 140)*.

all through the house

A heartfelt welcome is extended to your guests with more than mere words; it's reflected in the personal accents that are scattered all through your home. From the entryway to the guest room, crocheted touches offer silent invitations for visitors to make themselves at home. With these exciting selections, you'll discover a wealth of ideas for lending a cordial air to every room in the house.

IN THE LIVING ROOM

*E*stablish an atmosphere of warmth and hospitality beginning at the front door with these coordinating accessories. (Below) *Stitched with long-wearing worsted weight yarn, our handsome entry rug features eye-catching filet ripples. It's worked holding two strands of yarn, so you'll finish it fast. (Opposite) The lovely mantel skirt, fashioned with fabric and bedspread weight cotton thread, showcases a zigzag pattern that echoes the filet rug design. The elegant skirt can be customized to fit any size mantel, and ribbon woven through the eyelet border offers a charming finishing touch.*

Quick ENTRY RUG

Finished Size: Approximately 19" x 34"

MATERIALS

Worsted Weight Yarn, approximately:
12 ounces, (340 grams, 790 yards)
Crochet hook, size G (4.00 mm) **or** size needed for gauge

Note: Entire Rug is worked holding 2 strands of yarn together.

GAUGE: 12 dc and 6 rows = 4"

Ch 102 **loosely**.

Row 1 (Right side)**:** Dc in sixth ch from hook and in next 2 chs, (ch 1, skip next ch, dc in next 3 chs) 3 times, ch 4, skip next 4 chs, dc in next 7 chs, ch 4, skip next 4 chs, dc in next 3 chs, (ch 1, skip next ch, dc in next 3 chs) 8 times, ch 4, skip next 4 chs, dc in next 7 chs, ch 4, skip next 4 chs, (dc in next 3 chs, ch 1, skip next ch) 4 times, hdc in last ch.

Row 2: Ch 3 **(counts as first dc, now and throughout),** turn; (2 dc, ch 2, 3 dc) in first sp, ch 1, skip next 2 dc, dc in next 3 sts, (ch 1, skip next dc, dc in next 3 sts) twice, ch 4, 2 dc in next ch-4 sp, dc in next 5 dc, ch 4, 2 dc in next ch-4 sp, dc in next dc, (ch 1, skip next dc, dc in next 3 sts) 8 times, ch 1, skip next dc, dc in next dc, 2 dc in next ch-4 sp, ch 4, skip next 2 dc, dc in next 5 dc, 2 dc in next ch-4 sp, ch 4, skip next 2 dc, dc in next 3 sts, ch 1, (skip next dc, dc in next 3 sts, ch 1) twice, skip next 2 dc, (3 dc, ch 2, 3 dc) in last sp.

Row 3: Ch 2, turn; (3 dc, ch 2, 3 dc) in first sp, ch 1, skip next 2 dc, dc in next 3 sts, (ch 1, skip next dc, dc in next 3 sts) twice, ch 4, 2 dc in next ch-4 sp, dc in next 5 dc, ch 4, 2 dc in next ch-4 sp, dc in next dc, ch 1, (skip next dc, dc in next 3 sts, ch 1) 9 times, skip next dc, dc in next dc, 2 dc in next ch-4 sp, ch 4, skip next 2 dc, dc in next 5 dc, 2 dc in next ch-4 sp, ch 4, skip next 2 dc, dc in next 3 sts, ch 1, (skip next dc, dc in next 3 sts, ch 1) twice, skip next 2 dc, (3 dc, ch 2, 3 dc) in next sp, skip next 2 dc, hdc in last dc.

Row 4: Turn; slip st in next 3 dc and in next ch-2 sp, ch 3, (2 dc, ch 2, 3 dc) in same sp, ch 1, skip next 2 dc, dc in next 3 sts, (ch 1, skip next dc, dc in next 3 sts) twice, ch 4, 2 dc in next ch-4 sp, dc in next 5 dc, ch 4, 2 dc in next ch-4 sp, dc in next dc, ch 1, (skip next dc, dc in next 3 sts, ch 1) 10 times, skip next dc, dc in next dc, 2 dc in next ch-4 sp, ch 4, skip next 2 dc, dc in next 5 dc, 2 dc in next ch-4 sp, ch 4, skip next 2 dc, dc in next 3 sts, (ch 1, skip next dc, dc in next 3 sts) twice, ch 1, skip next 2 dc, (3 dc, ch 2, 3 dc) in last sp.

Row 5: Ch 2, turn; (3 dc, ch 2, 3 dc) in first sp, ch 1, skip next 2 dc, dc in next 3 sts, (ch 1, skip next dc, dc in next 3 sts) twice, ch 4, 2 dc in next ch-4 sp, dc in next 5 dc, ch 4, 2 dc in next ch-4 sp, dc in next dc, ch 1, (skip next dc, dc in next 3 sts, ch 1) 11 times, skip next dc, dc in next dc, 2 dc in next ch-4 sp, ch 4, skip next 2 dc, dc in next 5 dc, 2 dc in next ch-4 sp, ch 4, skip next 2 dc, dc in next 3 sts, ch 1, (skip next dc, dc in next 3 sts, ch 1) twice, skip next 2 dc, (3 dc, ch 2, 3 dc) in next sp, skip next 2 dc, hdc in last dc.

Row 6: Turn; slip st in next 3 dc and in next ch-2 sp, ch 3, 2 dc in same sp, ch 1, skip next 2 dc, dc in next 3 sts, (ch 1, skip next dc, dc in next 3 sts) twice, ch 1, skip next dc, dc in next dc, 2 dc in next ch-4 sp, ch 4, skip next 2 dc, dc in next 5 dc, 2 dc in next ch-4 sp, ch 4, skip next 2 dc, dc in next 3 sts, (ch 1, skip next dc, dc in next 3 sts) 11 times, ch 4, 2 dc in next ch-4 sp, dc in next 5 dc, ch 4, 2 dc in next ch-4 sp, dc in next dc, (ch 1, skip next dc, dc in next 3 sts) 3 times, ch 1, skip next 2 dc, 3 dc in last sp.

Row 7: Ch 2, turn; 3 dc in first ch-1 sp, ch 1, skip next 2 dc, (dc in next 3 sts, ch 1, skip next dc) 3 times, dc in next dc, 2 dc in next ch-4 sp, ch 4, skip next 2 dc, dc in next 5 dc, 2 dc in next ch-4 sp, ch 4, skip next 2 dc, dc in next 3 sts, (ch 1, skip next dc, dc in next 3 sts) 10 times, ch 4, 2 dc in next ch-4 sp, dc in next 5 dc, ch 4, 2 dc in next ch-4 sp, dc in next dc, (ch 1, skip next dc, dc in next 3 sts) 3 times, ch 1, skip next 2 dc, 3 dc in next ch-1 sp, skip next 2 dc, hdc in last dc.

Row 8: Turn; slip st in next 3 dc and in next ch-1 sp, ch 3, 2 dc in same sp, ch 1, skip next 2 dc, (dc in next 3 sts, ch 1, skip next dc) 3 times, dc in next dc, 2 dc in next ch-4 sp, ch 4, skip next 2 dc, dc in next 5 dc, 2 dc in next ch-4 sp, ch 4, skip next 2 dc, dc in next 3 sts, (ch 1, skip next dc, dc in next 3 sts) 9 times, ch 4, 2 dc in next ch-4 sp, dc in next 5 dc, ch 4, 2 dc in next ch-4 sp, dc in next dc, (ch 1, skip next dc, dc in next 3 sts) 3 times, ch 1, skip next 2 dc, 3 dc in last ch-1 sp.

Row 9: Ch 2, turn; 3 dc in first ch-1 sp, ch 1, skip next 2 dc, (dc in next 3 sts, ch 1, skip next dc) 3 times, dc in next dc, 2 dc in next ch-4 sp, ch 4, skip next 2 dc, dc in next 5 dc, 2 dc in next ch-4 sp, ch 4, skip next 2 dc, dc in next 3 sts, (ch 1, skip next dc, dc in next 3 sts) 8 times, ch 4, 2 dc in next ch-4 sp, dc in next 5 dc, ch 4, 2 dc in next ch-4 sp, dc in next dc, (ch 1, skip next dc, dc in next 3 sts) 3 times, ch 1, skip next 2 dc, 3 dc in next ch-1 sp, skip next 2 dc, hdc in last dc.

Row 10: Turn; slip st in next 3 dc and in next ch-1 sp, ch 3, 2 dc in same sp, ch 1, skip next 2 dc, (dc in next 3 sts, ch 1, skip next dc) 3 times, dc in next dc, 2 dc in next ch-4 sp, ch 4, skip next 2 dc, dc in next 5 dc, 2 dc in next ch-4 sp, ch 4, skip next 2 dc, dc in next 3 sts, (ch 1, skip next dc, dc in next 3 sts) 7 times, ch 4, 2 dc in next ch-4 sp, dc in next 5 dc, ch 4, 2 dc in next ch-4 sp, dc in next dc, (ch 1, skip next dc, dc in next 3 sts) 3 times, ch 1, skip next 2 dc, 3 dc in last ch-1 sp.

Row 11: Ch 2, turn; 3 dc in first ch-1 sp, ch 1, skip next 2 dc, dc in next 3 sts, (ch 1, skip next dc, dc in next 3 sts) twice, ch 4, 2 dc in next ch-4 sp, dc in next 5 dc, ch 4, 2 dc in next ch-4 sp, dc in next dc, (ch 1, skip next dc, dc in next 3 sts) 7 times, ch 1, skip next dc, dc in next dc, 2 dc in next ch-4 sp, ch 4, skip next 2 dc, dc in next 5 dc, 2 dc in next ch-4 sp, ch 4, skip next 2 dc, dc in next 3 sts, (ch 1, skip next dc, dc in next 3 sts) twice, ch 1, skip next 2 dc, 3 dc in next ch-1 sp, skip next 2 dc, hdc in last dc.

Rows 12-29: Repeat Rows 2-11 once, then repeat Rows 2-9 once **more**.
Finish off.

MANTEL SKIRT

Finished Size: Edging - approximately 6¹/₂" wide

MATERIALS
Bedspread Weight Cotton Thread (size 10), approximately
    130 yards for each foot of length
Steel crochet hook, size 7 (1.65 mm) **or** size needed for gauge
Linen - equal to depth and length of mantel to be covered
    plus 1"
¹/₂" wide satin ribbon equal to desired length of Skirt plus 1"
Pins
Sewing needle and thread

GAUGE: 18 dc and 9 rows = 2"

EDGING
Ch 55 **loosely**.

Row 1: 3 Dc in fourth ch from hook, dc in next ch, ch 3, skip next 2 chs, sc in next ch, ch 3, skip next 2 chs, dc in next 2 chs, ch 2, skip next 2 chs, dc in next 3 chs, ch 5, skip next 5 chs, dc in next 9 chs, ch 5, skip next 5 chs, (dc in next 3 chs, ch 1, skip next ch) 4 times, dc in next 2 chs, (dc, ch 3, 3 dc) in last ch.

Row 2: Ch 2, turn; (3 dc, ch 3, 3 dc) in first ch-3 sp, (ch 1, 3 dc in next ch-1 sp) 4 times, ch 5, 2 dc in next loop, dc in next 7 dc, ch 5, 3 dc in next loop, ch 1, skip next 2 dc, dc in next dc, ch 2, dc in next 2 dc, ch 5, skip next sc, dc in next 2 dc, leave remaining sts unworked.

Row 3: Ch 3, turn; 3 dc in first dc, dc in next dc, ch 3, sc in next loop, ch 3, dc in next 2 dc, ch 2, skip next dc, 3 dc in next ch-1 sp, ch 1, skip next 3 dc, 3 dc in next ch, ch 5, skip next 2 dc, dc in next 7 dc, 2 dc in next loop, ch 5, (3 dc in next ch-1 sp, ch 1) 4 times, (3 dc, ch 3, 3 dc) in next ch-3 sp.

Row 4: Ch 2, turn; (3 dc, ch 3, 3 dc) in first ch-3 sp, (ch 1, 3 dc in next ch-1 sp) 4 times, ch 5, 2 dc in next loop, dc in next 7 dc, ch 5, 3 dc in next loop, ch 1, 3 dc in next ch-1 sp, ch 1, skip next 2 dc, dc in next dc, ch 2, dc in next 2 dc, ch 5, skip next sc, dc in next 2 dc, leave remaining sts unworked.

Row 5: Ch 3, turn; 3 dc in first dc, dc in next dc, ch 3, sc in next loop, ch 3, dc in next 2 dc, ch 2, skip next dc, (3 dc in next ch-1 sp, ch 1) twice, skip next 3 dc, 3 dc in next ch, ch 5, skip next 2 dc, dc in next 7 dc, 2 dc in next loop, ch 5, (3 dc in next ch-1 sp, ch 1) 4 times, (3 dc, ch 3, 3 dc) in next ch-3 sp.

Row 6: Ch 2, turn; (3 dc, ch 3, 3 dc) in first ch-3 sp, (ch 1, 3 dc in next ch-1 sp) 4 times, ch 5, 2 dc in next loop, dc in next 7 dc, ch 5, 3 dc in next loop, ch 1, (3 dc in next ch-1 sp, ch 1) twice, skip next 2 dc, dc in next dc, ch 2, dc in next 2 dc, ch 5, skip next sc, dc in next 2 dc, leave remaining sts unworked.

Row 7: Ch 3, turn; 3 dc in first dc, dc in next dc, ch 3, sc in next loop, ch 3, dc in next 2 dc, ch 2, skip next dc, (3 dc in next ch-1 sp, ch 1) 3 times, skip next 3 dc, 3 dc in next ch, ch 5, skip next 2 dc, dc in next 7 dc, 2 dc in next loop, ch 5, (3 dc in next ch-1 sp, ch 1) 4 times, (3 dc, ch 3, 3 dc) in next ch-3 sp.

Row 8: Ch 2, turn; (3 dc, ch 3, 3 dc) in first ch-3 sp, (ch 1, 3 dc in next ch-1 sp) 4 times, ch 5, 2 dc in next loop, dc in next 7 dc, ch 5, 3 dc in next loop, ch 1, (3 dc in next ch-1 sp, ch 1) 3 times, skip next 2 dc, dc in next dc, ch 2, dc in next 2 dc, ch 5, skip next sc, dc in next 2 dc, leave remaining sts unworked.

Row 9: Ch 3, turn; 3 dc in first dc, dc in next dc, ch 3, sc in next loop, ch 3, dc in next 2 dc, ch 2, skip next dc, (3 dc in next ch-1 sp, ch 1) 4 times, skip next 3 dc, 3 dc in next ch, ch 5, skip next 2 dc, dc in next 7 dc, 2 dc in next loop, ch 5, (3 dc in next ch-1 sp, ch 1) 4 times, (3 dc, ch 3, 3 dc) in next ch-3 sp.

Row 10: Ch 2, turn; (3 dc, ch 3, 3 dc) in first ch-3 sp, (ch 1, 3 dc in next ch-1 sp) 4 times, ch 5, 2 dc in next loop, dc in next 7 dc, ch 5, 3 dc in next loop, ch 1, (3 dc in next ch-1 sp, ch 1) 4 times, skip next 2 dc, dc in next dc, ch 2, dc in next 2 dc, ch 5, skip next sc, dc in next 2 dc, leave remaining sts unworked.

Row 11: Ch 3, turn; 3 dc in first dc, dc in next dc, ch 3, sc in next loop, ch 3, dc in next 2 dc, ch 2, skip next dc, (3 dc in next ch-1 sp, ch 1) 5 times, skip next 3 dc, 3 dc in next ch, ch 5, skip next 2 dc, dc in next 7 dc, 2 dc in next loop, ch 5, (3 dc in next ch-1 sp, ch 1) 4 times, 3 dc in next ch-3 sp, leave remaining sts unworked.

Row 12: Ch 3, turn; 3 dc in first ch-1 sp, ch 1, (3 dc in next ch-1 sp, ch 1) 3 times, skip next 3 dc, 3 dc in next ch, ch 5, skip next 2 dc, dc in next 7 dc, 2 dc in next loop, ch 5, (3 dc in next ch-1 sp, ch 1) 5 times, skip next 2 dc, dc in next dc, ch 2, dc in next 2 dc, ch 5, skip next sc, dc in next 2 dc, leave remaining sts unworked.

Row 13: Ch 3, turn; 3 dc in first dc, dc in next dc, ch 3, sc in next loop, ch 3, dc in next 2 dc, ch 2, skip next dc, 3 dc in next ch-1 sp, (ch 1, 3 dc in next ch-1 sp) 4 times, ch 5, 2 dc in next loop, dc in next 7 dc, ch 5, 3 dc in next loop, (ch 1, 3 dc in next ch-1 sp) 4 times.

Continued on page 43.

FOR THE DINING ROOM

Radiant starflowers create a dramatic effect on this exquisite tablecloth. Crafted with bedspread weight cotton thread, the topper is created using a join-as-you-go technique that allows you to adjust the size and shape of the cloth to fit your table. Our handy placement diagrams show six possible arrangements for the versatile motifs.

STARFLOWER TABLECLOTH

Finished Size: Small Rectangle - approximately 51" x 74"
Large Rectangle - approximately 69" x 88"
Small Oval - approximately 54" x 69"
Large Oval - approximately 68" x 86"
Small Hexagon - approximately 69" x 73"
Large Hexagon - approximately 86" x 92"

MATERIALS

Bedspread Weight Cotton Thread (size 10), approximately:
Small Rectangle - 4,285 yards
Large Rectangle - 6,950 yards
Small Oval - 3,800 yards
Large Oval - 5,830 yards
Small Hexagon - 4,480 yards
Large Hexagon - 7,190 yards
Note: Each Motif requires approximately 26 yards of thread.
Steel crochet hook, size 6 (1.80 mm) **or** size needed for gauge

GAUGE: One Motif = 4³⁄₄" (from straight edge to straight edge)

PATTERN STITCHES
CLUSTER
★ YO twice, insert hook in ring, YO and pull up a loop, (YO and draw through 2 loops on hook) twice; repeat from ★ 2 times **more**, YO and draw through all 4 loops on hook *(Figs. 9a & b, page 134)*.
BEGINNING SHELL
Ch 3, (dc, ch 3, 2 dc) in same st or sp.
SHELL
(2 Dc, ch 3, 2 dc) in st or sp indicated.
3-DC CLUSTER
† YO, insert hook in **next** ch-1 sp, YO and pull up a loop, YO and draw through 2 loops on hook †, YO, insert hook in **next** dc, YO and pull up a loop, YO and draw through 2 loops on hook; repeat from † to † once; YO and draw through all 4 loops on hook *(Figs. 10a & b, page 134)*.

FIRST MOTIF

Ch 8; join with slip st to form a ring.
Rnd 1 (Right side)**:** Ch 3, ★ YO twice, insert hook in ring, YO and pull up a loop, (YO and draw through 2 loops on hook) twice; repeat from ★ once **more**, YO and draw through all 3 loops on hook **(beginning Cluster made)**, (ch 3, work Cluster) 11 times, ch 1, hdc in top of beginning Cluster to form last sp: 12 sps.
Note: Loop a short piece of thread around any stitch to mark last round as **right** side.
Rnd 2: Ch 7, (dc in next ch-3 sp, ch 4) around; join with slip st to third ch of beginning ch-7.
Rnd 3: Ch 3 **(counts as first dc, now and throughout)**, 5 dc in next ch-4 sp, (dc in next dc, 5 dc in next ch-4 sp) around; join with slip st to first dc: 72 dc.
Rnd 4: Work beginning Shell, ch 1, (skip next dc, dc in next dc, ch 1) 5 times, skip next dc, ★ work Shell in next dc, ch 1, (skip next dc, dc in next dc, ch 1) 5 times, skip next dc; repeat from ★ around; join with slip st to first dc: 6 Shells.
Rnd 5: Slip st in next dc and in next ch-3 sp, work beginning Shell, ch 3, skip next ch-1 sp, dc in next ch-1 sp, (ch 1, dc in next ch-1 sp) 3 times, ch 3, skip next ch-1 sp, ★ work Shell in next Shell (ch-3 sp), ch 3, skip next ch-1 sp, dc in next ch-1 sp, (ch 1, dc in next ch-1 sp) 3 times, ch 3, skip next ch-1 sp; repeat from ★ around; join with slip st to first dc.
Rnd 6: Slip st in next dc and in next ch-3 sp, work beginning Shell, ch 5, skip next ch-3 sp, dc in next ch-1 sp, (ch 1, dc in next ch-1 sp) twice, ch 5, ★ work Shell in next Shell, ch 5, skip next ch-3 sp, dc in next ch-1 sp, (ch 1, dc in next ch-1 sp) twice, ch 5; repeat from ★ around; join with slip st to first dc.
Rnd 7: Slip st in next dc and in next ch-3 sp, work beginning Shell, ch 7, skip next loop, work 3-dc Cluster, ch 7, (work Shell in next Shell, ch 7, skip next loop, work 3-dc Cluster, ch 7) around; join with slip st to first dc, finish off.

ADDITIONAL MOTIFS

Work same as First Motif through Rnd 6.
Following Placement Diagram, work One-Sided or Two-Sided Joining to form strips for size and shape desired.

ONE-SIDED JOINING

Rnd 7: Slip st in next dc and in next ch-3 sp, work beginning Shell, ch 7, skip next loop, work 3-dc Cluster, ch 7, (work Shell in next Shell, ch 7, skip next loop, work 3-dc Cluster, ch 7) 3 times, 2 dc in next Shell, ch 1, with **right** side facing, sc in corresponding Shell on **previous Motif**, ch 1, 2 dc in same sp on **new Motif**, ch 7, skip next loop, work 3-dc Cluster, sc in top of next 3-dc Cluster on **previous Motif**, ch 7, 2 dc in next Shell on **new Motif**, ch 1, sc in next Shell on **previous Motif**, ch 1, 2 dc in same sp on **new Motif**, ch 7, skip next loop, work 3-dc Cluster, ch 7; join with slip st to first dc, finish off.

TWO-SIDED JOINING

Rnd 7: Slip st in next dc and in next ch-3 sp, work beginning Shell, ch 7, skip next loop, work 3-dc Cluster, ch 7, (work Shell in next Shell, ch 7, skip next loop, work 3-dc Cluster, ch 7) twice, 2 dc in next Shell, ch 1, with **right** side facing, sc in corresponding Shell on **previous Motif**, ch 1, 2 dc in same sp on **new Motif**, ch 7, skip next loop, work 3-dc Cluster, ★ sc in top of next 3-dc Cluster on **previous Motif**, ch 7, 2 dc in next Shell on **new Motif**, ch 1, sc in next Shell on **previous Motif**, ch 1, 2 dc in same sp on **new Motif**, ch 7, skip next loop, work 3-dc Cluster; repeat from ★ once **more**, ch 7; join with slip st to first dc, finish off.

EDGING

Rnd 1: With **right** side facing, join thread with slip st in any Shell; work beginning Shell, ch 5, work (Shell, ch 5) in center ch of each ch-7 loop **and** in each Shell **and** in each joining around; join with slip st to first dc.

Rnd 2: Slip st in next dc and in next ch-3 sp, work beginning Shell, ch 5, (work Shell in next Shell, ch 5) around; join with slip st to first dc.

Rnd 3: Slip st in next dc and in next ch-3 sp, work beginning Shell, ch 3, working **around** ch-5 loop of previous rnd, sc in loop below, ch 3, (work Shell in next Shell, ch 3, working **around** ch-5 loop of previous rnd, sc in loop below, ch 3) around; join with slip st to first dc, finish off.

See Washing and Blocking, page 140.

PLACEMENT DIAGRAMS

Small Hexagon

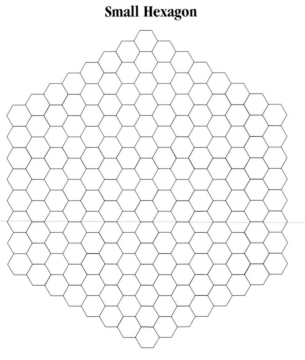

Large Hexagon

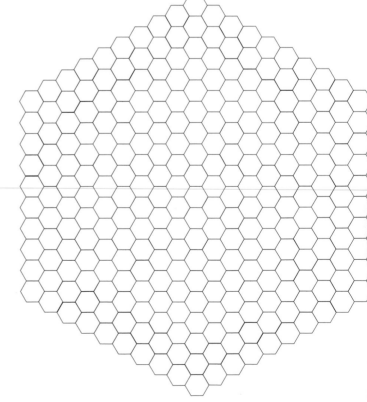

Small Oval

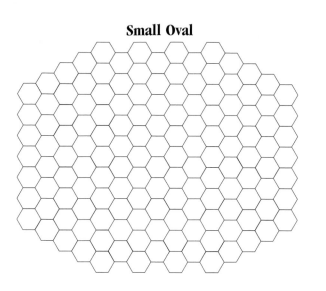

Large Oval

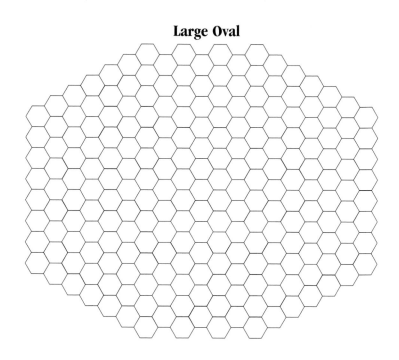

Small Rectangle

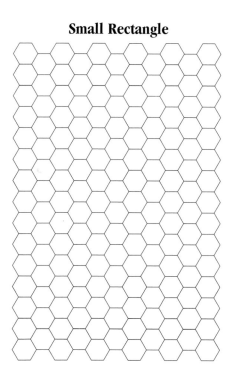

Large Rectangle

FOR THE BEDROOM

This lacy ensemble will encourage guests to drift off to dreamland. (Opposite) Our feminine throw brings to mind the romance of yesteryear. Stitched with soft worsted weight yarn, the pretty afghan is bordered with large scallops and has a double row of satin ribbon laced through its eyelet rounds. (Below) Designed to coordinate with our Victorian lace afghan, these dainty trims reflect its pretty scalloped edging in bedspread weight cotton thread. The trims are attached to a purchased sheet and pillowcases.

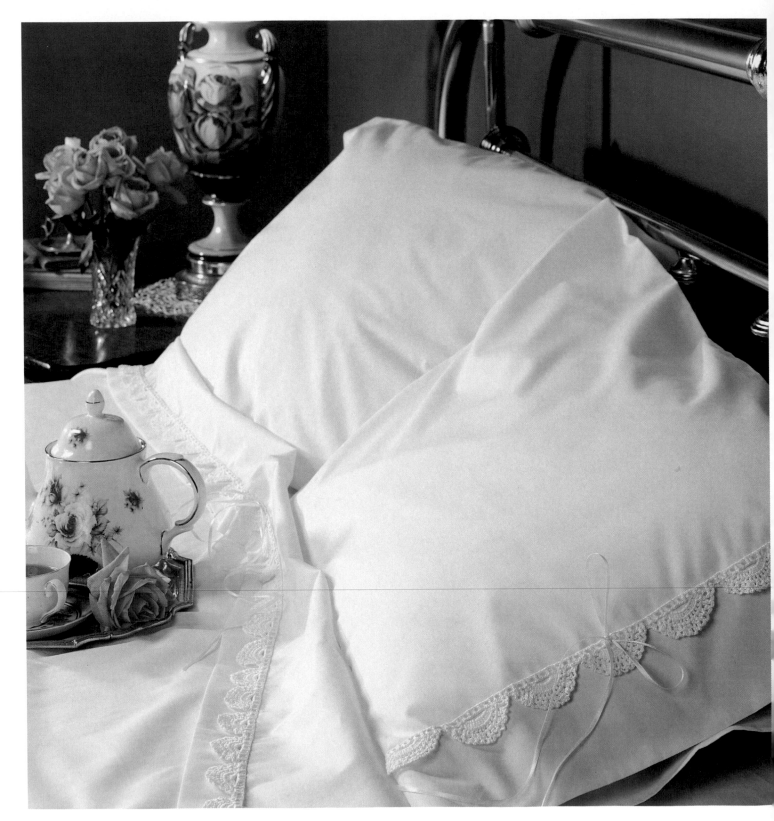

VICTORIAN LACE AFGHAN

Finished Size: Approximately 50" x 71"

MATERIALS

Worsted Weight Yarn, approximately:
39 ounces, (1,110 grams, 2,195 yards)
Crochet hook, size I (5.50 mm) **or** size needed for gauge
14 yards of 1/2" wide satin ribbon
Yarn needle

GAUGE: In pattern, 6 ch-1 sps = 3 1/2" and 4 rows = 3"
2 6-dc groups = 3 1/2"

BODY

Ch 148 **loosely**.

Row 1 (Right side): Dc in sixth ch from hook, (ch 1, skip next ch, dc in next ch) across: 72 sps.

Note: Loop a short piece of yarn around any stitch to mark last row as **right** side.

Row 2: Ch 4 **(counts as first dc plus ch 1, now and throughout)**, turn; (dc in next dc, ch 1) across to last sp, skip next ch, dc in next ch: 73 dc.

Rows 3-6: Ch 4, turn; dc in next dc, (ch 1, dc in next dc) across.

Row 7: Ch 4, turn; (dc in next dc, ch 1) 5 times, 3 dc in next dc, (skip next 2 dc, 6 dc in next dc) 19 times, skip next 2 dc, 3 dc in next dc, (ch 1, dc in next dc) 6 times: 19 6-dc groups.

Rows 8-78: Ch 4, turn; (dc in next dc, ch 1) 5 times, 3 dc in next dc, 6 dc in sp **between** center dc of each 6-dc group across to next 3-dc group, skip next 2 dc, 3 dc in next dc, (ch 1, dc in next dc) 6 times.

Row 79: Ch 4, turn; (dc in next dc, ch 1) 7 times, (skip next dc, dc in next dc, ch 1) across to next ch-1 sp, dc in next dc, (ch 1, dc in next dc) 5 times: 72 ch-1 sps.

Rows 80-84: Repeat Row 3, 5 times; at end of Row 84, do **not** finish off.

EDGING

TOP - FIRST SCALLOP

Row 1: Turn; slip st in first st, (slip st in next sp and in next st) 4 times, ch 7, skip next 4 sps, slip st in next st, slip st in next sp and in next st, leave remaining sts unworked.

Row 2: Turn; work 14 dc in loop, skip next sp, slip st in next st and in next sp, slip st in next st: 14 dc.

Row 3: Ch 1, turn; (dc in next dc, ch 1) 14 times, skip next sp, slip st in next st, slip st in next sp and in next st.

Row 4: Ch 4, turn; (sc in next ch-1 sp, ch 4) 15 times, skip next sp, slip st in next st, slip st in next sp and in next st.

Row 5: Ch 4, turn; (sc in next ch-4 sp, ch 4) 16 times, skip next sp, slip st in next st; do **not** finish off.

TOP - NEXT 5 SCALLOPS

Row 1: (Slip st in next sp and in next st) 4 times, ch 7, skip next 4 sps, slip st in next st, slip st in next sp and in next st, leave remaining sts unworked.

Rows 2-5: Work same as Top - First Scallop.

SIDE - FIRST SCALLOP

Row 1: Working across end of rows, slip st in first sp and in next st (top of dc), (slip st in next sp and in next st) 3 times, ch 7, skip next 4 sps, slip st in next st, slip st in next sp and in next st, leave remaining sts unworked.

Rows 2-5: Work same as Top - First Scallop.

SIDE - NEXT 6 SCALLOPS

Rows 1-5: Work same as Top - Next 5 Scallops.

BOTTOM - FIRST SCALLOP

Row 1: Working in free loops of beginning ch and in ch-1 sps **(Fig. 21b, page 138)**, slip st in first st, (slip st in next sp and in next st) 4 times, ch 7, skip next 4 sps, slip st in next st, slip st in next sp and in next st, leave remaining sts unworked.

Rows 2-5: Work same as Top - First Scallop.

BOTTOM - NEXT 5 SCALLOPS

Rows 1-5: Work same as Top - Next 5 Scallops.

SECOND SIDE

Work same as first Side.
Finish off.

FINISHING

Using photo as a guide for placement, weave ribbon through sps along outer sps of Body; sew ends together.

Leaving 4 sps free between outer ribbons and inner ribbons, weave ribbon through sps along inner sps of Body leaving 10" at each corner of afghan. Repeat for remaining 3 sides.

Tie ends in a bow at each corner.

SHEET AND PILLOWCASE EDGING

Finished Size: Approximately 1¼" wide

MATERIALS
Bedspread Weight Crochet Thread (size 10), approximately:
 200 yards for an Edging 82" (full size sheet)
 45 yards for an Edging 20" (one standard pillowcase)
Steel crochet hook, size 9 (1.40 mm) **or** size needed for gauge
Straight pins
Sewing needle and matching thread
Purchased sheet set
5 yards of ⅛" wide satin ribbon

GAUGE: 22 dc = 2"

BEGINNING CHAIN
Make a chain to fit across the sheet or the pillowcase. The number of chains must be divisible by 24 with 4 remaining. For example, as in our pillowcase, 220 (24 goes into 220, 9 times with 4 remaining). Count the chains and adjust as needed.

FOUNDATION ROW
Dc in sixth ch from hook, (ch 1, skip next ch, dc in next ch) across.

FIRST SCALLOP
Row 1: Turn; slip st in first dc, (slip st in next ch-1 sp and in next dc) 4 times, ch 8, skip next 4 ch-1 sps, slip st in next dc, slip st in next ch-1 sp and in next dc, leave remaining sts unworked.
Row 2: Turn; work 12 dc in loop, skip next ch-1 sp, slip st in next 3 sts: 12 dc.
Row 3: Ch 1, turn; (dc in next dc, ch 1) 12 times, skip next ch-1 sp, slip st in next dc, slip st in next ch-1 sp and in next dc.
Row 4: Ch 4, turn; (sc in next ch-1 sp, ch 4) 13 times, skip next ch-1 sp, slip st in next 3 sts.
Row 5: Ch 4, turn; (sc in next ch-4 sp, ch 4) 14 times, skip next ch-1 sp, slip st in next st; do **not** finish off.

REMAINING SCALLOPS
Row 1: (Slip st in next ch-1 sp and in next dc) 4 times, ch 8, skip next 4 ch-1 sps, slip st in next dc, slip st in next ch-1 sp and in next dc, leave remaining sts unworked.
Rows 2-5: Work same as First Scallop.
Finish off at end of last Scallop.

FINISHING
See Washing and Blocking, page 140.
Beginning at opposite ends, weave 2 separate pieces of ribbon through Foundation Row, working toward center; tack ribbon in place at each end and tie ends in a bow at center.
Using photo as a guide for placement, pin Edging to sheet and pillowcases along hem line.
Sew in place.

IN THE KITCHEN

*F*ashioned in ecru and shades of blue, these nostalgic kitchen accessories feature two favorite quilt patterns
— the Pinwheel and the Square in a Square. (Below) *The pot holders, stitched holding double strands of cotton
worsted weight yarn, are quick to make and extra durable.* (Opposite) *Perfect for everyday use, our long-lasting
dishcloths have old-fashioned charm. Pretty and practical, the nifty towel topper coordinates with our other
kitchen items. It's attached to a purchased kitchen towel and finished with a handy loop for easy hanging.*

Quick SQUARE IN A SQUARE POT HOLDER

Finished Size: Approximately 8³/₄" square

MATERIALS
100% Cotton Worsted Weight Yarn, approximately:
  Color A (Ecru) - 92 yards
  Color B (Dark Blue) - 32 yards
  Color C (Light Blue) - 32 yards
Crochet hook, size G (4.00 mm) **or** size needed for gauge

Note: Entire Pot Holder is worked holding 2 strands of yarn together.

GAUGE: 12 sc and 12 rows = 4"

CENTER
With Color A, ch 17 **loosely**.
Row 1 (Right side): Sc in second ch from hook and in each ch across: 16 sc.
Note: Loop a short piece of yarn around any stitch to mark last row as **right** side.
Rows 2-15: Ch 1, turn; sc in each sc across.
Row 16: Ch 1, turn; sc in each sc across changing to Color B in last sc *(Fig. 22a, page 138)*; do **not** finish off.

FIRST POINT
Row 1: Ch 1, turn; sc in each sc across.
Note: To **decrease**, pull up a loop in next 2 sc, YO and draw through all 3 loops on hook **(counts as one sc)**.
Rows 2-8: Ch 1, turn; decrease, sc in each sc across to last 2 sc, decrease: 2 sc.
Row 9: Ch 1, turn; decrease, finish off.

SECOND POINT
Row 1: With **right** side facing and working in free loops of beginning ch *(Fig. 21b, page 138)*, join Color B with slip st in first ch; ch 1, sc in same st and in each ch across: 16 sc.
Rows 2-9: Work same as First Point.

THIRD POINT
Row 1: With **right** side facing and working across end of rows, join Color C with slip st in first row; ch 1, sc in same row and in each row across: 16 sc.
Rows 2-9: Work same as First Point.

FOURTH POINT
Work same as Third Point.

EDGING
Rnd 1: With **right** side facing, join Color A with slip st in any corner; ch 1, (sc, ch 1) twice in same st, (sc, ch 1) evenly around working (sc, ch 1) twice in each corner; join with slip st to first sc.
Rnd 2: Slip st in first ch-1 sp, ch 1, (sc, ch 8, sc) in same sp, ch 1, (sc in next ch-1 sp, ch 1) across to next corner ch-1 sp, ★ (sc, ch 1) twice in corner ch-1 sp, (sc in next ch-1 sp, ch 1) across to next corner ch-1 sp; repeat from ★ around; join with slip st to first sc, finish off.

Quick PINWHEEL BLOCK POT HOLDER

Finished Size: Approximately 8³/₄" square

MATERIALS
100% Cotton Worsted Weight Yarn, approximately:
  MC (Light Blue) - 80 yards
  CC (Ecru) - 58 yards
Crochet hook, size G (4.00 mm) **or** size needed for gauge
Yarn needle

Note: Entire Pot Holder is worked holding 2 strands of yarn together.

GAUGE: 12 sc and 12 rows = 4"

BLOCK #1
With MC, ch 13 **loosely**.
Row 1 (Right side): Sc in second ch from hook and in next 10 chs changing to CC in last sc worked *(Fig. 22a, page 138)*, drop MC, do **not** cut yarn unless otherwise instructed, sc in last sc: 12 sc.
Note: Loop a short piece of yarn around any stitch to mark last row as **right** side.
Row 2: Ch 1, turn; sc in first 2 sc changing to MC in last sc worked, drop CC, sc in each sc across.
Row 3: Ch 1, turn; sc in each sc working one less sc in MC and changing to CC, drop MC, sc in last MC sc and in each sc across.
Row 4: Ch 1, turn; sc in each CC sc, sc in first MC sc changing to MC, drop CC, sc in each sc across.
Rows 5-11: Repeat Rows 3 and 4, 3 times, then repeat Row 3 once **more**; cut MC.
Row 12: Ch 1, turn; sc in each sc across; finish off.

BLOCK #2
Work same as Block #1 marking Row 2 as **right** side.

BLOCK #3
Work same as Block #1 reversing colors.

BLOCK #4

Work same as Block #1 reversing colors and marking Row 2 as **right** side.

ASSEMBLY

Following Placement Diagram as a guide, with **wrong** sides together and using MC, join Blocks together with Blanket Stitch **(Figs. 30a & b, page 141)** to form 2 strips, then join strips together using Blanket Stitch.

EDGING

With **right** side facing, join MC with slip st in any corner; ch 1, (sc, ch 8, sc) in same st, ch 1, (sc, ch 1) evenly around working (sc, ch 1) twice in each corner; join with slip st to first sc, finish off.

PLACEMENT DIAGRAM

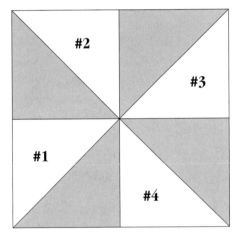

TOWEL TOPPER

Finished Size: Approximately 4¹/₂" square

MATERIALS

100% Cotton Worsted Weight Yarn, approximately:
  MC (Light Blue) - 25 yards
  CC (Ecru) - 18 yards
Crochet hook, size G (4.00 mm) **or** size needed for gauge
Ruler
Scissors
Fabric marking pen
Sewing needle and thread
Pins
Purchased kitchen towel: approximately 16" x 24¹/₂"

Note: Entire Towel Topper is worked holding 2 strands of yarn together.

GAUGE: 12 sc and 12 rows = 4"

With MC, ch 13 **loosely**.

Row 1 (Right side)**:** Sc in second ch from hook and in next 10 chs changing to CC in last sc worked **(Fig. 22a, page 138)**, drop MC, do **not** cut yarn unless otherwise instructed, sc in last sc: 12 sc.

Note: Loop a short piece of yarn around any stitch to mark last row as **right** side.

Row 2: Ch 1, turn; sc in first 2 sc changing to MC in last sc worked, drop CC, sc in each sc across.

Row 3: Ch 1, turn; sc in each sc working one less sc in MC and changing to CC, drop MC, sc in last MC sc and in each sc across.

Row 4: Ch 1, turn; sc in each CC sc, sc in first MC sc changing to MC, drop CC, sc in each sc across.

Rows 5-11: Repeat Rows 3 and 4, 3 times, then repeat Row 3 once **more**.

Row 12: Ch 1, turn; sc in each sc across changing to MC; cut CC.

Edging: Ch 1, turn; 3 sc in first sc, sc in each sc across to last sc, (2 sc, ch 10, slip st in side of last sc made, sc) in last sc **(Fig. 1, page 64)**; sc evenly around working 3 sc in each corner; join with slip st to first sc, finish off.

FINISHING

Trim length of towel to 16¹/₂". Fold towel in half lengthwise and use fabric marking pen to mark the center of the trimmed edge **(Fig. 1)**.

Fig. 1

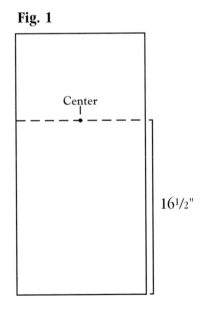

Machine baste close to trimmed edge. Using photo as a guide for placement, gather towel to fit Topper with marked center point matched with bottom point of Topper. Zig-zag over gathers to secure. Pin towel to back of Topper and stitch securely by hand.

Quick DISHCLOTH #1

Finished Size: Approximately 10" square

MATERIALS

100% Cotton Worsted Weight Yarn, approximately:
Dark Blue - 118 yards
Crochet hook, size G (4.00 mm) **or** size needed for gauge

GAUGE: In pattern, 7 V-Sts and 7 rows = 4"

PATTERN STITCHES

V-ST
(Dc, ch 1, dc) in st or sp indicated.

CLUSTER
★ YO, insert hook in ch-1 sp indicated, YO and pull up a loop, YO and draw through 2 loops on hook; repeat from ★ 2 times **more**, YO and draw through all 4 loops on hook (**Figs. 9a & b, page 134**).

Ch 36 **loosely**.

Row 1: Dc in fourth ch from hook, (skip next ch, work V-St in next ch) across to last 2 chs, skip next ch, 2 dc in last ch: 15 V-Sts.

Row 2 (Right side): Ch 3, turn; dc in first dc, ch 1, [work Cluster in next V-St (ch-1 sp), ch 1] across to last 2 sts, skip next dc, YO, insert hook in last st, YO and pull up a loop, YO and draw through 2 loops on hook, YO, insert hook in same st, YO and pull up a loop, YO and draw through 2 loops on hook, YO and draw through all 3 loops on hook: 15 Clusters.

Row 3: Ch 3, turn; work V-St in each ch-1 sp across, skip next dc, dc in top of turning ch: 16 V-Sts.

Row 4: Ch 3, turn; work Cluster in next V-St, (ch 1, work Cluster in next V-St) across, dc in top of turning ch: 16 Clusters.

Row 5: Ch 3, turn; dc in first dc, work V-St in each ch-1 sp across, skip next Cluster, 2 dc in top of turning ch.

Repeat Rows 2-5 until piece measures approximately 9½" from beginning ch, ending by working Row 3 or Row 5.

Edging: Ch 1, turn; 3 sc in first dc, sc evenly around working 3 sc in each corner; join with slip st to first sc, finish off.

Quick DISHCLOTH #2

Finished Size: Approximately 8" x 10"

MATERIALS

100% Cotton Worsted Weight Yarn, approximately:
Light Blue - 102 yards
Crochet hook, size G (4.00 mm) **or** size needed for gauge

GAUGE: 16 hdc and 11 rows = 4"

Ch 33 **loosely**.

Row 1: Hdc in second ch from hook and in each ch across: 32 hdc.

Note: To work **Cross Stitch**, skip next st, hdc in next st, working **around** hdc just worked, hdc in skipped st (**Figs. 14a & b, page 135**).

Row 2 (Right side): Ch 2, turn; hdc in first 10 hdc, work 6 Cross Sts, hdc in last 10 hdc.

Note: Loop a short piece of yarn around any stitch to mark last row as **right** side.

Repeat Row 2 until piece measures approximately 9¼" from beginning ch, ending by working a **wrong** side row.

Last Row: Ch 2, turn; hdc in each hdc across.

Edging: Ch 2, do **not** turn; 2 hdc in same st, work Cross Sts evenly around working 3 hdc in each corner; join with slip st to beginning ch-2, finish off.

Quick DISHCLOTH #3

Finished Size: Approximately 10½" x 10¾"

MATERIALS

100% Cotton Worsted Weight Yarn, approximately:
MC (Dark Blue) - 70 yards
CC (Ecru) - 62 yards
Crochet hook, size G (4.00 mm) **or** size needed for gauge

GAUGE: 16 sc and 16 rows = 4"

With MC, ch 42 **loosely**.

Row 1 (Right side): Sc in second ch from hook and in each ch across: 41 sc.

Row 2: Ch 1, turn; sc in each sc across to last sc changing to CC in last sc worked (**Fig. 22a, page 138**), drop MC, do **not** cut yarn unless otherwise instructed, sc in last sc.

Row 3: Ch 1, turn; sc in first 2 sc changing to MC in last sc worked, drop CC, sc in each sc across.

Row 4: Ch 1, turn; sc in each sc working one less sc in MC and changing to CC, drop MC, sc in last MC sc and in each sc across.

Row 5: Ch 1, turn; sc in each CC sc, sc in first MC sc changing to MC, drop CC, sc in each sc across.

Rows 6-41: Repeat Rows 4 and 5, 18 times.

Row 42: Ch 1, turn; sc in each sc across, finish off CC only.

Edging: With **right** side facing, insert hook in end of Row 40, YO and pull up a loop with MC, ch 1, (sc, ch 1) evenly around working (sc, ch 1) twice in each corner; join with slip st to first sc, finish off.

MANTEL SKIRT

Continued from page 29.

Row 14: Ch 3, turn; 3 dc in first ch-1 sp, ch 1, (3 dc in next ch-1 sp, ch 1) 3 times, skip next 3 dc, 3 dc in next ch, ch 5, skip next 2 dc, dc in next 7 dc, 2 dc in next loop, ch 5, (3 dc in next ch-1 sp, ch 1) 4 times, skip next 2 dc, dc in next dc, ch 2, dc in next 2 dc, ch 5, skip next sc, dc in next 2 dc, leave remaining sts unworked.

Row 15: Ch 3, turn; 3 dc in first dc, dc in next dc, ch 3, sc in next loop, ch 3, dc in next 2 dc, ch 2, skip next dc, 3 dc in next ch-1 sp, (ch 1, 3 dc in next ch-1 sp) 3 times, ch 5, 2 dc in next loop, dc in next 7 dc, ch 5, 3 dc in next loop, (ch 1, 3 dc in next ch-1 sp) 4 times, leave remaining sts unworked.

Row 16: Ch 3, turn; 3 dc in first ch-1 sp, ch 1, (3 dc in next ch-1 sp, ch 1) 3 times, skip next 3 dc, 3 dc in next ch, ch 5, skip next 2 dc, dc in next 7 dc, 2 dc in next loop, ch 5, (3 dc in next ch-1 sp, ch 1) 3 times, skip next 2 dc, dc in next dc, ch 2, dc in next 2 dc, ch 5, skip next sc, dc in next 2 dc, leave remaining sts unworked.

Row 17: Ch 3, turn; 3 dc in first dc, dc in next dc, ch 3, sc in next loop, ch 3, dc in next 2 dc, ch 2, skip next dc, 3 dc in next ch-1 sp, (ch 1, 3 dc in next ch-1 sp) twice, ch 5, 2 dc in next loop, dc in next 7 dc, ch 5, 3 dc in next loop, (ch 1, 3 dc in next ch-1 sp) 4 times, leave remaining sts unworked.

Row 18: Ch 3, turn; 3 dc in first ch-1 sp, ch 1, (3 dc in next ch-1 sp, ch 1) 3 times, skip next 3 dc, 3 dc in next ch, ch 5, skip next 2 dc, dc in next 7 dc, 2 dc in next loop, ch 5, (3 dc in next ch-1 sp, ch 1) twice, skip next 2 dc, dc in next dc, ch 2, dc in next 2 dc, ch 5, skip next sc, dc in next 2 dc, leave remaining sts unworked.

Row 19: Ch 3, turn; 3 dc in first dc, dc in next dc, ch 3, sc in next loop, ch 3, dc in next 2 dc, ch 2, skip next dc, 3 dc in next ch-1 sp, ch 1, 3 dc in next ch-1 sp, ch 5, 2 dc in next loop, dc in next 7 dc, ch 5, 3 dc in next loop, (ch 1, 3 dc in next ch-1 sp) 4 times, leave remaining sts unworked.

Row 20: Ch 3, turn; 3 dc in first ch-1 sp, ch 1, (3 dc in next ch-1 sp, ch 1) 3 times, skip next 3 dc, 3 dc in next ch, ch 5, skip next 2 dc, dc in next 7 dc, 2 dc in next loop, ch 5, 3 dc in next ch-1 sp, ch 1, skip next 2 dc, dc in next dc, ch 2, dc in next 2 dc, ch 5, skip next sc, dc in next 2 dc, leave remaining sts unworked.

Row 21: Ch 3, turn; 3 dc in first dc, dc in next dc, ch 3, sc in next loop, ch 3, dc in next 2 dc, ch 2, skip next dc, 3 dc in next ch-1 sp, ch 5, 2 dc in next loop, dc in next 7 dc, ch 5, 3 dc in next loop, (ch 1, 3 dc in next ch-1 sp) 4 times, leave remaining sts unworked.

Row 22: Ch 3, turn; 3 dc in first ch-1 sp, ch 1, (3 dc in next ch-1 sp, ch 1) 3 times, skip next 3 dc, 3 dc in next ch, ch 5, skip next 2 dc, dc in next 7 dc, 2 dc in next loop, ch 5, skip next 2 dc, dc in next dc, ch 2, dc in next 2 dc, ch 5, skip next sc, dc in next 2 dc, leave remaining sts unworked.

Row 23: Ch 3, turn; 3 dc in first dc, dc in next dc, ch 3, sc in next loop, ch 3, dc in next 2 dc, ch 2, skip next dc, 3 dc in next ch, ch 5, skip next 2 dc, dc in next 7 dc, 2 dc in next loop, ch 5, (3 dc in next ch-1 sp, ch 1) 4 times, (3 dc, ch 3, 3 dc) in last ch-3 sp.

Repeat Rows 2-23 for pattern until desired length, ending by working Row 22; finish off.

FINISHING

See Washing and Blocking, page 140.

Weave ribbon through sps at top of Edging. Turn ends under 1/2" and sew in place.

Make a 1/4" hem on all sides of linen.

Pin dc above ribbon to Edging along hem line of one long side of linen and sew in place.

gifts for all

Reminding friends and family that they're loved is one of life's simple pleasures. In this assortment of unique gifts, there are ideas for conveying this heartfelt message to Mom and Dad on their special days and thanking a best friend for always being there. You'll also find lots of all-occasion gifts and a pretty tote for delivering your presents. Most of these projects are quick to stitch, and all are sure to brighten someone's day.

Quick BASKET FRILLS

Creating personalized gifts is fun and easy with these frilly edgings. Stitched with bedspread weight cotton thread, they can be used to trim baskets brimming with bath pretties, flowers, or fresh-baked goodies.

Finished Size: Edging #1- approximately ⁵/₈" wide
Edging #2 - approximately 1¼" wide
Edging #3 - approximately 1½" wide

MATERIALS
Bedspread Weight Cotton Thread (size 10), approximately:
Edging #1 - 1¼ yards per inch
Edging #2 - 1²/₃ yards per inch
Edging #3 - 2 yards per inch
Steel crochet hook, size 6 (1.80 mm) **or** size needed for gauge
Glue gun
Basket

GAUGE: 8 sts = 1"

MULTIPLES
All 3 of these Edgings are written using multiples. This enables you to make the Edgings the length needed for use on any size basket.
For Edging #1 and Edging #2, the multiple plus the number of chains needed for the first row is given.
Make the beginning chain long enough to fit around the basket. The beginning chain must be divisible by the multiple with the amount indicated left over. Count the chains and adjust as needed.

For example, our basket for Edging #1 measures 16" around and requires a beginning chain of 130 chains (8 goes into 130, 16 times with 2 left over).
Edging #3 is worked for a multiple of 3 + 1 row to enable the Border on the end of rows to work.

EDGING #1
Make a chain with a multiple of 8 + 2 chs to fit around the basket; adjust chs as needed.
Row 1: Sc in second ch from hook and in each ch across.
Row 2 (Right side)**:** Ch 1, turn; sc in first sc, ★ skip next 3 sc, tr in next sc, (ch 1, tr in same sc) 5 times, skip next 3 sc, sc in next sc; repeat from ★ across.
Note: Loop a short piece of thread around any stitch to mark last row as **right** side.
Row 3: Ch 2, turn; (slip st in next ch-1 sp, ch 2) 5 times, slip st in next sc, ★ ch 2, (slip st in next ch-1 sp, ch 2) 5 times, slip st in next sc; repeat from ★ across; finish off.

See Washing and Blocking, page 140.
Glue Edging to basket.

You're Sweet!

EDGING #2

Make a chain with a multiple of 12 + 9 chs to fit around the basket; adjust chs as needed.

Row 1 (Right side): Dc in seventh ch from hook, (ch 1, skip next ch, dc in next ch) across.

Note: Loop a short piece of thread around any stitch to mark last row as **right** side.

Row 2: Ch 1, turn; sc in first ch-1 sp, ★ ch 3, sc in next ch-1 sp, ch 5, skip next ch-1 sp, sc in next ch-1 sp; repeat from ★ across to last sp, ch 1, hdc in last sp to form last sp.

Row 3: Ch 1, turn; sc in same sp, ch 3, sc in next ch-5 sp, (3 dc, ch 3, 3 dc) in next ch-3 sp, sc in next ch-5 sp, ★ (ch 3, sc in next sp) twice, (3 dc, ch 3, 3 dc) in next ch-3 sp, sc in next ch-5 sp; repeat from ★ across to last ch-3 sp, ch 3, sc in last ch-3 sp.

Row 4: Ch 1, turn; sc in first sc, ★ ch 3, sc in next ch-3 sp, ch 5, (sc, ch 3, sc) in next ch-3 sp (between 3-dc groups), ch 5, sc in next ch-3 sp; repeat from ★ across, ch 1, hdc in last sc to form last sp.

Row 5: Ch 1, turn; sc in same sp, ch 4, sc in next ch-5 sp and in next ch-3 sp, (ch 3, sc in same sp) 4 times, ★ (sc in next sp, ch 4) twice, sc in next ch-5 sp and in next ch-3 sp, (ch 3, sc in same sp) 4 times; repeat from ★ across to last 2 sps, sc in next ch-5 sp, ch 4, sc in last ch-3 sp; finish off.

See Washing and Blocking, page 140.
Glue Edging to basket.

EDGING #3

FOUNDATION

Ch 11 **loosely**.

Row 1: Dc in eighth ch from hook, ch 2, skip next 2 chs, dc in last ch: 2 sps.

Row 2: Ch 5, turn; dc in next dc, ch 2, skip next 2 chs, dc in next ch.

Repeat Row 2 for desired length, ending by working a multiple of 3 + 1 row; do **not** finish off.

BORDER

Ch 1, working in end of rows, sc in first row, ★ ch 10, slip st in sixth ch from hook to form a ring, (sc, hdc, 9 dc, hdc, sc) in ring, ch 4, skip next 2 rows, sc in next row; repeat from ★ across; working in sps and in free loops of beginning ch *(Fig. 21b, page 138)*, sc evenly across; 3 sc in end of each row across; sc evenly across last row of Foundation; join with slip st to first sc, finish off.

See Washing and Blocking, page 140.
Glue Edging to basket.

COZY LAP ROBE

Smaller than traditional afghans, our cozy lap robe is ideal for wrapping the legs in an extra layer of warmth. This handsome piece is crocheted with worsted weight yarn in deep autumn hues. Leaf stitches create its distinctive pattern, which is sure to appeal to a special gentleman.

Finished Size: Approximately 34" x 39"

MATERIALS

Worsted Weight Yarn, approximately:
  Color A (Green) - 12 ounces, (340 grams, 770 yards)
  Color B (Rust) - 11 ounces, (310 grams, 705 yards)
  Crochet hook, size I (5.50 mm) **or** size needed for guage

GAUGE: 14 sc and 14 rows = 4"

PATTERN STITCH
LEAF

Working **below** next sc, insert hook in sc one row **below** and 2 sc to the **right**, YO and pull up a loop *(Fig. 1a)*, insert hook in sc 2 rows **below** and one sc to the **right**, YO and pull up a loop, insert hook in sc 3 rows **below**, YO and pull up a loop, insert hook in sc 2 rows **below** and one sc to the **left**, YO and pull up a loop, insert hook in sc one row **below** and 2 sc to the **left**, YO and pull up a loop, YO and draw through all 6 loops on hook *(Fig. 1b)*. Skip sc behind Leaf.

Fig. 1a

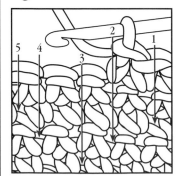

Fig. 1b

BODY

With Color B, ch 114 **loosely**.

Row 1 (Right side)**:** Sc in second ch from hook and in each ch across: 113 sc.

Note: Loop a short piece of yarn around any stitch to mark last row as **right** side.

Rows 2-4: Ch 1, turn; sc in each sc across changing to Color A in last sc worked on Row 4 ***(Fig. 22a, page 138)***.

Row 5: Ch 1, turn; sc in first 4 sc, work Leaf, (sc in next 7 sc, work Leaf) across to last 4 sc, sc in last 4 sc: 14 Leaves.

Rows 6-8: Ch 1, turn; sc in each st across changing to Color B in last sc worked on Row 8.

Row 9: Ch 1, turn; sc in first 8 sc, work Leaf, (sc in next 7 sc, work Leaf) across to last 8 sc, sc in last 8 sc: 13 Leaves.

Rows 10-132: Repeat Rows 2-9, 15 times, then repeat Rows 2-4 once **more**; do **not** finish off.

EDGING

Rnd 1: Ch 1, turn; 3 sc in first sc, sc in next 3 sc, work Leaf, (sc in next 7 sc, work Leaf) across to last 4 sc, sc in next 3 sc, 3 sc in last sc; sc in end of each row across; working in free loops of beginning ch ***(Fig. 21b, page 138)***, 3 sc in first ch, sc in each ch across to last ch, 3 sc in last ch; sc in end of each row across; join with slip st to first sc.

Rnd 2: Ch 1, do **not** turn; sc in same st, ch 1, sc in side of sc just worked ***(Fig. 1, page 64)***, skip next st, (sc in next st, ch 1, sc in side of sc just worked, skip next st) around; join with slip st to first sc, finish off.

RUFFLED PEACOCK SHAWL

This ruffled shawl will please the woman who prefers classic elegance. Featuring rows of lacy pineapples, the extra-full wrap is perfect for days when just a light cover-up is needed.

Finished Measurement: Approximately 26" across
top edge x 31" long

MATERIALS

Worsted Weight Yarn, approximately:
   23 ounces, (650 grams, 1,340 yards)
Crochet hook, size F (3.75 mm) **or** size needed for gauge
³/₈" Button
Sewing needle and thread

GAUGE: 18 sc = 4"

BODY

Ch 132 **loosely.**

Row 1 (Right side)**:** Dc in fourth ch from hook, ★ ch 7, skip next 5 chs, sc in next ch, ch 3, skip next 2 chs, sc in next ch, ch 7, skip next 5 chs, dc in next 2 chs; repeat from ★ across: 16 ch-5 loops.

Note: Loop a short piece of yarn around any stitch to mark last row as **right** side.

Row 2: Ch 3 **(counts as first dc, now and throughout)**, turn; dc in next dc, ★ ch 3, sc in next loop, ch 6, skip next ch-3 sp, sc in next loop, ch 3, dc in next 2 dc; repeat from ★ across.

Row 3: Ch 3, turn; dc in next dc, ★ skip next ch-3 sp, 11 tr in next loop, dc in next 2 dc; repeat from ★ across: 8 tr groups.

Row 4: Ch 3, turn; dc in next dc, ★ ch 1, sc in next tr, (ch 3, skip next tr, sc in next tr) 5 times, ch 1, dc in next 2 dc; repeat from ★ across: 40 ch-3 sps.

Row 5: Ch 3, turn; dc in next dc, ★ ch 2, skip next ch-1 sp, sc in next ch-3 sp, (ch 3, sc in next ch-3 sp) 4 times, ch 2, dc in next 2 dc; repeat from ★ across: 48 sps.

Row 6: Ch 3, turn; dc in next dc, ch 3, skip next ch-2 sp, (sc in next ch-3 sp, ch 3) 4 times, ★ dc in next dc, ch 6, dc in next dc, ch 3, skip next ch-2 sp, (sc in next ch-3 sp, ch 3) 4 times; repeat from ★ across to last 2 dc, dc in last 2 dc.

Row 7: Ch 3, turn; dc in next dc, ch 4, skip next ch-3 sp, sc in next ch-3 sp, (ch 3, sc in next ch-3 sp) twice, ★ ch 2, 2 dc in next ch-3 sp, 11 tr in next loop, 2 dc in next ch-3 sp, ch 2, sc in next ch-3 sp, (ch 3, sc in next ch-3 sp) twice; repeat from ★ across to last ch-3 sp, ch 4, dc in last 2 dc: 7 tr groups.

Row 8: Ch 3, turn; dc in next dc, ch 7, skip next ch-4 sp, sc in next ch-3 sp, ch 3, sc in next ch-3 sp, ch 7, dc in next 2 dc, ★ ch 1, sc in next tr, (ch 3, skip next tr, sc in next tr) 5 times, ch 1, dc in next 2 dc, ch 7, skip next ch-2 sp, sc in next ch-3 sp, ch 3, sc in next ch-3 sp, ch 7, dc in next 2 dc; repeat from ★ across.

Row 9: Ch 3, turn; dc in next dc, ch 3, sc in next loop, ch 6, skip next ch-3 sp, sc in next loop, ch 3, dc in next 2 dc, ★ ch 2, skip next ch-1 sp, sc in next ch-3 sp, (ch 3, sc in next ch-3 sp) 4 times, ch 2, dc in next 2 dc, ch 3, sc in next loop, ch 6, skip next ch-3 sp, sc in next loop, ch 3, dc in next 2 dc; repeat from ★ across.

Row 10: Ch 3, turn; dc in next dc, skip next ch-3 sp, 11 tr in next loop, dc in next 2 dc, ★ ch 3, skip next ch-2 sp, (sc in next ch-3 sp, ch 3) 4 times, dc in next 2 dc, skip next ch-3 sp, 11 tr in next loop, dc in next 2 dc; repeat from ★ across: 8 tr groups.

Row 11: Ch 3, turn; dc in next dc, ch 1, sc in next tr, (ch 3, skip next tr, sc in next tr) 5 times, ch 1, dc in next 2 dc, ★ ch 4, skip next ch-3 sp, sc in next ch-3 sp, (ch 3, sc in next ch-3 sp) twice, ch 4, dc in next 2 dc, ch 1, sc in next tr, (ch 3, skip next tr, sc in next tr) 5 times, ch 1, dc in next 2 dc; repeat from ★ across.

Row 12: Ch 3, turn; dc in next dc, ch 2, skip next ch-1 sp, sc in next ch-3 sp, (ch 3, sc in next ch-3 sp) 4 times, ch 2, dc in next 2 dc, ★ ch 7, skip next ch-4 sp, sc in next ch-3 sp, ch 3, sc in next ch-3 sp, ch 7, dc in next 2 dc, ch 2, skip next ch-1 sp, sc in next ch-3 sp, (ch 3, sc in next ch-3 sp) 4 times, ch 2, dc in next 2 dc; repeat from ★ across.

Row 13: Ch 3, turn; dc in next dc, ch 3, skip next ch-2 sp, (sc in next ch-3 sp, ch 3) 4 times, dc in next 2 dc, ★ ch 3, sc in next loop, ch 6, skip next ch-3 sp, sc in next loop, ch 3, dc in next 2 dc, ch 3, skip next ch-2 sp, (sc in next ch-3 sp, ch 3) 4 times, dc in next 2 dc; repeat from ★ across.

Row 14: Ch 3, turn; dc in next dc, ch 4, skip next ch-3 sp, sc in next ch-3 sp, (ch 3, sc in next ch-3 sp) twice, ch 4, dc in next 2 dc, ★ skip next ch-3 sp, 11 tr in next loop, dc in next 2 dc, ch 4, skip next ch-3 sp, sc in next ch-3 sp, (ch 3, sc in next ch-3 sp) twice, ch 4, dc in next 2 dc; repeat from ★ across: 7 tr groups.

Row 15: Ch 3, turn; dc in next dc, ch 7, skip next ch-4 sp, sc in next ch-3 sp, ch 3, sc in next ch-3 sp, ch 7, dc in next 2 dc, ★ ch 1, sc in next tr, (ch 3, skip next tr, sc in next tr) 5 times, ch 1, dc in next 2 dc, ch 7, skip next ch-4 sp, sc in next ch-3 sp, ch 3, sc in next ch-3 sp, ch 7, dc in next 2 dc; repeat from ★ across.

Rows 16-24: Repeat Rows 9-15 once, then repeat Rows 9 and 10 once **more.**

Row 25: Ch 3, turn; dc in next dc, ch 1, sc in next tr, (ch 3, skip next tr, sc in next tr) 5 times, ch 1, ★ dc in next dc, ch 6, dc in next dc, ch 4, skip next ch-3 sp, sc in next ch-3 sp, (ch 3, sc in next ch-3 sp) twice, ch 4, dc in next dc, ch 6, dc in next dc, ch 1, sc in next tr, (ch 3, skip next tr, sc in next tr) 5 times, ch 1; repeat from ★ across to last 2 dc, dc in last 2 dc.

Row 26: Ch 3, turn; dc in next dc, ch 2, skip next ch-1 sp, sc in next ch-3 sp, (ch 3, sc in next ch-3 sp) 4 times, ch 2, ★ 2 dc in next ch-1 sp, 11 tr in next loop, 2 dc in next ch-4 sp, ch 7, sc in next ch-3 sp, ch 3, sc in next ch-3 sp, ch 7, 2 dc in next ch-4 sp, 11 tr in next loop, 2 dc in next ch-1 sp, ch 2, sc in next ch-3 sp, (ch 3, sc in next ch-3 sp) 4 times, ch 2; repeat from ★ across to last ch-1 sp, dc in last 2 dc: 14 tr groups.

Row 27: Ch 3, turn; dc in next dc, ch 3, skip next ch-2 sp, (sc in next ch-3 sp, ch 3) 4 times, dc in next 2 dc, ★ ch 1, sc in next tr, (ch 3, skip next tr, sc in next tr) 5 times, ch 1, dc in next 2 dc, ch 3, sc in next loop, ch 6, skip next ch-3 sp, sc in next loop, ch 3, dc in next 2 dc, ch 1, sc in next tr, (ch 3, skip next tr, sc in next tr) 5 times, ch 1, dc in next 2 dc, ch 3, skip next ch-2 sp, (sc in next ch-3 sp, ch 3) 4 times, dc in next 2 dc; repeat from ★ across: 124 ch-3 sps.

Row 28: Ch 3, turn; dc in next dc, ch 4, skip next ch-3 sp, sc in next ch-3 sp, (ch 3, sc in next ch-3 sp) twice, ch 4, dc in next 2 dc, ★ ch 2, skip next ch-1 sp, sc in next ch-3 sp, (ch 3, sc in next ch-3 sp) 4 times, ch 2, dc in next 2 dc, 11 tr in next loop, dc in next 2 dc, ch 2, skip next ch-1 sp, sc in next ch-3 sp, (ch 3, sc in next ch-3 sp) 4 times, ch 2, dc in next 2 dc, ch 4, skip next ch-3 sp, sc in next ch-3 sp, (ch 3, sc in next ch-3 sp) twice, ch 4, dc in next 2 dc; repeat from ★ across: 7 tr groups.

Row 29: Ch 3, turn; dc in next dc, ch 7, skip next ch-4 sp, sc in next ch-3 sp, ch 3, sc in next ch-3 sp, ch 7, dc in next 2 dc, ★ ch 3, skip next ch-2 sp, (sc in next ch-3 sp, ch 3) 4 times, dc in next 2 dc, ch 1, sc in next tr, (ch 3, skip next tr, sc in next tr) 5 times, ch 1, dc in next 2 dc, ch 3, skip next ch-2 sp, (sc in next ch-3 sp, ch 3) 4 times, dc in next 2 dc, ch 7, skip next ch-4 sp, sc in next ch-3 sp, ch 3, sc in next ch-3 sp, ch 7, dc in next 2 dc; repeat from ★ across.

Row 30: Ch 3, turn; dc in next dc, ch 3, sc in next loop, ch 6, skip next ch-3 sp, sc in next loop, ch 3, dc in next 2 dc, ★ ch 4, skip next ch-3 sp, sc in next ch-3 sp, (ch 3, sc in next ch-3 sp) twice, ch 4, dc in next 2 dc, ch 2, skip next ch-1 sp, sc in next ch-3 sp, (ch 3, sc in next ch-3 sp) 4 times, ch 2, dc in next 2 dc, ch 4, skip next ch-3 sp, sc in next ch-3 sp, (ch 3, sc in next ch-3 sp) twice, ch 4, dc in next 2 dc, ch 3, sc in next loop, ch 6, skip next ch-3 sp, sc in next loop, ch 3, dc in next 2 dc; repeat from ★ across.

Row 31: Ch 3, turn; dc in next dc, 11 tr in next loop, dc in next 2 dc, ★ ch 7, skip next ch-4 sp, sc in next ch-3 sp, ch 3, sc in next ch-3 sp, ch 7, dc in next 2 dc, ch 3, skip next ch-2 sp, (sc in next ch-3 sp, ch 3) 4 times, dc in next 2 dc, ch 7, skip next ch-4 sp, sc in next ch-3 sp, ch 3, sc in next ch-3 sp, ch 7, dc in next 2 dc, 11 tr in next loop, dc in next 2 dc; repeat from ★ across: 8 tr groups.

Row 32: Ch 3, turn; dc in next dc, ch 1, sc in next tr, (ch 3, skip next tr, sc in next tr) 5 times, ch 1, dc in next 2 dc, ★ ch 3, sc in next loop, ch 6, skip next ch-3 sp, sc in next loop, ch 3, dc in next 2 dc, ch 4, skip next ch-3 sp, sc in next ch-3 sp, (ch 3, sc in next ch-3 sp) twice, ch 4, dc in next 2 dc, ch 3, sc in next loop, ch 6, skip next ch-3 sp, sc in next loop, ch 3, dc in next 2 dc, ch 1, sc in next tr, (ch 3, skip next tr, sc in next tr) 5 times, ch 1, dc in next 2 dc; repeat from ★ across.

Row 33: Ch 3, turn; dc in next dc, ch 2, skip next ch-1 sp, sc in next ch-3 sp, (ch 3, sc in next ch-3 sp) 4 times, ch 2, dc in next 2 dc, ★ 11 tr in next loop, dc in next 2 dc, ch 7, skip next ch-4 sp, sc in next ch-3 sp, ch 3, sc in next ch-3 sp, ch 7, dc in next 2 dc, 11 tr in next loop, dc in next 2 dc, ch 2, skip next ch-1 sp, sc in next ch-3 sp, (ch 3, sc in next ch-3 sp) 4 times, ch 2, dc in next 2 dc; repeat from ★ across: 14 tr groups.

Rows 34-47: Repeat Rows 27-33 twice; do **not** finish off.

EDGING

Rnd 1: Ch 4, do **not** turn; 2 dc in same st; work 96 dc evenly spaced across end of rows; working in skipped ch-sps of beginning ch, work 76 sc evenly spaced across; work 96 dc evenly spaced across end of rows; working in Back Loop Only of each st and in each ch across last row *(Fig. 20, page 138)*, (2 dc, tr) in first dc, 2 tr in next st, (tr in next st, 2 tr in next st) across; join with slip st to top of beginning ch-4.

Rnd 2: (Ch 3, skip next st, slip st in Back Loop Only of next st) around, working last slip st in same st as joining; finish off.

Sew on button.

Quick PRETTY BOOKMARKS

A friend who loves to read will treasure this novel gift idea! Our pretty bookmarks, stitched with bedspread weight cotton thread and accented with satin ribbon, are sweet tokens that work up quickly. As an added surprise, present one of the page-keepers tucked inside a special book.

Finished Size: Bookmark #1 - approximately 1¹/₂" x 6¹/₂"
Bookmark #2 - approximately 1¹/₂" x 6³/₄"

MATERIALS
Bedspread Weight Cotton Thread (size 10),
approximately 20 yards **each**
Steel crochet hook, size 8 (1.50 mm) **or** size needed for gauge
Bookmark #1 - 10" length of ³/₈" wide ribbon
Bookmark #2 - 20" length of ¹/₈" wide ribbon

GAUGE: 20 dc and 8 rows = 2"

BOOKMARK #1

Foundation Row (Right side)**:** Ch 60; tr in eighth ch from hook and in next ch, ch 2, (skip next 2 chs, tr in next 2 chs, ch 2) across to last 3 chs, skip next 2 chs, tr in last ch: 14 sps.

Rnd 1: Ch 3, dc in sp at end of Foundation Row, (ch 3, dc in third ch from hook) twice, 2 dc in same sp, † (ch 3, dc in third ch from hook) twice, dc in same sp, dc in sp **between** next 2 tr, ★ dc in next sp, (ch 3, dc in third ch from hook) twice, dc in same sp, dc in sp **between** next 2 tr; repeat from ★ across to last sp †, dc in last sp, [(ch 3, dc in third ch from hook) twice, 2 dc in same sp] twice; repeat from † to † once, dc in same sp as beginning ch-3, (ch 3, dc in third ch from hook) twice; join with slip st to top of beginning ch-3.

Rnd 2: Slip st in first ch-3 sp, ch 1, sc in same sp, (ch 5, sc in next ch-3 sp) twice, (ch 4, sc in next ch-3 sp) 27 times, (ch 5, sc in next ch-3 sp) 3 times, (ch 4, sc in next ch-3 sp) across, ch 5; join with slip st to first sc, finish off.

FINISHING
See Washing and Blocking, page 140.
Using photo as a guide for placement, weave ribbon through center sps.

BOOKMARK #2
Row 1 (Right side)**:** Ch 18, dc in sixth ch from hook, (ch 1, skip next ch, dc in next ch) across: 7 sps.

Row 2: Ch 4 **(counts as first dc plus ch 1, now and throughout)**, turn; (skip next ch, dc in next dc, ch 1) twice, skip next ch and next dc, 3 dc in next ch-1 sp, ch 1, skip next dc and next ch, dc in next dc, (ch 1, skip next ch, dc in next dc) twice: 9 dc.

Row 3: Ch 4, turn; skip next ch, dc in next dc, ch 1, skip next ch and next dc, 3 dc in next ch-1 sp, ch 1, skip next 3 dc, 3 dc in next ch-1 sp, ch 1, skip next dc and next ch, dc in next dc, ch 1, skip next ch, dc in last dc: 10 dc.

Row 4: Ch 4, turn; skip next ch and next dc, 3 dc in next ch-1 sp, ch 1, skip next 2 dc, dc in next dc, ch 1, skip next ch, dc in next dc, ch 1, skip next 2 dc, 3 dc in next ch-1 sp, ch 1, skip next dc and next ch, dc in last dc.

Row 5: Ch 3 **(counts as first dc, now and throughout)**, turn; 2 dc in next ch-1 sp, ch 1, skip next 2 dc, dc in next dc, ch 1, (skip next ch, dc in next dc, ch 1) 3 times, skip next 2 dc, 3 dc in last ch-1 sp.

Row 6: Ch 4, turn; skip next 2 dc, 3 dc in next ch-1 sp, ch 1, skip next dc and next ch, dc in next dc, ch 1, skip next ch, dc in next dc, ch 1, skip next ch and next dc, 3 dc in next ch-1 sp, ch 1, skip next 2 dc, dc in last dc.

Row 7: Ch 4, turn; skip next ch, dc in next dc, ch 1, (skip next 2 dc, 3 dc in next ch-1 sp, ch 1) twice, skip next 2 dc, dc in next dc, ch 1, skip next ch, dc in last dc.

Row 8: Ch 4, turn; (skip next ch, dc in next dc, ch 1) twice, skip next 2 dc, 3 dc in next ch-1 sp, ch 1, skip next 2 dc, dc in next dc, (ch 1, skip next ch, dc in next dc) twice: 9 dc.

Rows 9-26: Repeat Rows 3-8, 3 times.

Row 27: Ch 4, turn; (skip next ch, dc in next dc, ch 1) 3 times, skip next dc, dc in next dc, (ch 1, skip next ch, dc in next dc) across: 8 dc.

Edging: Do **not** turn; † ch 5, working in end of rows, skip first row, sc in next row, ch 5, (skip next row, sc in next row, ch 5) across to last row, skip last row †; working in free loops of beginning ch *(Fig. 21b, page 138)* and in sps, sc in first ch, (sc in next ch-1 sp, sc in next ch) across, repeat from † to † once; working across last row, sc in first dc, (sc in next ch-1 sp, sc in next dc) across; join with slip st to first ch of beginning ch-5, finish off.

ROMANTIC DOILY

*R*eflecting the elegance of the Victorian Era, this enchanting doily is a charming remembrance *for someone who's a romantic at heart. The light, airy creation is fashioned with cotton thread.*

Finished Size: Approximately 13¹/₂" in diameter

MATERIALS
Bedspread Weight Cotton Thread (size 10),
   approximately 162 yards
Steel crochet hook, size 7 (1.65 mm) **or** size needed for gauge

GAUGE: Rnds 1-3 = 2¹/₂"

PATTERN STITCHES
BEGINNING CLUSTER
Ch 4, ★ YO twice, insert hook in st or sp indicated, YO and pull up a loop, (YO and draw through 2 loops on hook) twice; repeat from ★ once **more**, YO and draw through all 3 loops on hook *(Figs. 9a & b, page 134)*.
CLUSTER
★ YO twice, insert hook in st or sp indicated, YO and pull up a loop, (YO and draw through 2 loops on hook) twice; repeat from ★ 2 times **more**, YO and draw through all 4 loops on hook.

CENTER
Ch 6; join with slip st to form a ring.
Rnd 1 (Right side): Ch 3, 11 dc in ring; join with slip st to top of beginning ch-3: 12 sts.
Note: Loop a short piece of thread around any stitch to mark last round as **right** side.
Rnd 2: Working in Back Loops Only *(Fig. 20, page 138)*, work beginning Cluster in same st, ch 3, (work Cluster in next dc, ch 3) around; join with slip st to top of beginning Cluster: 12 Clusters.

Rnd 3: Slip st in first ch-3 sp, ch 1, sc in same sp, ch 3, work Cluster in next ch-3 sp, (ch 2, work Cluster) twice in same sp, ch 3, ★ sc in next ch-3 sp, ch 3, work Cluster in next ch-3 sp, (ch 2, work Cluster) twice in same sp, ch 3; repeat from ★ around; join with slip st to first sc: 18 Clusters.
Rnd 4: Slip st in first ch-3 sp, ch 1, sc in same sp, (ch 6, sc in next sp) around, ch 3, dc in first sc to form last loop: 24 loops.
Rnd 5: Ch 1, sc in same loop, (ch 6, sc in next loop) around, ch 3, dc in first sc to form last loop.
Rnds 6 and 7: Ch 1, sc in same loop, (ch 8, sc in next loop) around, ch 4, tr in first sc to form last loop.
Rnd 8: Ch 1, sc in same loop, ch 10, (sc in next loop, ch 10) around; join with slip st to first sc.
Rnd 9: Slip st in first loop, ch 1, (5 sc, ch 5, 5 sc) in same loop and in each loop around; join with slip st to first sc, finish off: 24 loops.

CLUSTER RING
Ch 5; join with slip st to form a ring.
Row 1: Work beginning Cluster in ring, ch 3, work (Cluster, ch 4, Cluster, ch 3, Cluster) in ring, ch 5, with **right** side of Center facing, sc in any loop.
Row 2: Ch 5, turn; skip first loop and next ch-3 sp, in next ch-4 sp work (Cluster, ch 3, Cluster, ch 4, Cluster, ch 3, Cluster).
Row 3: Ch 5, turn; skip first ch-3 sp, in next ch-4 sp work (Cluster, ch 3, Cluster, ch 4, Cluster, ch 3, Cluster), ch 5, sc in next loop on Center.
Rows 4-47: Repeat Rows 2 and 3, 22 times.
Row 48: Ch 5, turn; skip first loop and next ch-3 sp, work (Cluster, ch 3, Cluster) in next ch-4 sp, ch 2, slip st in beginning ring on Row 1, ch 2, work (Cluster, ch 3, Cluster) in same ch-4 sp, ch 5; join with slip st to top of beginning Cluster on Row 1, finish off.

FINISHING
See Washing and Blocking, page 140.
Using photo as a guide for placement, weave ribbon through sps, criss-crossing ends at bottom.

BORDER

Rnd 1: With **right** side facing and working in end of rows on Cluster Ring, join thread with slip st in last ch-5 loop worked; ch 8, tr in same loop, ch 10, skip next ch-3 sp, ★ (tr, ch 4, tr) in next ch-5 loop, ch 10, skip next ch-3 sp; repeat from ★ around; join with slip st to fourth ch of beginning ch-8: 24 ch-10 loops.

Rnd 2: Slip st in first ch-4 sp, ch 1, (2 sc, ch 5, 2 sc) in same sp, (5 sc, ch 5, 5 sc) in next loop, ★ (2 sc, ch 5, 2 sc) in next ch-4 sp, (5 sc, ch 5, 5 sc) in next loop; repeat from ★ around; join with slip st to first sc: 48 loops.

Rnd 3: Slip st in next sc and in next loop, work beginning Cluster in same loop, ch 3, work (Cluster, ch 3) 3 times in same loop, sc in next loop, ch 3, ★ work (Cluster, ch 3) 4 times in next loop, sc in next loop, ch 3; repeat from ★ around; join with slip st to top of beginning Cluster: 24 4-Cluster groups.

Rnd 4: Slip st in first ch-3 sp, ch 1, (2 sc, ch 5, 2 sc) in same sp and in each of next 2 sps, 4 sc in each of next 2 sps, ★ (2 sc, ch 5, 2 sc) in each of next 3 sps, 4 sc in each of next 2 sps; repeat from ★ around; join with slip st to first sc, finish off.

See Washing and Blocking, page 140.

Quick FRIENDSHIP CUP

Give this whimsical teacup and saucer to a dear friend as a reminder of the special bond you share. Crocheted with blue and white fabric strips, the cup can be filled with tea bags and presented with a thoughtful friendship verse.

Finished Size: Approximately 7" in diameter x 3¹/₂" high

MATERIALS

100% Cotton Fabric, 44/45" wide, approximately:
   MC (White) - ³/₄ yard
   CC (Blue) - ¹/₄ yard
Crochet hook, size K (6.50 mm)

Prepare fabric and cut into 1" wide strips *(see Preparing Fabric Strips and Joining Fabric Strips, page 139)*.

SAUCER - Rnd 1 (Right side): With MC, ch 4, 11 dc in fourth ch from hook; join with slip st to Back Loop Only of beginning ch *(Fig. 20, page 138)*: 12 sts.
Note: Loop a scrap piece of fabric around any stitch to mark last round as **right** side.
Rnd 2: Ch 3 **(counts as first dc, now and throughout)**, working in Back Loops Only, dc in same st, 2 dc in next dc and in each dc around; join with slip st to both loops of first dc: 24 dc.
Rnd 3: Ch 3, working in both loops, 2 dc in next dc, (dc in next dc, 2 dc in next dc) around; join with slip st to first dc, finish off: 36 dc.

Rnd 4: With **right** side facing, join CC with slip st in any st; ch 1, sc in same st and in next 4 dc, 2 sc in next dc, (sc in next 5 dc, 2 sc in next dc) around; join with slip st to first sc, finish off: 42 sc.
CUP - Rnd 1: With **wrong** side facing, Rnds 2-4 forward, and working in free loops on Rnd 1 *(Fig. 21a, page 138)*, join MC with slip st in top of beginning ch; ch 1, 2 sc in same st, sc in next dc, (2 sc in next dc, sc in next dc) around; do **not** join, place marker *(see Markers, page 138)*: 18 sc.
Rnd 2: (Sc in next 2 sc, 2 sc in next sc) around: 24 sc.
Rnd 3: (Sc in next 3 sc, 2 sc in next sc) around: 30 sc.
Rnd 4: (Sc in next 14 sc, 2 sc in next sc) twice: 32 sc.
Rnd 5: Sc in each sc around; slip st in next sc, finish off.
Rnd 6: With **outside** of Cup facing, join CC with slip st in same st; ch 1, sc in each sc around; join with slip st to first sc, finish off.
HANDLE - With MC, ch 8 **loosely**; drop loop from hook, keeping last slip st worked on Cup at back, insert hook from **inside** to **outside** of Rnd 3 on side of Cup, hook dropped loop and pull through, drop loop from hook, insert hook from **outside** to **inside** through st to the left, hook dropped loop and pull through, slip st in each ch across; slip st in st on Rnd 5 directly above, finish off.

~~Quick~~ ROSY COASTER

*A pretty rose motif makes this delicate coaster a lovely accent. Fashioned with
dainty bedspread weight cotton thread, it's a nice pick-me-up anytime.*

Finished Size: Approximately 4¹/₂" (from point to point)

MATERIALS

Bedspread Weight Cotton Thread (size 10), approximately:

   MC (White) - 17 yards **each**

   Color A (Pink) - 6 yards **each**

   Color B (Green) - 4 yards **each**

Steel crochet hook, size 8 (1.50 mm) **or** size needed for gauge

GAUGE: Rnds 1-5 = 2"

PATTERN STITCHES

CLUSTER

★ YO twice, insert hook in sc indicated, YO and pull up a
loop, (YO and draw through 2 loops on hook) twice; repeat
from ★ 2 times **more**, YO and draw through all 4 loops on
hook *(Figs. 9a & b, page 134)*.

PICOT

Ch 3, slip st in third ch from hook.

With Color A, ch 6; join with slip st to form a ring.

Rnd 1 (Right side): Ch 2, 11 hdc in ring; join with slip st to top
of beginning ch-2: 12 sts.

Note: Loop a short piece of thread around any stitch to mark
last round as **right** side.

Rnd 2: Ch 1, sc in same st, ch 3, skip next hdc, (sc in next
hdc, ch 3, skip next hdc) around; join with slip st to first sc:
6 ch-3 sps.

Rnd 3: Slip st in first ch-3 sp, ch 1, (sc, 5 dc, sc) in same sp
and in each ch-3 sp around; join with slip st to first sc: 6 petals.

Rnd 4: Ch 1, sc in same st, ch 7, (sc in first sc of next petal,
ch 7) around; join with slip st to first sc: 6 loops.

Rnd 5: Slip st in first loop, ch 1, (sc, 7 dc, sc) in same loop and
in each loop around; join with slip st to first sc, finish off: 6 petals.

Rnd 6: With **right** side facing, join Color B with slip st in center
dc of any 7-dc group; ch 1, sc in same st, ch 3, work (Cluster,
ch 5, Cluster) in first sc of next petal, ch 3, ★ sc in center dc of
next 7-dc group, ch 3, work (Cluster, ch 5, Cluster) in first sc of
next petal, ch 3; repeat from ★ around; join with slip st to first
sc, finish off: 12 Clusters.

Rnd 7: With **right** side facing, join MC with slip st in first ch-3 sp; ch 1, 4 sc in same sp, 7 sc in next loop, (4 sc in each of next 2 ch-3 sps, 7 sc in next loop) around to last ch-3 sp, 4 sc in last ch-3 sp; join with slip st to first sc: 90 sc.

Rnd 8: Slip st in next sc, ch 4, skip next sc, (dc in next sc, ch 1, skip next sc) twice, (dc, ch 1) 3 times in next sc, (skip next sc, dc in next sc, ch 1) 3 times, skip next 2 sc, ★ (dc in next sc, ch 1, skip next sc) 3 times, (dc, ch 1) 3 times in next sc, (skip next sc, dc in next sc, ch 1) 3 times, skip next 2 sc; repeat from ★ around; join with slip st to third ch of beginning ch-4: 54 ch-1 sps.

Rnd 9: Ch 2, hdc in next ch-1 sp, (hdc in next dc and in next ch-1 sp) 3 times, (hdc, ch 2, hdc) in next dc, ★ hdc in next ch-1 sp, (hdc in next dc and in next ch-1 sp) 8 times, (hdc, ch 2, hdc) in next dc; repeat from ★ around to last 5 ch-1 sps, hdc in next ch-1 sp, (hdc in next dc and in next ch-1 sp) 4 times; join with slip st to top of beginning ch-2.

Rnd 10: Ch 6, slip st in third ch from hook, dc in same st, skip next 2 hdc, [(dc, work Picot, dc) in next hdc, skip next 2 hdc] twice, (dc, work Picot, dc) in next ch-2 sp, ★ skip next hdc, [(dc, work Picot, dc) in next hdc, skip next 2 hdc] 6 times, (dc, work Picot, dc) in next ch-2 sp; repeat from ★ around to last 10 hdc, skip next hdc, [(dc, work Picot, dc) in next hdc, skip next 2 hdc] 3 times; join with slip st to third ch of beginning ch-6, finish off.

See Washing and Blocking, page 140.

SOFT AND ROOMY TOTE

Here's a fun gift that can be enjoyed long after the special occasion is over! Our roomy tote is a fast-to-finish project that's worked with fabric strips and a jumbo hook. Fill the holder with surprises for two gifts in one.

Finished Size: Approximately 10" high x 14" wide

MATERIALS

100% Cotton Fabric, 44/45" wide, approximately:
MC (Multi) - 5 yards
CC (Blue) - 1 yard
Crochet hook, size Q (15.00 mm) **or** size needed for gauge

Prepare fabric and tear into 2" wide strips **(see Preparing Fabric Strips and Joining Fabric Strips, page 139)**.

GAUGE: 6 sc = 5½" and 5 rows = 4"
Rnds 1-3 = 5" x 11½"

With MC, ch 10 **loosely**.

Rnd 1 (Right side)**:** 3 Sc in second ch from hook, sc in next 7 chs, 3 sc in last ch; working in free loops of beginning ch **(Fig. 21b, page 138)**, sc in next 7 chs; join with slip st to first sc: 20 sc.

Rnd 2: Ch 1, sc in same st, 3 sc in next sc, sc in next 9 sc, 3 sc in next sc, sc in each sc around; join with slip st to first sc: 24 sc.

Rnd 3: Ch 1, 2 sc in same st, (sc in next sc, 2 sc in next sc) twice, sc in next 7 sc, 2 sc in next sc, (sc in next sc, 2 sc in next sc) twice, sc in each sc around; join with slip st to Back Loop Only of first sc **(Fig. 20, page 138)**: 30 sc.

Rnd 4: Ch 1, sc in Back Loop Only of each sc around; join with slip st to both loops of first sc.

Rnds 5-13: Ch 1, sc in both loops of each sc around; join with slip st to first sc changing to CC at end of Rnd 13 **(Fig. 22b, page 138)**.

Rnd 14: Ch 1, sc in each sc around; join with slip st to first sc.

Rnd 15: Ch 1, sc in first 10 sc, ch 20 (handle), skip next 5 sc, sc in next 10 sc, ch 20 (handle), skip last 5 sc; join with slip st to first sc: 20 sc.

Edging: Slip st in each sc and in each ch around; join with slip st to first slip st, finish off.

just for fun

You don't need a special reason to create these lighthearted projects! Assembled just for the fun of it, our assortment includes a wall accent that will have you all abuzz, a comical clown who'll keep you in stitches, and a handy stadium cushion to help you enjoy your favorite sporting events. Turn to these pleasing patterns for hours of stitching amusement!

Quick COLORFUL CLOWN

Something funny is going on, and it all starts when you stitch our whimsical stuffed clown! Holding a bright red balloon, he's guaranteed to bring lots of smiles. This playtime pal is a great scrap-yarn project!

Finished Size: Approximately 13" tall

MATERIALS
Worsted Weight Yarn, approximately:
    Black - 35 yards
    Pink - 14 yards
    White - 32 yards
    Green - 30 yards
    Blue - 50 yards
    Orange - 1 yard
    Peach - 34 yards
    Yellow - 5 yards
    Red - 10 yards
    Turquiose - 9 yards
Crochet hook, size G (4.00 mm) **or** size needed for gauge
Polyester fiberfill
Yarn and tapestry needles
Cardboard - 1½" wide x 5" long
Glue gun
2 - 6 mm black beads
1 - 6" length 22 gauge white wire

GAUGE: 4 sc and 4 rows = 1"

LEFT LEG
With Black, ch 3; being careful not to twist ch, join with slip st to form a ring.

Rnd 1 (Right side)**:** Ch 1, 2 sc in each ch around; do **not** join, place marker *(see Markers, page 138)*: 6 sc.

Rnd 2: 2 Sc in each sc around: 12 sc.

Rnds 3 and 4: Sc in each sc around changing to White in last sc worked on Rnd 4 *(Fig. 22a, page 138)*.

Rnd 5: Sc in Back Loop Only of each sc around changing to Pink in last sc worked *(Fig. 20, page 138)*; drop White.

Rnd 6: Sc in both loops of each sc around changing to White in last sc worked; drop Pink.

Rnd 7: Sc in each sc around changing to Pink in last sc worked; drop White.

Rnds 8-10: Repeat Rnds 6 and 7 once, then repeat Rnd 6 once **more**; at end of Rnd 10, cut Pink.

Rnds 11-23: Sc in each sc around; at end of Rnd 23, slip st in next sc, finish off.
Stuff Leg with polyester fiberfill.

RIGHT LEG
Work same as Left Leg; at end of Rnd 23, do **not** finish off.

BODY

Rnd 1: Holding Legs together, sc in seventh st of Left Leg, sc in each sc around Left Leg, sc in each sc around Right Leg; do **not** join, place marker: 24 sc.

Rnds 2 and 3: Sc in each sc around changing to Green in last sc worked on Rnd 3.

Rnds 4-8: Sc in each sc around.

Note: To **decrease**, pull up a loop in next 2 sts, YO and draw through all 3 loops on hook **(counts as one sc)**.

Rnd 9: (Sc in next 4 sc, decrease) around: 20 sc.

Rnd 10: (Sc in next 3 sc, decrease) around: 16 sc.

Rnds 11 and 12: Sc in each sc around.

Rnd 13: (Sc in next 2 sc, decrease) around: 12 sc.

Rnd 14: Sc in each sc around.

Stuff Body with polyester fiberfill.

Rnd 15: (Sc in next sc, decrease) around changing to Peach in last st worked; do **not** finish off: 8 sc.

HEAD

Rnd 1: 2 Sc in Back Loop Only of each sc around: 16 sc.

Rnd 2: Working in both loops, (sc in next sc, 2 sc in next sc) around: 24 sc.

Rnds 3-8: Sc in each sc around.

Stuff Head with polyester fiberfill before closing.

Rnd 9: (Sc in next 2 sc, decrease) around: 18 sc.

Rnd 10: (Sc in next sc, decrease) around: 12 sc.

Rnd 11: Decrease around: 6 sc.

Rnd 12: (Skip next st, slip st in next st) 3 times; finish off: 3 sts.

RUFFLE

Rnd 1 (Right side)**:** With Head toward you and working in free loops of Rnd 15 on Body *(Fig. 21a, page 138)*, join Yellow with slip st in any st at center back; ch 3, 3 dc in same st, 4 dc in next st and in each st around; join with slip st to top of beginning ch-3, finish off: 32 sts.

Rnd 2: With **right** side facing, join Pink with slip st in same st as joining; ch 3, dc in same st, 2 dc in next dc and in each dc around; join with slip st to top of beginning ch-3, finish off: 64 sts.

ARM AND SLEEVE (Make 2)

With Peach, ch 3; being careful not to twist ch, join with slip st to form a ring.

Rnd 1 (Right side)**:** Ch 1, 2 sc in each ch around; do **not** join, place marker: 6 sc.

Rnd 2: (Sc in next 2 sc, 2 sc in next sc) twice: 8 sc.

Rnds 3-18: Sc in each sc around changing to Green in last sc worked on Rnd 18.

Rnds 19 and 20: Sc in each sc around.

Rnd 21: Slip st in next sc, ch 1, **turn**; working in Back Loops Only, (sc in next sc, 2 sc in next sc) around: 12 sc.

Rnd 22: Sc in both loops of each sc around.

Rnd 23: (Sc in next 3 sc, 2 sc in next sc) around: 15 sc.

Rnd 24: Sc in each sc around.

Rnd 25: (Sc in next 4 sc, 2 sc in next sc) around: 18 sc.

Rnds 26-28: Sc in each sc around; at end of Rnd 28, slip st in next st, finish off.

Stuff Arm with polyester fiberfill.

Sew opening on Rnd 20 closed.

SHOE (Make 2)

With Black, ch 3; being careful not to twist ch, join with slip st to form a ring.

Rnd 1 (Right side)**:** Ch 1, 2 sc in each ch around; do **not** join, place marker: 6 sc.

Rnds 2 and 3: 2 Sc in each sc around: 24 sc.

Rnds 4 and 5: Sc in each sc around.

Rnd 6: (Sc in next 2 sc, decrease) around: 18 sc.

Rnd 7: Sc in each sc around.

Rnd 8: (Sc in next sc, decrease) around: 12 sc.

Rnds 9 and 10: Sc in each sc around; at end of Rnd 10, slip st in next sc, finish off leaving a long end for sewing.

SHOELACE (Make 2)

With Turquoise, ch 82; finish off.

Knot and trim ends.

EAR (Make 2)

With Peach, ch 2, 6 sc in second ch from hook; finish off leaving a long end for sewing.

MOUTH

With Turquoise, ch 8 **loosely**.

Rnd 1 (Right side)**:** 2 Sc in second ch from hook, sc in next 5 chs, 4 sc in last ch; working in free loops of beginning ch *(Fig. 21b, page 138)*, sc in next 5 chs, 2 sc in next ch; join with slip st to first sc, finish off leaving a long end for sewing: 18 sc.

NOSE

With Red, ch 3; being careful not to twist ch, join with slip st to form a ring.

Rnd 1 (Right side)**:** Ch 1, 2 sc in each ch around; join with slip st to first sc, finish off leaving a long end for sewing: 6 sc.

POLKA DOT (Make 6)

Work same as Nose, making one in each of the following colors: Yellow, Pink, Green, Orange, Red, and Turquoise.

Continued on page 67.

Quick STADIUM CUSHION

Show your team spirit with this comfortable stadium cushion stitched in your favorite team's colors! A quick project, the sporty pad is worked with slip stitches and treble crochets using a jumbo hook and holding four strands of yarn together.

Finished Size: Approximately 17" wide x 14½" deep

MATERIALS
Worsted Weight Yarn, approximately:
  Color A (Gold) - 5 ounces, (140 grams, 330 yards)
  Color B (Blue) - 3 ounces, (90 grams, 195 yards)
Crochet hook, size Q (15.00 mm)

Note: *Cushion is worked holding 4 strands of yarn together.*

GAUGE: In pattern, 4 sts and 4 rows = 3"

With Color A, ch 22 **loosely**.

Row 1 (Right side): Sc in second ch from hook, tr in next ch, (slip st in next ch pushing tr to **right** side, tr in next ch) across to last ch, sc in last ch: 21 sts.

Note: Loop a short piece of yarn around any stitch to mark last row as **right** side.

Row 2: Ch 1, turn; sc in first sc, slip st in next tr, (tr in next slip st, slip st in next tr pushing tr to **right** side) across to last sc, sc in last sc; finish off.

Row 3: With **right** side facing, join Color B with sc in first sc *(see Joining With Sc, page 138)*, tr in next slip st, (slip st in next tr pushing tr to **right** side, tr in next slip st) across to last sc, sc in last sc.

Row 4: Repeat Row 2.

Row 5: With Color A, repeat Row 3.

Rows 6-17: Repeat Rows 2-5, 3 times.

Row 18: Repeat Row 2; do **not** finish off.

Edging: Ch 1, turn; sc evenly around working 3 sc in each corner; join with slip st to first sc, finish off.

Quick VICTORIAN CHARMERS

Small in size, these Victorian miniatures are big on possibilities! The dainty designs are quick to work up with cotton thread. Accent them with ribbon and charms to make a necklace, a bookmark, a lapel pin, package ties, and other romantic keepsakes.

MATERIALS

Bedspread Weight Cotton Thread (size 10), approximately 5 to 15 yards **total** for each Charmer of the following colors: Ecru, Pink, Rose, Brown, Dark Brown, and Green

Steel crochet hook, size 7 (1.65 mm)

Tapestry needle

Sewing needle and thread

Finishing materials: Glue gun, ribbon, pin backing, charms, etc.

Note: Gauge is not important. Charmers can be smaller or larger without changing the overall effect.

PATTERN STITCHES

SC DECREASE

Pull up a loop in next 2 sts, YO and draw through all 3 loops on hook **(counts as one sc)**.

DC DECREASE (uses next 2 sts)

★ YO, insert hook in **next** st, YO and pull up a loop, YO and draw through 2 loops on hook; repeat from ★ once **more**, YO and draw through all 3 loops on hook **(counts as one dc)**.

LADY

HEAD

Rnd 1: With Ecru, ch 4, 11 dc in fourth ch from hook; join with slip st to top of beginning ch: 12 sts.

Rnd 2: Ch 1, sc in same st and in each dc around; join with slip st to first sc.

Rnd 3: Ch 2, dc in next sc, work dc decrease 5 times; skip beginning ch-2 and join with slip st to first dc, finish off: 6 dc.

DRESS

Rnd 1: With **right** side facing, join Rose with slip st same st as joining; ch 1, 2 sc in same st and in each dc around; join with slip st to first sc: 12 sc.

Rnd 2: Ch 3 **(counts as first dc, now and throughout)**, dc in next 2 sc, ch 1, dc in next 6 sc, ch 1, dc in last 3 sc; join with slip st to first dc: 12 dc and 2 ch-1 sps.

Rnd 3: Ch 1, sc in same st, work sc decrease, sc in next ch-1 sp, work sc decrease 3 times, sc in next ch-1 sp, work sc decrease, sc in last dc; join with slip st to Front Loop Only of first sc *(Fig. 20, page 138)*: 9 sc.

Rnd 4: Ch 3, working in Front Loops Only, dc in same st, 2 dc in next sc and in each sc around; join with slip st to first dc, finish off: 18 dc.

Rnd 5: With **right** side facing and working behind previous rnd and in free loops of Rnd 3 *(Fig. 21a, page 138)*, join Green with slip st in same st as joining; ch 3, dc in same st, (3 dc in next st, 2 dc in next st) around; join with slip st to first dc: 22 dc.

Rnds 6 and 7: Ch 3, dc in next dc and in each dc around; join with slip st to first dc.

Rnd 8: Ch 3, dc in same st, skip next dc, ★ (slip st, ch 3, dc) in next dc, skip next dc; repeat from ★ around; join with slip st to base of beginning ch-3, finish off: 11 scallops.

BONNET

Rnd 1 (Right side): With Green, ch 2, 6 sc in second ch from hook; join with slip st to first sc.

Note: Loop a short piece of thread around any stitch to mark last round as **right** side.

Rnd 2: Ch 3, dc in same st, 2 dc in next sc and in each sc around; join with slip st to first dc: 12 dc.

Rnd 3: Ch 3, (2 dc in next dc, dc in next dc) 4 times, leave remaining 3 dc unworked: 13 dc.

Edging: Ch 1, turn; working in Back Loops Only, (slip st in next dc, ch 1) across, slip st in end of Rnd 3, sc in next 3 dc, slip st in end of Rnd 3; finish off.

ARMS

With Rose, ch 18 **loosely**; slip st in back ridge of second ch from hook and in each ch across *(Fig. 2a, page 133)*; finish off.

Insert Arms through ch-1 sps on Dress. Tack in place at back. With Dark Brown, add Straight St eyes *(Fig. 28, page 141)*. Sew a group of six 1½" strands of Brown to top of Head, leaving one end free on face to form bangs. Form bun by wrapping remaining length around Head, overlapping to cover sewing stitches. Tuck remaining loose ends under bun and secure at back of Head. Trim bangs and fray.

Place Bonnet on Head with sc of last round at neck; thread needle with Green and insert needle through slip st at each end of Rnd 4; tie ends in a bow to secure.

FAN

With Pink, ch 8 **loosely**.

Row 1: Sc in back ridge of second ch from hook and in each ch across *(Fig. 2a, page 133)*: 7 sc.

Note: Do not cut thread unless otherwise instructed; carry thread **loosely** along the sides when not being used.

Row 2 (Right side): Ch 3, turn; sc in Back Loop Only of each sc across *(Fig. 20, page 138)* changing to Green in last sc worked *(Fig. 22a, page 138)*, drop Pink.

Note: Loop a short piece of thread around any stitch to mark last row as **right** side.

Row 3: Ch 1, turn; sc in both loops of each sc across.

Row 4: Ch 3, turn; sc in Back Loop Only of each sc across changing to Pink in last sc worked, drop Green.

Row 5: Ch 1, turn; sc in both loops of each sc across.

Rows 6-13: Repeat Rows 2-5 twice; cut Green at end of Row 12.

Row 14: Ch 3, turn; sc in Back Loop Only of each sc across; do **not** cut Pink.

BASE

Row 1: Ch 1, working in end of rows, skip first row, sc in next row, (skip next row, sc in next row) across: 7 sc.

Row 2: Ch 1, turn; work sc decrease, sc in next 3 sc, work sc decrease: 5 sc.

Row 3: Ch 1, turn; work sc decrease, sc in next sc, work sc decrease: 3 sc.

Row 4: Ch 3, turn; skip first 2 sc, slip st in last sc; finish off.

Fold six 1¹/₂" strands of Green in half. With **wrong** side facing, draw the folded end up through ch-3 sp on Row 4 of Base and pull the loose ends through the folded end; draw the knot up **tightly**. Trim ends.

QUILT BLOCK

CENTER

With Rose, ch 5 **loosely**.

Row 1: Sc in second ch from hook and in each ch across: 4 sc.

Rows 2-4: Ch 1, turn; sc in each sc across changing to Ecru in last sc worked on Row 4 *(Fig. 22a, page 138)*.

BORDER

Rnd 1 (Right side): Ch 3 **(counts as first dc, now and throughout)**, dc in end of next 3 rows, ch 5; working in free loops of beginning ch *(Fig. 21b, page 138)*, dc in each ch across, ch 5; dc in end of each row across, ch 5; dc in each sc across, ch 5; join with slip st to first dc, finish off: 16 dc and 4 loops.

Note: Loop a short piece of thread around any stitch to mark last round as **right** side.

Rnd 2: With **right** side facing and working in **front** of corner loops, join Green with slip st in any corner on Center; ch 3, 4 dc in same st, ch 4, (5 dc in next corner on Center, ch 4) around; join with slip st to first dc, finish off.

Rnd 3: With **right** side facing and working **around** loops on Rnds 1 and 2, join Rose with slip st in center dc of any corner; ch 1, 3 sc in same st, sc in next 8 dc, (3 sc in next dc, sc in next 8 dc) around; join with slip st to first sc: 44 sc.

Rnd 4: Ch 1, sc in same st, ch 1, sc in side of sc just worked *(Fig. 1)*, skip next sc, (sc in next sc, ch 1, sc in side of sc just worked, skip next sc) around; join with slip st to first sc, finish off.

Fig. 1

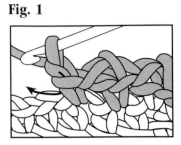

HAT

Rnd 1 (Right side): With Ecru, ch 4, 11 dc in fourth ch from hook; join with slip st to top of beginning ch: 12 sts.

Note: Loop a short piece of thread around any stitch to mark last round as **right** side.

Rnd 2: Ch 3 **(counts as first dc, now and throughout)**, dc in same st, 2 dc in next dc and in each dc around; join with slip st to first dc changing to Brown *(Fig. 22b, page 138)*, do **not** cut Ecru: 24 dc.

Rnd 3: Ch 1, sc in each dc around; join with slip st to first sc.

Rnd 4: Ch 1, sc in each sc around; join with slip st to Front Loop Only of first sc changing to Ecru *(Fig. 20, page 138)*, cut Brown.

Rnd 5: Ch 3, working in Front Loops Only, dc in same st, 2 dc in next sc and in each sc around; join with slip st to both loops of first dc: 48 dc.

Rnd 6: Ch 1, working in both loops, sc in same st, ch 1, sc in side of sc just worked *(Fig. 1)*, skip next dc, (sc in next dc, ch 1, sc in side of sc just worked, skip next dc) around; join with slip st to first sc, finish off.

BOW

With Brown, ch 15, slip st in ninth ch from hook, ch 9, slip st in ninth ch from hook, ch 6; finish off.

FLOWER

With Pink, ch 4, slip st in fourth ch from hook, (ch 3, slip st) 4 times in same st; finish off leaving a long end for sewing.

LEAVES

With Green, ch 3, slip st in second ch from hook, (sc, slip st) in next ch, ch 6, slip st in second ch from hook, sc in next ch, slip st in next ch; finish off.

With **right** side facing, sew Bow at joining on Rnd 4 of Hat. Sew Leaves and Flower to opposite side of Hat, twisting one petal of Flower to center.

THIMBLE

Rnd 1 (Right side): With Ecru, ch 4, 7 dc in fourth ch from hook; join with slip st to top of beginning ch: 8 sts.

Note: Loop a short piece of thread around any stitch to mark last round as **right** side.

Rnd 2: Ch 3 **(counts as first dc, now and throughout)**, 2 dc in next dc, (dc in next dc, 2 dc in next dc) around; join with slip st to first dc: 12 dc.

Rnd 3: Ch 3, dc in next dc, 2 dc in next dc, (dc in next 2 dc, 2 dc in next dc) around; join with slip st to first dc: 16 dc.

Rnd 4: Ch 3, dc in next dc and in each dc around; join with slip st to first dc.

Rnd 5: Ch 1, turn; working in Back Loops Only *(Fig. 20, page 138)*, sc in same st, ch 3, (sc in next dc, ch 3) around; join with slip st to first sc, finish off.

FLOWER AND LEAVES

Work same as Hat.

Sew Leaves and Flower to front of Thimble, twisting one petal of Flower to center.

HEART

Rnd 1 (Right side): With Pink, ch 5, (dc, ch 1) 6 times in fifth ch from hook; join with slip st to fourth ch of beginning ch: 7 ch-1 sps.

Rnd 2: Ch 1, sc in same st, ch 3, sc in next ch-1 sp, ch 3, (sc in next dc, ch 3, sc in next ch-1 sp, ch 3) around; join with slip st to first sc: 14 ch-3 sps.

Rnd 3: Slip st in first ch-3 sp, ch 1, sc in same sp, 3 dc in each of next 3 ch-3 sps, sc in next 3 ch-3 sps, 3 dc in next sc, sc in next 3 ch-3 sps, 3 dc in each of next 3 ch-3 sps, sc in last ch-3 sp; do **not** join, finish off: 29 sts.

Rnd 4: With **right** side facing, join Ecru with slip st in last sc worked; ch 1, sc in same st, ch 3, working **around** previous rnds, slip st in center beginning ch, ch 3, sc in next sc on Rnd 3, ch 3, (skip next st, sc in next st, ch 3) 6 times, skip next dc, (sc, ch 3) twice in next dc (point), (skip next st, sc in next st, ch 3) 6 times, skip last dc; join with slip st to first sc, finish off.

CRESCENT

Rnd 1 (Right side): With Ecru, ch 2, 6 sc in second ch from hook; join with slip st to first sc: 6 sc.

Note: Loop a short piece of thread around any stitch to mark last round as **right** side.

Rnd 2: Ch 1, sc in same st, ch 3, (sc in next sc, ch 3) around; join with slip st to first sc: 6 ch-3 sps.

Rnd 3: Slip st in first ch-3 sp, ch 3, 3 dc in same sp, 4 dc in next ch-3 sp and in each ch-3 sp around; join with slip st to top of beginning ch-3: 24 sts.

Rnd 4: Ch 4, (dc in next dc, ch 1) around; join with slip st to third ch of beginning ch-4, finish off: 24 ch-1 sps.
Edging: Fold piece in half with **wrong** side together and joining at center back; working through **both** thicknesses and matching sts, join Rose with slip st in first dc; ch 1,

sc in same st, ch 3, (sc in next ch-1 sp, ch 3) 11 times, sc in next dc; finish off.

With Ecru, make a 1" tassel *(Figs. 27a & b, page 141)*; tie to center bottom of Crescent.

BANDANNA AFGHAN

Cover yourself in classic cowboy style with this Western wrap. Stitched with worsted weight yarn in red, white, and black, the bold afghan resembles an oversize bandanna.

Finished Size: Approximately 49" x 64"

MATERIALS
Worsted Weight Yarn, approximately:
    MC (Red) - 35 ounces, (990 grams, 2,300 yards)
    Color A (White) - 11 ounces, (310 grams, 725 yards)
    Color B (Black) - 5 ounces, (140 grams, 330 yards)
Crochet hook, size I (5.50 mm) **or** size needed for gauge
Yarn needle

GAUGE: Rnds 1-5 = 3¾"
        One Square = 7½"

SQUARE (Make 48)
Rnd 1 (Right side): With Color A, ch 5, (dc, ch 1) 7 times in fifth ch from hook; join with slip st to fourth ch of beginning ch-5, finish off: 8 ch-1 sps.
Note: Loop a short piece of yarn around any stitch to mark last round as **right** side.
Rnd 2: With **right** side facing, join MC with slip st in any ch-1 sp; ch 3 **(counts as first dc, now and throughout)**, 2 dc in same sp, (dc, ch 1, tr, ch 1, dc) in next ch-1 sp, ★ 3 dc in next ch-1 sp, (dc, ch 1, tr, ch 1, dc) in next ch-1 sp; repeat from ★ around; join with slip st to first dc, finish off: 5 dc **each** side.

Rnd 3: With **wrong** side facing, join Color B with sc in ch to **right** of any corner tr *(see Joining With Sc, page 138)*; ch 3, ★ skip next corner tr, sc in next ch, working in dc and in chs, (ch 1, skip next dc, sc in next st) 3 times, ch 3; repeat from ★ 2 times **more**, skip next corner tr, (sc in next st, ch 1, skip next dc) 3 times; join with slip st to first sc, finish off.

Rnd 4: With **right** side facing, join MC with sc in sc to **right** of any corner ch-3 sp; ★ † working in **front** of next ch-3, (dc, ch 1, tr, ch 1, dc) in corner tr on rnd **below**, (sc in next sc, working **behind** next ch-1, dc in skipped dc on rnd **below**) 3 times †, sc in next sc; repeat from ★ 2 times **more**, then repeat from † to † once; join with slip st to first sc: 48 sts.

Rnd 5: Ch 1, sc in same st and in next 2 sts, ch 3, (skip next corner tr, sc in next 11 sts, ch 3) 3 times, skip next corner tr, sc in last 8 sts; join with slip st to first sc, finish off: 11 sc **each** side.

Rnd 6: With **wrong** side facing, join Color A with slip st in sc to **right** of any corner ch-3 sp; ch 3, 5 dc in next corner ch-3 sp, dc in next sc, ★ (ch 1, skip next sc, dc in next sc) 5 times, 5 dc in next corner ch-3 sp, dc in next sc; repeat from ★ 2 times **more**, ch 1, (skip next sc, dc in next sc, ch 1) 4 times, skip next sc; join with slip st to first dc, finish off.

Rnd 7: With **right** side facing, join MC with sc in dc to **right** of first dc of any corner 5-dc group; sc in next 2 dc, ★ † (dc, ch 2, dc) in next dc, sc in next 3 dc, working in **front** of next ch-1, tr in skipped sc on rnd **below**, sc in next dc, (working **behind** next ch-1, tr in skipped sc on rnd **below**, sc in next dc) 3 times, working in **front** of next ch-1, tr in skipped sc on rnd **below** †, sc in next 3 dc; repeat from ★ 2 times **more**, then repeat from † to † once; join with slip st to first sc, finish off.

Rnd 8: With **wrong** side facing, join Color B with sc in dc to **right** of any corner ch-2 sp; ch 3, skip next corner ch-2 sp, sc in next dc, ★ (ch 1, skip next sc, sc in next st) 8 times, ch 3, skip next ch-2 sp, sc in next dc; repeat from ★ 2 times **more**, ch 1, (skip next sc, sc in next st, ch 1) 7 times, skip last sc; join with slip st to first sc, finish off.

Rnd 9: With **right** side facing, join MC with sc in sc to **right** of any corner ch-3 sp; ★ † working **behind** next ch-3, (dc, ch 1, tr, ch 1, dc) in corner ch-2 sp on rnd **below**, (sc in next sc, working **behind** next ch-1, dc in skipped sc on rnd **below**) twice, (sc in next sc, working in **front** of next ch-1, dc in skipped sc on rnd **below**) 4 times, (sc in next sc, working **behind** next ch-1, dc in skipped sc on rnd **below**) twice †, sc in next sc; repeat from ★ 2 times **more**, then repeat from † to † once; join with slip st to first sc, finish off: 88 sts.

Rnd 10: With **wrong** side facing, join Color A with sc in ch to **right** of any corner tr; ch 3, skip next corner tr, sc in next ch, ★ working in sc and in chs, (ch 1, skip next dc, sc in next st) 10 times, ch 3, skip next corner tr, sc in next ch; repeat from

★ 2 times **more**, ch 1, skip next dc, (sc in next st, ch 1, skip next dc) 9 times; join with slip st to first sc, finish off.

Rnd 11: With **right** side facing, join MC with sc in sc to **right** of any corner ch-3 sp; ★ † working **behind** next ch-3, (dc, ch 3, dc) in corner tr on rnd **below**, (sc in next sc, working **behind** next ch-1, dc in skipped dc on rnd **below**) 3 times, (sc in next sc, working in **front** of next ch-1, dc in skipped dc on rnd **below**) 4 times, (sc in next sc, working **behind** next ch-1, dc in skipped dc on rnd **below**) 3 times †, sc in next sc; repeat from ★ 2 times **more**, then repeat from † to † once; join with slip st to first sc, finish off.

ASSEMBLY

With **wrong** sides together and MC, and working through **both** loops, whipstitch Squares together, forming 6 vertical strips of 8 Squares each *(Fig. 25a, page 140)*; then whipstitch strips together.

BORDER

Rnd 1: With **right** side facing, join MC with sc in any corner ch-3 sp; ch 2, sc in same sp, ★ † sc in next 23 sts, (sc in next ch-3 sp, hdc in joining, sc in next ch-3 sp, sc in next 23 sts) across to next corner ch-3 sp †, (sc, ch 2, sc) in corner ch-3 sp; repeat from ★ 2 times **more**, then repeat from † to † once; join with slip st to first sc, finish off.

Rnd 2: With **wrong** side facing, join Color A with sc in sc to **right** of any corner ch-2 sp; ch 3, ★ skip next corner ch-2 sp, sc in next sc, (ch 1, skip next st, sc in next st) across to next corner ch-2 sp, ch 3; repeat from ★ 2 times **more**, skip next corner ch-2 sp, (sc in next st, ch 1, skip next st) across; join with slip st to first sc, finish off.

Rnd 3: With **right** side facing, join MC with sc in sc to **right** of any corner ch-3 sp; working **behind** next ch-3, (dc, ch 1, tr, ch 1, dc) in ch-2 sp on rnd **below**, ★ sc in next sc, (working **behind** next ch-1, dc in skipped st on rnd **below**, sc in next sc) across to next corner ch-3 sp, working **behind** next ch-3, (dc, ch 1, tr, ch 1, dc) in ch-2 sp on rnd **below**; repeat from ★ 2 times **more**, (sc in next sc, working **behind** next ch-1, dc in skipped st on rnd **below**) across; join with slip st to first sc, finish off.

Rnd 4: With **wrong** side facing, join Color B with sc in ch to **right** of any corner tr; ch 3, skip next corner tr, sc in next ch, ★ working in sc and in chs, (ch 1, skip next dc, sc in next st) across to next corner tr, ch 3, skip corner tr, sc in next ch; repeat from ★ 2 times **more**, ch 1, skip next dc, (sc in next st, ch 1, skip next dc) across; join with slip st to first sc, finish off.

Rnd 5: With **right** side facing, join MC with sc in sc to **right** of any ch-3 sp; ★ † working **behind** next ch-3, (dc, ch 1, tr, ch 1, dc) in corner tr on rnd **below**, sc in next sc, working **behind** next ch-1, dc in skipped dc on rnd **below**, sc in next sc, (working in **front** of next ch-1, dc in skipped dc on rnd below, sc in next sc) 4 times, (working **behind** next ch-1, dc in skipped dc on rnd **below**, sc in next sc) 4 times, [(working in **front** of next ch-1, dc in skipped dc on rnd **below**, sc in next sc) 9 times, (working **behind** next ch-1, dc in skipped sc on rnd **below**, sc in next sc) 4 times] across to last 5 ch-1 sps, (working in **front** of next ch-1, dc in skipped dc on rnd **below**, sc in next sc) 4 times, working **behind** next ch-1, dc in skipped dc on rnd **below** †, sc in next sc; repeat from ★ 2 times **more**, then repeat from † to † once; join with slip st to first sc, finish off.

Rnd 6: With Color A, repeat Rnd 4.

Rnd 7: With **right** side facing, join MC with sc in sc to **right** of any corner ch-3 sp; working **behind** next ch-3, (dc, ch 1, tr, ch 1, dc) in corner tr on rnd **below**, ★ sc in next sc, (working **behind** next ch-1, dc in skipped dc on rnd **below**, sc in next sc) across to next corner ch-3 sp, working **behind** corner ch-3, (dc, ch 1, tr, ch 1, dc) in corner tr on rnd **below**; repeat from ★ 2 times **more**, (sc in next sc, working **behind** next ch-1, dc in skipped dc on rnd **below**) across; join with slip st to first sc.

Rnd 8: Ch 2, slip st in next ch-1 sp, ch 3, slip st in next ch-1 sp, ★ ch 2, skip next dc, (slip st in next sc, ch 2, skip next dc) across to next corner ch-1 sp, slip st in corner ch-1 sp, ch 3, slip st in next ch-1 sp; repeat from ★ 2 times **more**, ch 2, skip next dc, (slip st in next sc, ch 2, skip next dc) across; join with slip st to joining, finish off.

COLORFUL CLOWN

Continued from page 60.

PANTS

With Blue, ch 32 **loosely**; being careful not to twist ch, join with slip st to form a ring.

Rnd 1 (Right side): Ch 1, sc in back ridge of each ch around *(Fig. 2a, page 133)*; do **not** join, place marker: 32 sc.

Rnds 2-9: Sc in each sc around.

RIGHT PANT LEG

Rnd 1: Sc in next 16 sc, leave remaining 16 sc unworked: 16 sc.

Rnds 2 and 3: Sc in each sc around.

Rnd 4: (Sc in next 7 sc, 2 sc in next sc) twice: 18 sc.

Rnds 5-8: Sc in each sc around.

Rnd 9: (Sc in next 8 sc, 2 sc in next sc) twice: 20 sc.

Rnds 10 and 11: Sc in each sc around.

Rnd 12: (Sc in next 9 sc, 2 sc in next sc) twice: 22 sc.

Rnd 13: Sc in next 8 sc, slip st in next sc, leave remaining sc unworked; finish off.

LEFT PANT LEG

Rnd 1: With **right** side facing, join Blue with slip st in first unworked st on Rnd 9; ch 1, sc in each sc around: 16 sc.

Rnds 2-12: Work same as Right Pant Leg.

Rnd 13: Sc in next 17 sc, leave remaining 4 sc unworked; slip st in next sc, finish off.

WAISTBAND AND STRAPS

With **right** side facing and working in beginning ch on Pants, join Blue with slip st in st at center back; ch 1, sc in same st and in next 2 sts, ch 24 **loosely**; sc in second ch from hook and in each ch across (Strap), sc in next 26 sts, ch 24 **loosely**; sc in second ch from hook and in each ch across (Strap), sc in last 3 sts; join with slip st to first sc, finish off.

HAT

With Black, ch 3; being careful not to twist ch, join with slip st to form a ring.

Rnd 1 (Right side): Ch 1, 2 sc in each ch around; do **not** join, place marker: 6 sc.

Rnd 2: 2 Sc in each sc around: 12 sc.

Rnd 3: (Sc in next sc, 2 sc in next sc) around: 18 sc.

Rnds 4-7: Sc in each sc around.

Rnd 8 (Brim): Slip st in next st, ch 1, working in Front Loops Only, (sc in next sc, 2 sc in next sc) around; join with slip st to first sc, finish off leaving a long end for sewing: 27 sc.

Stuff Hat with polyester fiberfill.

BALLOON

With Red, ch 3; being careful not to twist ch, join with slip st to form a ring.

Rnd 1 (Right side): Ch 1, 2 sc in each ch around; do **not** join, place marker: 6 sc.

Rnd 2: 2 Sc in each sc around: 12 sc.

Rnd 3: (Sc in next sc, 2 sc in next sc) around: 18 sc.

Rnds 4 and 5: Sc in each sc around.

Rnd 6: (Sc in next 4 sc, decrease) around: 15 sc.

Rnd 7: Sc in each sc around.

Rnd 8: (Sc in next 3 sc, decrease) around: 12 sc.

Rnd 9: Decrease around: 6 sc.

Stuff Balloon with polyester fiberfill.

Rnd 10: Decrease around: 3 sc.

Rnd 11: 2 Sc in each sc around; slip st in next sc, finish off: 6 sc.

FINISHING

Using photo as a guide for placement, sew Ears, Nose, Mouth, and Hat to Head.

Holding one strand of Yellow, Pink, Blue and Green together, wrap yarn around Hat above Brim and tie in a knot, positioning knot over right Ear. Fray ends.

Sew Arms to Body.

Using photo as a guide for placement, sew Polka Dots to Pants.

Put Pants on Clown and sew Straps to front of Waistband, leaving 1/4" free at ends of Straps.

Lace Shoelaces into each Shoe and tie ends in a bow.

Stuff Shoes with polyester fiberfill and sew to bottom front of Legs.

HAIR

Wind Orange loosely and evenly around width of cardboard until card is filled, then cut across one end; repeat as needed. Thread yarn needle with a long strand of Orange. Holding 6 strands of Orange together at a time, sew each group to Head, forming 3 rows across back of Head beginning above one Ear and ending above other Ear. Fray yarn ends and trim to desired length.

With Black, add mouth using Back St *(Figs. 31a & b, page 142)* and Straight St *(Fig. 28, page 141)*.

Glue beads to Head for eyes.

Insert one end of wire into Balloon; glue in place. Glue wire to right Arm. Fold end of each Arm to form hand and sew in place.

Quick BLOOMER MAGNETS

A touch of nostalgia is in store with our old-fashioned bloomer magnets. Created with bedspread weight cotton thread, these humorous designs are sure to draw attention to your notes and reminders.

Finished Size: Boy's - approximately 3 1/4" x 1 3/4"
Girl's - approximately 3 3/4" x 2"

MATERIALS

Bedspread Weight Cotton Thread (size 10), approximately:
Color A (Red) - 40 yards
Color B (White) - 35 yards
Steel crochet hooks, sizes 8 (1.50 mm) **and** 10 (1.30 mm) **or** sizes needed for gauge
Tapestry needle
Sewing needle and thread
Magnetic strips
Girl's: 1 1/2" length of white 1/8" wide ribbon
Boy's: 2 red seed beads

GAUGE: With larger size hook, 10 hdc = 1"
With smaller size hook, 12 sc = 1"

GIRL'S BLOOMERS

BODY

With smaller size hook and Color A, ch 48 **loosely**; being careful not to twist ch, join with slip st to form a ring.

Rnd 1 (Right side)**:** Ch 1, sc in each ch around; join with slip st to BLO of first sc *(Fig. 20, page 138)*: 48 sc.

Note: Loop a short piece of thread around any stitch to mark last round as **right** side.

Rnd 2: Ch 1, sc in BLO of same st, sc in FLO of next sc, (sc in BLO of next sc, sc in FLO of next sc) 5 times, ch 1, (sc in BLO of next sc, sc in FLO of next sc) 12 times, ch 1, (sc in BLO of next sc, sc in FLO of next sc) around; join with slip st to BLO of first sc: 48 sc.

Rnd 3: Ch 1, sc in BLO of same st, sc in FLO of next sc, (sc in BLO of next sc, sc in FLO of next sc) 5 times, (sc, ch 1, sc) in next ch-1 sp, (sc in BLO of next sc, sc in FLO of next sc) 12 times, (sc, ch 1, sc) in next ch-1 sp, (sc in BLO of next sc, sc in FLO of next sc) around; join with slip st to BLO of first sc: 52 sc.

Rnd 4: Ch 1, sc in BLO of same st, ★ (sc in FLO of next sc, sc in BLO of next sc) around to next ch-1 sp, (sc, ch 1, sc) in ch-1 sp; repeat from ★ once **more**, sc in FLO of next sc, (sc in BLO of next sc, sc in FLO of next sc) around; join with slip st to BLO of first sc: 56 sc.

Rnd 5: Ch 1, sc in BLO of same st, sc in FLO of next sc, ★ (sc in BLO of next sc, sc in FLO of next sc) around to next ch-1 sp, (sc, ch 1, sc) in ch-1 sp; repeat from ★ once **more**, (sc in BLO of next sc, sc in FLO of next sc) around; join with slip st to BLO of first sc: 60 sc.

Rnds 6-10: Repeat Rnds 4 and 5, twice, then repeat Rnd 4 once **more**; do **not** finish off: 80 sc.

RIGHT LEG

Rnd 1: Ch 1, sc in BLO of same st, sc in FLO of next sc, (sc in BLO of next sc, sc in FLO of next sc) 9 times; flattening piece so that ch-1 sps are together and skipping 40 sc in between, sc through **both** sps, (sc in BLO of next sc, sc in FLO of next sc) 10 times; join with slip st to BLO of first sc: 41 sc.

Rnd 2: Ch 1, sc in BLO of same st, † sc in FLO of next sc, (sc in BLO of next sc, sc in FLO of next sc) 9 times †, sc in BLO of next 2 sc, repeat from † to † once; join with slip st to BLO of first sc.

Note: To **decrease**, working in FLO or BLO as indicated, pull up a loop in next 2 sc, YO and draw through all 3 loops on hook **(counts as one sc)**.

Rnd 3: Ch 1, sc in BLO of same st, sc in FLO of next sc, (sc in BLO of next sc, sc in FLO of next sc) 9 times, decrease in BLO, sc in FLO of next sc, (sc in BLO of next sc, sc in FLO of next sc) 9 times; join with slip st to BLO of first sc: 40 sc.

Rnd 4: Ch 1, sc in BLO of same st, decrease in BLO, sc in FLO of next sc, (sc in BLO of next sc, sc in FLO of next sc) around; join with slip st to BLO of first sc: 39 sc.

Rnd 5: Ch 1, sc in BLO of same st, decrease in FLO, (sc in BLO of next sc, sc in FLO of next sc) around; join with slip st to BLO of first sc: 38 sc.

Rnd 6: Ch 1, sc in BLO of same st, sc in FLO of next sc, (sc in BLO of next sc, sc in FLO of next sc) around; join with slip st to BLO of first sc, finish off.

LEFT LEG

Rnd 1: With **right** side facing, join Color A with slip st in same center sp on Body as Right Leg; ch 1, sc in same sp, (sc in BLO of next sc, sc in FLO of next sc) around; join with slip st to BLO of first sc: 41 sc.

Rnd 2: Ch 1, sc in BLO of same st, (sc in BLO of next sc, sc in FLO of next sc) around; join with slip st to BLO of first sc.

Rnd 3: Work same as Rnd 5 of Right Leg: 40 sc.

Rnds 4-6: Work same as Rnds 4-6 of Right Leg: 38 sc.

RUFFLES

Rnd 1: With **right** side facing, join Color B with slip st in any st on Rnd 6 of Right Leg; ch 1, sc in same st, ch 3, skip next sc, (sc in next sc, ch 3, skip next 2 sc) around; join with slip st to first sc: 13 ch-3 sps.

Rnd 2: (Sc, hdc, sc) in first ch-3 sp, ch 1, slip st in next sc, ★ (sc, hdc, sc) in next ch-3 sp, ch 1, slip st in next sc; repeat from ★ around.

Note: To work **Back Post single crochet *(abbreviated BPsc)***, insert hook from **back** to **front** around post of st indicated *(Fig. 15, page 136)*, YO and pull up a loop, YO and draw through both loops on hook **(counts as one sc)**.

Rnd 3: Ch 1, work BPsc around sc in rnd **below** first slip st, ch 3, (work BPsc around sc in rnd **below** next slip st, ch 3) around; join with slip st to first BPsc: 13 ch-3 sps.

Rnds 4-6: Repeat Rnds 2 and 3 once, then repeat Rnd 2 once **more**.

Finish off.

Repeat for Left Leg.

WAIST EDGING

With **right** side facing, join Color B with slip st in free loop of beginning ch at center back *(Fig. 21b, page 138)*; ch 1, sc in same st, ch 1, skip next ch, (sc in next ch, ch 1, skip next ch) around; join with slip st to first sc, finish off.

FINISHING

Using photo as a guide for placement and using Color B, make 3 cross stitches on center front.

Tie ribbon in a bow and sew to top of Bloomers above cross stitches.

Attach magnetic strip to back.

BOY'S BLOOMERS

BODY

With larger size hook and Color B, ch 40 **loosely**; being careful not to twist ch, join with slip st to form a ring.

Rnd 1 (Right side): Ch 2 **(counts as first hdc, now and throughout)**, hdc in next ch and in each ch around; join with slip st to first hdc: 40 hdc.

Note: Loop a short piece of thread around any stitch to mark last round as **right** side.

Rnd 2: Ch 2, hdc in next 9 hdc, ch 1, hdc in next 20 hdc, ch 1, hdc in last 10 hdc; join with slip st to first hdc changing to Color A *(Fig. 22b, page 138)*: 40 hdc.

Note: Work in the following Color Sequence: (1 Rnd Color A, 2 rnds Color B) twice, changing to Color A at end of Rnd 8.

Rnds 3-8: Ch 2, ★ hdc in next hdc and in each hdc across to next ch-1 sp, (hdc, ch 1, hdc) in ch-1 sp; repeat from ★ once **more**, hdc in each hdc across; join with slip st to first hdc: 64 hdc.

RIGHT LEG

Rnd 1: Ch 2, hdc in next 15 hdc; flattening piece so that ch-1 sps are together and skipping 32 hdc in between, hdc through **both** sps, hdc in each hdc around; join with slip st to first hdc changing to Color B: 33 hdc.

Note: Work in the following Color Sequence: 2 Rnds Color B, 1 rnd Color A, 1 rnd Color B.

Rnds 2-4: Ch 2, hdc in next hdc and in each hdc around; join with slip st to first hdc.

Rnd 5: Ch 1, sc in each hdc around; join with slip st to first sc, finish off.

LEFT LEG

Rnd 1: With **right** side facing, join Color A with slip st in same center sp on Body as Right Leg; ch 2, hdc in next hdc and in each hdc around; join with slip st to first hdc changing to Color B: 33 hdc.

Rnds 2-5: Work same as Right Leg in the same Color Sequence.

FINISHING

Using photo as a guide for placement, sew beads to center front.

Attach magnetic strip to back.

Quick SUMMER-FRESH BROOM

A curious bumblebee is all abuzz about the colorful flowers on our decorative whisk broom. Displayed on a wall, this charming piece will bring a summer-fresh feeling to your home.

MATERIALS

Bedspread Weight Cotton Thread (size 10), approximately:

Coneflower
  MC (White or Pink) - 14 yards **each**
  CC (Gold) - 4 yards **each**

Brown-eyed Susan
  Brown - 4 yards
  Gold - 6 yards

Bumble Bee
  Black - 8 yards
  Yellow - 5 yards
  White - 4 yards

Steel crochet hook, size 8 (1.50 mm)
12" Craft broom

Tapestry needle
Polyester fiberfill
3" length wire
Glue gun
Silk ivy
Various ribbons

Note: Gauge is not important. Pieces can be smaller or larger without changing the overall effect.

PATTERN STITCH

DECREASE (uses next 2 sts)

★ YO, insert hook in **next** st, YO and pull up a loop, YO and draw through 2 loops on hook; repeat from ★ once **more**, YO and draw through all 3 loops on hook **(counts as one dc)**.

CONEFLOWER (Make 2)
CENTER
With CC, ch 5; join with slip st to form a ring.

Rnd 1 (Right side): Ch 3 **(counts as first dc, now and throughout)**, 11 dc in ring; join with slip st to first dc: 12 dc.

Note: Loop a short piece of thread around any stitch to mark last round as **right** side and front.

Rnd 2: Ch 3, 2 dc in next dc, (dc in next dc, 2 dc in next dc) around; join with slip st to first dc: 18 dc.

Rnd 3: Ch 1, sc in each dc around; join with slip st to Back Loop Only of first sc *(Fig. 20, page 138)*.

Rnd 4: Ch 2, working in Back Loops Only, dc in next sc, decrease around; skip beginning ch-2 and join with slip st to first dc, finish off leaving a long end for sewing: 9 dc.

Thread needle with end and weave through remaining dc; gather tightly and secure.

PETALS
Rnd 1: With front facing and working in free loops on Rnd 3 *(Fig. 21a, page 138)*, join MC with slip st in any sc; ★ ch 12 **loosely**, sc in second ch from hook, hdc in next ch, dc in last 9 chs, skip next sc, slip st in next sc; repeat from ★ around to last sc, leave last sc unworked: 8 Petals.

Rnd 2: Working in remaining free loops on Rnd 3, ★ ch 12 **loosely**, sc in second ch from hook, hdc in next ch, dc in last 9 chs, slip st in skipped sc **behind** next Petal; repeat from ★ around, finish off.

BROWN-EYED SUSAN
CENTER
With Brown, ch 5; join with slip st to form a ring.

Rnd 1 (Right side): Ch 3 **(counts as first dc, now and throughout)**, 11 dc in ring; join with slip st to first dc: 12 dc.

Note: Loop a short piece of thread around any stitch to mark last round as **right** side.

Rnd 2: Ch 3, dc in same st, 2 dc in next dc and in each dc around; join with slip st to first dc: 24 dc.

Rnd 3: Ch 1, sc in same st, 2 sc in next dc, (sc in next dc, 2 sc in next dc) around; join with slip st to first sc, finish off: 36 sc.

PETALS
Rnd 1: With **right** side facing, join Gold with slip st in any sc; ★ ch 7 **loosely**, sc in second ch from hook, hdc in next ch, dc in next ch, tr in last 3 chs, skip next 2 sc, slip st in next sc; repeat from ★ around working last slip st in same st as first slip st; finish off: 12 Petals.

BUMBLE BEE

BODY

With Black, ch 5; join with slip st to form a ring.

Rnd 1 (Right side): Ch 3 **(counts as first dc, now and throughout)**, 11 dc in ring; join with slip st to first dc: 12 dc.

Rnd 2: Ch 1, sc in same st and in next dc, 2 sc in next dc, (sc in next 2 dc, 2 sc in next dc) around; join with slip st to first sc: 16 sc.

Rnd 3: Ch 1, sc in each sc around, drop Black; join with slip st to first sc changing to Yellow *(Fig. 22b, page 138)*.

Rnd 4: Ch 3, 2 dc in next sc, (dc in next sc, 2 dc in next sc) around, drop Yellow; join with slip st to first dc changing to Black: 24 dc.

Rnd 5: Ch 1, sc in each dc around; join with slip st to first sc.

Rnd 6: Ch 1, sc in each sc around, drop Black; join with slip st to first sc changing to Yellow.

Rnd 7: Ch 3, dc in next sc and in each sc around, drop Yellow; join with slip st to first dc changing to Black.

Rnd 8: Ch 1, sc in each dc around; join with slip st to first sc.

Rnd 9: Ch 3, dc in next sc and in each sc around, drop Black; join with slip st to first dc changing to Yellow.

Rnd 10: Ch 3, dc in next dc, decrease, (dc in next 2 dc, decrease) around, cut Yellow; join with slip st to first dc changing to Black: 18 dc.

Rnd 11: Ch 1, sc in each dc around; join with slip st to first sc.

Rnd 12: Ch 3, dc in next sc and in each sc around; join with slip st to first dc.

Rnd 13: Ch 2, dc in next dc, decrease around; skip beginning ch-2 and join with slip st to first dc, finish off leaving a long end for sewing: 9 dc.

Stuff Body **lightly** with polyester fiberfill.

Thread needle with end and weave through remaining dc; gather tightly and secure.

WING (Make 2)

With White, ch 11 **loosely**.

Foundation Row: Sc in fifth ch from hook, (ch 1, skip next ch, sc in next ch) 3 times: 4 sps.

Rnd 1: Ch 4, (dc, ch 1) 5 times around post of last sc worked; working over beginning ch, dc in next sp, ch 1, hdc in next sp, (ch 1, hdc) twice in next sp, ch 2, slip st in second ch from hook, (hdc, ch 1) twice in same sp, hdc in next sp, ch 1, dc in next sp, ch 1, dc in same sp as beginning ch-4, ch 1; join with slip st to third ch of beginning ch-4, finish off.

Using photo as guide for placement, sew Wings to Rnd 9 of Body. Add Yellow French Knots on Rnd 12 for eyes *(Fig. 32, page 142)*. Insert wire into top of head; bend ends up, then bend tip of each end in a small loop.

FINISHING

Tie ribbons in a bow. Using photo as guide for placement, glue bow, ivy, Flowers and Bumblebee to broom.

RAINBOW RIVERS RUG

Brighten a child's room with the rainbow of colors on our fun floor covering! Flowing against a black background, the vivid stripes of this deep-pile rug are stitched into a cushiony foundation.

Finished Size: Foundation - approximately 25" x 34"
Rug with Stripes - approximately 25" x 36"

MATERIALS

Worsted Weight Yarn, approximately:
MC (Black) - 18 ounces, (510 grams, 1,015 yards)
Color A (Red) - 26 yards
Color B (Orange) - 26 yards
Color C (Yellow) - 26 yards
Color D (Green) - 26 yards
Color E (Blue) - 26 yards
Color F (Purple) - 26 yards
Crochet hooks, sizes G (4.00 mm) **and** K (6.50 mm) **or** sizes needed for gauge

GAUGE: With double strand of MC and smaller size hook, 6 dc and 3 rows = 2"

Note: Each row is worked across length of Rug.

FOUNDATION

Holding 2 strands of MC together and using smaller size hook, ch 104 **loosely**.

Row 1: Dc in fourth ch from hook and in each ch across **(3 skipped chs count as first dc)**: 102 dc.

Row 2 (Right side): Ch 3 **(counts as first dc, now and throughout)**, turn; dc in next dc and in each dc across.

Note: Loop a short piece of yarn around any stitch to mark last row as **right** side and bottom.

Rows 3-38: Repeat Row 2, 36 times. Finish off.

STRIPES

COLOR SEQUENCE

★ One row each Color A, Color B, Color C, Color D, Color E, and Color F; repeat from ★ throughout.

Row 1: With **right** side facing, using larger size hook, and bottom toward you, join one strand of Color A with sc around post of second dc on Row 2 *(see Joining With Sc, page 138)*; sc around same st, (ch 2, 2 sc around post of next dc) across to last dc, leave last dc unworked; finish off.

Note: Stripes will be worked beginning at alternate ends.

Row 2: With **right** side facing and larger size hook, join one strand of next color with sc around post of second dc on next row at **same** end as last sc worked on previous row; sc around same st, (ch 2, 2 sc around post of next dc) across to last dc, leave last dc unworked; finish off.

Repeat Row 2 until 36 Stripes are completed.

rock-a-bye collection

Few things bring us more joy than a precious little one. Soft and cuddly, these tiny bundles fill us with love and inspire our crochet creativity. As we looked for new ways to shower infants with handmade tokens, we were especially pleased with this adorable collection, which includes lots of warming wraps, a pair of handy thumbless mittens, and a colorful caterpillar that's cute as a bug!

GRANNY SQUARE LAYETTE

Granny squares are the focus of this cozy layette. The tiny floral blocks, crocheted with baby fingering weight yarn, are used to create the sacque, bonnet, afghan, and booties. Gently textured ridges separate the squares, which are worked individually and then slip stitched together.

Finished Size: Layette - Newborn
Afghan - approximately 34" x 45"

MATERIALS
Baby Fingering Weight Yarn, approximately:
Complete Set
MC (White) - 18 ounces, (510 grams, 3,150 yards)
Color A (Green) - 5¼ ounces, (150 grams, 920 yards)
Color B (Pink) - 1½ ounces, (40 grams, 265 yards)
Color C (Yellow) - 1½ ounces, (40 grams, 265 yards)
Afghan
MC (White) - 16 ounces, (450 grams, 2,800 yards)
Color A (Green) - 2¼ ounces, (65 grams, 395 yards)
Color B (Pink) - 1¼ ounces, (35 grams, 220 yards)
Color C (Yellow) - 1¼ ounces, (35 grams, 220 yards)
Bonnet
MC (White) - ¾ ounce, (20 grams, 130 yards)
Color A (Green) - 20 yards
Color B (Pink) - 10 yards
Color C (Yellow) - 10 yards

Sacque
MC (White) - 1 ounce, (30 grams, 175 yards)
Color A (Green) - 2¾ ounces, (80 grams, 480 yards)
Color B (Pink) - 10 yards
Color C (Yellow) - 10 yards
Booties
MC (White) - 55 yards
Color A (Green) - 5 yards
Color B (Pink) - 5 yards
Crochet hook, size D (3.25 mm) **or** size needed for gauge
Yarn needle
Sewing needle and thread
2 - ⅜" buttons

GAUGE: One Square = 3"

PATTERN STITCHES

BEGINNING POPCORN

Ch 3, 4 dc in sp indicated, drop loop from hook, insert hook in top of beginning ch-3, hook dropped loop and draw through.

POPCORN

5 Dc in sp indicated, drop loop from hook, insert hook in first dc of 5-dc group, hook dropped loop and draw through *(Fig. 13, page 135)*.

SC DECREASE

Pull up a loop in next 2 sts, YO and draw through all 3 loops on hook **(counts as one sc)**.

HDC DECREASE (uses next 2 sts)

(YO, insert hook in **next** st, YO and pull up a loop) twice, YO and draw through all 5 loops on hook **(counts as one hdc)**.

DC DECREASE (uses next 2 sts)

★ YO, insert hook in **next** st, YO and pull up a loop, YO and draw through 2 loops on hook; repeat from ★ once **more**, YO and draw through all 3 loops on hook **(counts as one dc)**.

SQUARE

With Color B or Color C as indicated in each design, ch 4; join with slip st to form a ring.

Rnd 1 (Right side)**:** Work beginning Popcorn in ring, ch 2, (work Popcorn in ring, ch 2) 3 times; join with slip st to top of beginning Popcorn, finish off: 4 Popcorns.

Rnd 2: With **right** side facing and working behind Popcorns, join Color A with slip st in any ch-2 sp; ch 3 **(counts as first dc, now and throughout)**, (2 dc, ch 1, 3 dc) in same sp, ch 1, (3 dc, ch 1) twice in next ch-2 sp and in each ch-2 sp around; join with slip st to first dc, finish off: 24 dc.

Rnd 3: With **right** side facing, join MC with slip st in first ch-1 sp (corner); ch 3, (2 dc, ch 1, 3 dc) in same sp, ch 1, 3 dc in next ch-1 sp, ch 1, ★ (3 dc, ch 1) twice in next ch-1 sp, 3 dc in next ch-1 sp, ch 1; repeat from ★ around; join with slip st to first dc: 36 dc.

Rnd 4: Slip st in next 2 dc and in next ch-1 sp, ch 3, (2 dc, ch 1, 3 dc) in same sp, ch 1, (3 dc in next ch-1 sp, ch 1) twice, ★ (3 dc, ch 1) twice in next corner ch-1 sp, (3 dc in next ch-1 sp, ch 1) twice; repeat from ★ around; join with slip st to first dc: 48 dc.

Rnd 5: Ch 1, sc in same st and in each dc and each ch-1 sp around working 3 sc in each corner ch-1 sp; join with slip st to first sc, finish off: 72 sc.

AFGHAN

Make 96 Squares using Color B for Rnd 1 and 96 Squares using Color C for Rnd 1.

ASSEMBLY

Alternating colors, join Squares into 12 vertical strips of 16 Squares each.

Note: **Join Squares** as follows: With **wrong** sides together and working through **inside** loops of **both** pieces, join MC with slip st in any corner sc; slip st in each sc across to next corner sc; finish off.

Alternating colors, join strips in same manner.

EDGING

Rnd 1: With **wrong** side facing, join MC with slip st in any corner sc; ch 1, ★ 3 sc in corner sc, sc in next 18 sc on same Square, sc in 19 sc across each Square to last Square, sc in next 18 sc; repeat from ★ around; join with slip st to first sc.

Rnd 2: Ch 1, turn; sc in same st, skip next 2 sc, 5 dc in next sc, skip next 2 sc, (sc in next sc, skip next 2 sc, 5 dc in next sc, skip next 2 sc) around; join with slip st to first sc, finish off.

BONNET

Make 4 Squares using Color B for Rnd 1 and 4 Squares using Color C for Rnd 1.

ASSEMBLY

Alternating colors, join Squares into 2 vertical strips of 4 Squares each, following joining instructions for afghan.
Alternating colors, join strips in same manner.
Fold piece in half widthwise and join Squares together to form Bonnet.

EDGING

Rnd 1: With **wrong** side facing, join MC with slip st in any unworked corner sc; ch 1, ★ 3 sc in corner sc, sc in next 18 sc on same Square, sc in 19 sc across each of next 2 Squares, sc in next 18 sc; repeat from ★ once **more**; join with slip st to first sc: 154 sc.

Rnd 2: Ch 1, turn; sc in same st, skip next 2 sc, 5 dc in next sc, (skip next 2 sc, sc in next sc, skip next 2 sc, 5 dc in next sc) 12 times, hdc in next 7 sc, hdc decrease, (hdc in next 5 sc, hdc decrease) across to last 6 sc, hdc in last 6 sc: 13 5-dc groups and 68 hdc.

Note: Begin working in rows.

Row 1: Ch 1, turn; sc in first 7 hdc, sc decrease, (sc in next 2 hdc, sc decrease) across to last 7 hdc, sc in last 7 hdc, leave remaining sts unworked: 54 sc.

Row 2: Ch 1, turn; sc in first 6 sc, (sc decrease, sc in next 6 sc) across; do **not** finish off: 48 sc.

TIES

Ch 68 **loosely**; sc in second ch from hook and in each ch across; slip st in end of row, finish off.

With **right** side facing, join MC with slip st in end of Row 2 on opposite side; ch 68 **loosely**; sc in second ch from hook and in each ch across; slip st in first sc, finish off.

Continued on page 86.

THUMBLESS MITTENS

Sized for baby's tiny hands, these classic thumbless mittens will protect infants from frosty weather. We crafted them with variegated baby fingering weight yarn in a pleasing blend of pastels and white, so they're ideal for boys or girls.

Finished Size: Infant

MATERIALS
Baby Fingering Weight Yarn, approximately:
½ ounce, (20 grams, 75 yards)
Crochet hook, size C (2.75 mm) **or** size needed for gauge
Yarn needle
1 yard of ⅛" wide ribbon

GAUGE: 15 sc and 19 rnds = 2"

BODY
Ch 39 **loosely**; being careful not to twist ch, join with slip st to form a ring.
Rnd 1 (Right side)**:** Sc in each ch around; do **not** join, place marker *(see Markers, page 138)*: 39 sc.
Rnds 2-27: Sc in each sc around.
Note: To **decrease**, pull up a loop in next 2 sc, YO and draw through all 3 loops on hook **(counts as one sc)**.
Rnd 28: Sc in next 3 sc, (decrease, sc in next 2 sc) around: 30 sc.
Rnd 29: (Sc in next 3 sc, decrease) around: 24 sc.

Rnd 30: (Sc in next 4 sc, decrease) around; slip st in next sc, finish off leaving a long end for sewing: 20 sc.

Thread yarn needle with end and weave through remaining sts; gather tightly and secure.

EDGING
Rnd 1: With **right** side facing and working in free loops of beginning ch *(Fig. 21b, page 138)*, join yarn with slip st in first ch; ch 1, sc in each ch around to last ch, 2 sc in last ch; join with slip st to first sc: 40 sc.
Rnd 2: Ch 1, sc in same st, (ch 3, skip next sc, sc in next sc) around to last sc, ch 1, skip last sc, hdc in first sc to form last sp: 20 sps.
Rnds 3 and 4: Ch 1, sc in same sp, (ch 3, sc in next ch-3 sp) around, ch 1, hdc in first sc to form last sp.
Rnd 5: Ch 1, sc in same st, ch 1, (2 dc, ch 1) twice in center ch of next ch-3 sp, ★ sc in center ch of next ch-3 sp, ch 1, (2 dc, ch 1) twice in center ch of next ch-3 sp; repeat from ★ around; join with slip st to first sc, finish off.

Weave ribbon through sps on Rnd 2 of Edging and tie in a bow.

Wrapped in the softness of one of these adorable afghans, a little one is sure to have sweet dreams. Fast to finish in worsted weight yarn, the pattern is designed for solid or striped styles, so it's a snap to coordinate your blanket with the nursery decor.

Finished Size: Approximately 34" x 45"

MATERIALS

Worsted Weight Brushed Acrylic Yarn, approximately:

Solid

21 ounces, (600 grams, 1,620 yards)

Striped

MC (White) - 10 ounces, (280 grams, 770 yards)
Color A (Yellow) - 5½ ounces, (160 grams, 425 yards)
Color B (Blue) - 5½ ounces, (160 grams, 425 yards)

Crochet hook, size H (5.00 mm) **or** size needed for gauge

GAUGE: In pattern, 3 repeats and 9 rows = 3"

PATTERN STITCH

PUFF ST

★ YO, insert hook in sp indicated, YO and pull up a loop even with loop on hook; repeat from ★ 2 times **more**, YO and draw through all 7 loops on hook *(Fig. 12, page 135)*.

SOLID AFGHAN

BODY

Ch 128 **loosely**.

Row 1 (Right side)**:** Sc in second ch from hook and in each ch across: 127 sc.

Note: Loop a short piece of yarn around any stitch to mark last row as **right** side.

Row 2: Ch 1, turn; sc in first sc, (ch 1, skip next sc, sc in next sc) across: 64 sc.

Row 3: Ch 3 **(counts as first dc, now and throughout)**, turn; work Puff St in first ch-1 sp, (ch 3, slip st in next ch-1 sp, ch 3, work Puff St in next ch-1 sp) across to last sc, ch 1, dc in last sc: 32 Puff Sts.

Row 4: Ch 1, turn; sc in first dc and in next Puff St, ★ sc in next ch-3 sp, ch 1, sc in next ch-3 sp and in next Puff St; repeat from ★ across to last dc, sc in last dc: 127 sts.

Row 5: Ch 1, turn; sc in first sc, (ch 1, skip next st, sc in next sc) across: 64 sc.

Rows 6-122: Repeat Rows 3-5, 39 times; do **not** finish off at end of Row 122.

EDGING

Rnd 1: Ch 1, turn; sc in first st, ch 3, (skip next 3 sts, sc in next st, ch 3) twice, (skip next 2 sts, sc in next st, ch 3) across to last 4 sts, skip next 3 sts, (sc, ch 3, sc) in last st, † ch 3;

working in end of rows, skip first row, [(sc in next row, ch 3) twice, skip next row] 3 times, [(sc in next row, ch 3) twice, skip next 2 rows, (sc in next row, ch 3) twice, skip next row] across †; working in free loops of beginning ch *(Fig. 21b, page 138)*, (sc, ch 3, sc) in first ch, ch 3, (skip next 3 sts, sc in next st, ch 3) twice, (skip next 2 chs, sc in next ch, ch 3) across to last 4 chs, skip next 3 chs, (sc, ch 3, sc) in last ch; repeat from † to † once; sc in same st as first sc, ch 3; join with slip st to first sc: 228 ch-3 sps.

Rnd 2: Slip st in first ch-3 sp, ch 3, work Puff St in next ch-3 sp, ch 3, ★ slip st in next ch-3 sp, ch 3, work Puff St in next ch-3 sp, ch 3; repeat from ★ around; join with slip st to first slip st, finish off.

STRIPED AFGHAN

BODY

COLOR SEQUENCE

2 Rows MC *(Fig. 22a, page 138)*, ★ 1 row Color A, 2 rows MC, 1 row Color B, 2 rows MC; repeat from ★ throughout.

With MC, ch 128 **loosely**.

Row 1 (Right side)**:** Sc in second ch from hook and in each ch across: 127 sc.

Note: Loop a short piece of yarn around any stitch to mark last row as **right** side.

Row 2: Ch 1, turn; sc in first sc, (ch 1, skip next sc, sc in next sc) across changing colors in last sc: 64 sc.

Row 3: Ch 3 **(counts as first dc, now and throughout)**, turn; work Puff St in first ch-1 sp, (ch 3, slip st in next ch-1 sp, ch 3, work Puff St in next ch-1 sp) across to last sc, ch 1, dc in last sc; finish off: 32 Puff Sts.

Row 4: With **right** side facing, join MC with slip st in first dc; ch 1, sc in same st and in next Puff St, ★ sc in next ch-3 sp, ch 1, sc in next ch-3 sp and in next Puff St; repeat from ★ across to last dc, sc in last dc: 127 sts.

Row 5: Ch 1, turn; sc in first sc, (ch 1, skip next st, sc in next sc) across changing colors in last sc: 64 sc.

Rows 6-122: Repeat Rows 3-5, 39 times; do **not** finish off or change colors at end of Row 122.

EDGING

Work same as Solid Afghan.

RECEIVING BLANKET EDGING

Mama and baby will receive these warming wraps with open arms! A delicate picot edging, worked in bedspread weight cotton thread, is crocheted into the edge of cotton flannel or seersucker fabric to fashion these precious blankets.

Finished Size: Approximately 1" wide

MATERIALS

Bedspread Weight Cotton Thread (size 10), approximately 205 yards for **one** Edging

Steel crochet hook, size 7 (1.65 mm) **or** size needed for gauge

1¹/₈ yards cotton flannel **or** seersucker for **each** blanket

6" diameter cardboard circle

Scissors

Fabric marking pen

PREPARING BLANKET

Wash, dry, and press fabric. Trim fabric to a 36" square. To round corners, place cardboard circle on one corner of fabric with edge of circle even with edges of fabric. Use fabric marking pen to draw along edge of circle in corner; cut away excess fabric along drawn line. Repeat for remaining corners. Press all edges of blanket ¹/₄" to wrong side. Turn raw edge under to meet crease and press again.

GAUGE: 9 sc = 1"

EDGING

Note: When working stitches on first round, insert hook through blanket along second pressed edge.

Rnd 1 (Right side)**:** With **right** side of blanket facing, join thread with slip st in center of any side; ch 1, sc evenly around (total sc must be a multiple of 8); join with slip st to first sc.

Rnd 2: ★ Ch 3, skip next 3 sc, slip st in next sc, ch 6 **loosely**; sc in second ch from hook, hdc in next ch, dc in last 3 chs, skip next 3 sc, slip st in next sc; repeat from ★ around working last slip st in same sc as beginning ch-3.

Rnd 3: Slip st in first ch-3 sp, ch 1, sc in same sp, ★ † ch 1, working in free loops of ch-6 *(Fig. 21b, page 138)*, [sc in next ch, ch 2, sc in side of sc just worked *(Fig. 1, page 64)*, skip next ch] twice, (sc, ch 2, sc in side of sc just worked) twice at top of point, skip next hdc, sc in next dc, ch 2, sc in side of sc just worked, skip next dc, sc in next dc, ch 1 †, sc in next ch-3 sp; repeat from ★ around to last point, then repeat from † to † once; join with slip st to first sc, finish off.

Quick CRIB CATERPILLAR

This cute snuggle bug will inch its way into your heart — and baby's, too! Fashioned with brushed acrylic yarn, the caterpillar's roly-poly body is formed by increasing and decreasing your stitches. The toy's child-safe face is embroidered.

Finished Size: Approximately 11¹/₂" long

MATERIALS
Worsted Weight Brushed Acrylic Yarn, approximately:
  MC (Lavender) - 1 ounce, (30 grams, 75 yards)
  CC (Yellow) - ¹/₂ ounce, (20 grams, 40 yards)
  Small amounts of Aqua, Dark Lavender, and Pink for facial features
Crochet hook, size G (4.00 mm) **or** size needed for gauge
Polyester fiberfill
Yarn needle

GAUGE: 8 sc and 8 rnds = 2"

HEAD AND BODY
With MC, ch 3; being careful not to twist ch, join with slip st to form a ring.
Rnd 1: Ch 1, 2 sc in each ch around; do **not** join, place marker *(see Markers, page 138)*: 6 sc.

Rnd 2: 2 Sc in each sc around: 12 sc.
Rnd 3: (Sc in next sc, 2 sc in next sc) around: 18 sc.
Rnd 4: (Sc in next 2 sc, 2 sc in next sc) around: 24 sc.
Rnd 5: (Sc in next 3 sc, 2 sc in next sc) around: 30 sc.
Rnds 6-11: Sc in each sc around.
Stuff Head with polyester fiberfill.
Note: To **decrease**, pull up a loop in next 2 sc, YO and draw through all 3 loops on hook **(counts as one sc)**.
Rnd 12: (Sc in next 3 sc, decrease) around: 24 sc.
Rnd 13: Decrease around changing to CC in last st *(Fig. 22a, page 138)*: 12 sc.
Rnd 14: 2 Sc in each sc around: 24 sc.
Rnd 15: (Sc in next 3 sc, 2 sc in next sc) around: 30 sc.
Rnds 16-20: Sc in each sc around.
Stuff Body with polyester fiberfill.
Rnd 21: (Sc in next 3 sc, decrease) around: 24 sc.
Rnd 22: Decrease around changing to MC in last st: 12 sc.
Rnds 23-31: Repeat Rnds 14-22 changing to CC in last st on Rnd 31.

Rnds 32-48: Repeat Rnds 14-30.
Rnds 49 and 50: Decrease around: 6 sc.
Finish off leaving a long end for sewing.
Thread needle with end and weave through remaining sts; gather tightly and secure.

ANTENNA (Make 2)

With CC, ch 3; being careful not to twist ch, join with slip st to form a ring.
Rnd 1: Ch 1, 2 sc in each ch around; do **not** join, place marker: 6 sc.
Rnds 2-6: Sc in each sc around; at end of Rnd 6, slip st in next sc, finish off leaving a long end for sewing.
Stuff Antenna with polyester fiberfill.

LEG (Make 16)

With MC, work same as Antenna through Rnd 4; at end of Rnd 4, slip st in next sc, finish off leaving a long end for sewing.

FINISHING

Using photo as a guide for placement, sew Antennae to top of Head, spacing 3 sts apart.
Sew two Legs to each side of each segment of Body.
With Blue, add Satin St for eyes *(Fig. 29, page 141)*. With Pink, add Satin Stitch for nose.
With Dark Lavender, add Straight Stitch for eye lashes *(Fig. 28, page 141)*.

Quick GUMDROP BOTTLE COVER

Goody, goody gumdrop for this sweet bottle cover! Created with baby fingering weight yarn, it's a darling shower gift. The puffy "gumdrops" are made using popcorn stitches.

Finished Size: To fit an 8 ounce bottle

MATERIALS

Baby Fingering Weight Yarn, approximately:
MC (White) - 55 yards
Color A (Yellow) - 40 yards
Color B (Green) - 40 yards
Color C (Pink) - 35 yards
Color D (Blue) - 35 yards
Crochet hook, size C (2.75 mm) **or** size needed for gauge
1/2 yard of 1/8" wide ribbon
Yarn needle

GAUGE: Rnds 1-3 of Bottom = 2 1/2"
          10 dc and 6 rows = 2"

PATTERN STITCHES
EXTENDED SINGLE CROCHET *(abbreviated Ex sc)*
Pull up a loop in next sc, (YO and draw through first loop on hook) 3 times, YO and draw through both loops on hook *(Fig. 1)*, pushing Ex sc to **right** side.

Fig. 1

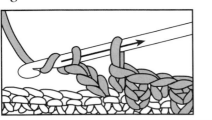

POPCORN
5 Dc in st indicated changing to MC in last dc worked; do **not** cut yarn unless otherwise instructed, drop loop from hook, insert hook in first dc of 5-dc group, hook dropped loop and draw through *(Fig. 13, page 135)*.

BOTTOM

With MC, ch 3; join with slip st to form a ring.
Rnd 1 (Right side)**:** Ch 3 **(counts as first dc, now and throughout)**, 11 dc in ring; join with slip st to first dc: 12 dc.
Note: Loop a short piece of yarn around any stitch to mark last round as **right** side.
Rnd 2: Ch 3, dc in same st, 2 dc in each dc around; join with slip st to first dc: 24 dc.
Rnd 3: Ch 3, 2 dc in next dc, (dc in next dc, 2 dc in next dc) around; join with slip st to first dc: 36 dc.

SIDES

Rnd 1: Slip st from **back** to **front** around post of first dc, ch 3, work BPdc around next dc and around each dc around *(Fig. 17, page 136)*; join with slip st to first dc.
Rnds 2-4: Ch 3, dc in next dc and in each dc around; join with slip st to first dc changing to Color A at end of Rnd 4 *(Fig. 22b, page 138)*, do **not** cut MC.
Rnd 5: Ch 1, **turn**; sc in each st around; drop Color A, join with slip st to first sc changing to Color B.
Rnd 6: Ch 1, turn; sc in same st, work Ex sc in next sc, (sc in next sc, work Ex sc in next sc) around; cut Color B, join with slip st to first sc changing to Color A: 18 Ex sc.

Rnd 7: Ch 1, turn; sc in each st around; cut Color A, join with slip st to first sc changing to MC: 36 sc.

Rnds 8 and 9: Ch 1, turn; sc in each sc around; join with slip st to first sc.

Rnd 10: Ch 3, turn; dc in next 2 sc changing to Color C in last dc worked, work Popcorn in next sc, ★ dc in next 3 sc changing to Color C in last dc worked, work Popcorn in next sc; repeat from ★ around; cut Color C, join with slip st to first dc: 9 Popcorns.

Rnd 11: Ch 1, turn; sc in each st around; join with slip st to first sc: 36 sc.

Rnd 12: Ch 2, drop MC, with Color B, ch 1, turn; work Popcorn in next sc, ★ dc in next 3 sc changing to Color B in last dc worked, work Popcorn in next sc; repeat from ★ 7 times **more**, cut Color B, dc in last 2 sc; join with slip st to top of beginning ch: 9 Popcorns.

Rnd 13: Repeat Rnd 11.

Rnd 14: Ch 3, turn; dc in next 2 sc changing to Color A in last dc worked, work Popcorn in next sc, ★ dc in next 3 sc changing to Color A in last dc worked, work Popcorn in next sc; repeat from ★ around; cut Color A, join with slip st to first dc.

Rnd 15: Repeat Rnd 11.

Rnd 16: Ch 2, drop MC, with Color D, ch 1, turn; work Popcorn in next sc, ★ dc in next 3 sc changing to Color D in last dc worked, work Popcorn in next sc; repeat from ★ 7 times **more**, cut Color D, dc in last 2 sc; join with slip st to top of beginning ch.

Rnd 17: Repeat Rnd 11.

Rnd 18: Ch 1, turn; sc in each sc around; join with slip st to first sc changing to Color A, do **not** cut MC.

Rnds 19-21: Repeat Rnds 5-7.

Rnd 22: Ch 3, turn; dc in next sc and in each sc around; join with slip st to first dc.

Rnds 23-25: Ch 3, do **not** turn; dc in next dc and in each dc around; join with slip st to first dc.

Rnd 26: Ch 1, sc in same st, ch 1, skip next dc, (dc, ch 1) 3 times in next dc, skip next dc, ★ sc in next dc, ch 1, skip next dc, (dc, ch 1) 3 times in next dc, skip next dc; repeat from ★ around; join with slip st to first sc, finish off.

Weave ribbon through dc on Rnd 25 and tie in a bow.

ROCK-A-BYE RIPPLES

Rock-a-bye your little one off to sleep beneath this cuddly cover-up. Stitched in baby-soft pastels, the naptime throw features a familiar ripple pattern worked in worsted weight yarn. What a charming way to show your overflowing love for baby!

Finished Size: Approximately 36" x 49"

MATERIALS

Worsted Weight Yarn, approximately:
  MC (White) - 12 ounces, (340 grams, 925 yards)
  Color A (Lavender) - 4 ounces, (110 grams, 310 yards)
  Color B (Pink) - 2½ ounces, (70 grams, 195 yards)
Crochet hooks, sizes F (3.75 mm) **and** G (4.00 mm) **or** sizes needed for gauge

GAUGE: With larger size hook, 8 dc = 2"
    In pattern, 1 repeat = 3½" and 6 rows = 4"

Gauge Swatch: (7" x 4")
Ch 39 **loosely**.
Rows 1-6: Work same as Body.
Finish off.

PATTERN STITCHES
BEGINNING DECREASE
Ch 2, turn; skip next st, dc in next dc **(counts as one dc)**.
DECREASE
† YO, insert hook in **next** st, YO and pull up a loop, YO and draw through 2 loops on hook †, skip next 3 sts, repeat from † to † once, YO and draw through all 3 loops on hook **(counts as one dc)**.
ENDING DECREASE
† YO, insert hook in **next** st, YO and pull up a loop, YO and draw through 2 loops on hook †, skip next st, repeat from † to † once, YO and draw through all 3 loops on hook **(counts as one dc)**.

COLOR SEQUENCE
4 Rows MC **(Fig. 22a, page 138)**, ★ 1 row Color B, 1 row Color A, 4 rows MC; repeat from ★ throughout.

BODY

With larger size hook and MC, ch 199 **loosely**.
Row 1: Dc in fifth ch from hook **(4 skipped chs count as first dc plus ch 1)**, ch 1, (skip next ch, dc in next ch, ch 1) twice, skip next ch, (dc, ch 3, dc) in next ch, ★ ch 1, (skip next ch, dc in next ch, ch 1) 3 times, skip next ch, decrease, ch 1, (skip next ch, dc in next ch, ch 1) 3 times, skip next ch, (dc, ch 3, dc) in next ch; repeat from ★ across to last 8 chs, (ch 1, skip next ch, dc in next ch) across: 91 dc.

Row 2 (Right side): Work beginning decrease, (dc in next ch-1 sp, dc in next dc) 3 times, (2 dc, ch 3, 2 dc) in next ch-3 sp, (dc in next dc, dc in next ch-1 sp) 3 times, ★ decrease, (dc in next ch-1 sp, dc in next dc) 3 times, (2 dc, ch 3, 2 dc) in next ch-3 sp, (dc in next dc, dc in next ch-1 sp) 3 times; repeat from ★ across to last 2 dc, work ending decrease: 171 dc.

Note: Loop a short piece of yarn around any stitch to mark last row as **right** side.

Row 3: Work beginning decrease, ch 1, (skip next dc, dc in next dc, ch 1) 3 times, (dc, ch 3, dc) in next ch-3 sp, ch 1, (dc in next dc, ch 1, skip next dc) 3 times, ★ decrease, ch 1, (skip next dc, dc in next dc, ch 1) 3 times, (dc, ch 3, dc) in next ch-3 sp, ch 1, (dc in next dc, ch 1, skip next dc) 3 times; repeat from ★ across to last 3 dc, work ending decrease: 91 dc.

Rows 4-70: Repeat Rows 2 and 3, 33 times, then repeat Row 2 once **more**.
Finish off.

EDGING

With **right** side facing and smaller size hook, join Color A with slip st in end of last row; ch 3, 4 dc in same row, working in end of rows, (sc, 5 dc) in next row, sc in next row, (5 dc in next row, sc in next row) across to last row, 7 dc in last row; working in skipped chs and in free loops of beginning ch **(Fig. 21b, page 138)**, sc in first ch, (skip next 2 sts, 5 dc in next st, skip next 2 sts, sc in next st) twice, † skip next 2 sts, 7 dc in next ch-3 sp, skip next 2 sts, sc in next st, (skip next 2 sts, 5 dc in next st, skip next 2 sts, sc in next st) twice †; repeat from † to † across; working in end of rows, 7 dc in first row, (sc in next row, 5 dc in next row) across to last row, (sc, 5 dc) in last row; working across last row, skip next 2 dc, sc in next dc, skip next 2 dc, 5 dc in next dc, skip next 2 dc, sc in next dc, ★ 7 dc in next ch-3 sp, skip next 2 dc, sc in next dc, (skip next 2 dc, 5 dc in next dc, skip next 2 dc, sc in next dc) twice, skip next 2 dc; repeat from ★ across to last ch-3 sp, 7 dc in next ch-3 sp, sc in next dc, skip next 2 dc, 5 dc in next dc, skip next 2 dc, sc in next dc, skip last 2 dc; join with slip st to top of beginning ch-3, finish off.

GRANNY SQUARE LAYETTE

Continued from page 76.

SACQUE

YOKE

MINI-SQUARE

Working same as Square, page 76, through Rnd 3, make
5 Mini-Squares using Color B for Rnd 1 and 5 Mini-Squares
using Color C for Rnd 1; do **not** finish off.

Rnd 4: Ch 1, sc in same st and in each dc and each ch-1 sp
around working 3 sc in each corner ch-1 sp; join with slip st to
first sc, finish off: 56 sc.

ASSEMBLY

Join Mini-Squares following Placement Diagram and joining
instructions for afghan.

PLACEMENT DIAGRAM

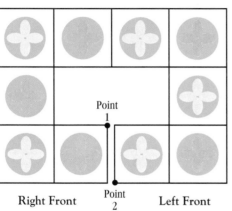

Point
1

Right Front   Point   Left Front
2

NECK EDGING

Row 1: With **right** side facing, join MC with slip st in corner sc
as indicated by Point 1 on Diagram; ch 1, sc in 15 sc across
each of next 6 Squares working sc in each joining: 95 sc.

Row 2: Ch 3, turn; dc in next 2 sc, † dc decrease, dc in next
4 sc, dc decrease, dc in next 2 sc, dc decrease twice, dc in next
2 sc †, repeat from † to † once **more**, dc decrease, dc in next
4 sc, (dc decrease, dc in next 3 sc) twice, repeat from † to †
twice, (dc decrease, dc in next 4 sc) twice: 74 dc.

Row 3: Ch 3, turn; dc in next 4 dc, dc decrease, dc in next
4 dc, † dc decrease twice, dc in next 3 dc, dc decrease, dc in
next 3 dc, dc decrease twice, dc in next 3 dc †, (dc decrease,
dc in next 4 dc) 3 times, repeat from † to † once, dc decrease,
dc in last 5 dc: 59 dc.

Row 4: Ch 3, turn; † dc in next 7 dc, dc decrease twice, dc in
next 5 dc, dc decrease twice †, dc in next 7 dc, dc decrease,
repeat from † to † once, dc in last 9 dc: 50 dc.

Row 5: Ch 1, turn; sc in each dc across; finish off.

BODY

Row 1: With **right** side facing, join Color A with slip st in
corner sc as indicated by Point 2 on diagram; ch 1, sc in same
st and in next 7 sc, 2 sc in next sc, sc in next 6 sc, 2 sc in
joining, sc in next 6 sc, 2 sc in next sc, sc in next 22 sc, sc in
joining, sc in next 14 sc, sc in joining, sc in next 19 sc, (2 sc in
next sc, sc in next 4 sc) twice, sc in joining, [sc in next 3 sc,
(2 sc in next sc, sc in next 3 sc) 3 times, sc in joining] twice,
(sc in next 4 sc, 2 sc in next sc) twice, sc in next 19 sc, sc in
joining, sc in next 14 sc, sc in joining, sc in next 22 sc, 2 sc
in next sc, sc in next 6 sc, 2 sc in joining, sc in next 6 sc, 2 sc in
next sc, sc in next 8 sc: 229 sc.

Row 2: Ch 3, turn; 2 dc in first sc, skip next 2 sc, sc in
next sc, (skip next 2 sc, 5 dc in next sc, skip next 2 sc, sc in
next sc) across to last 3 sc, skip next 2 sc, 3 dc in last sc:
37 5-dc groups.

Row 3: Ch 1, turn; sc in first dc, skip next 2 dc, 5 dc in next sc,
(skip next 2 dc, sc in next dc, skip next 2 dc, 5 dc in next sc) 5
times, skip next 7 5-dc groups and next 2 dc (armhole), sc in
next dc, place marker around sc just worked for Sleeve
placement, (skip next 2 dc, 5 dc in next sc, skip next 2 dc, sc in
next dc) 12 times, place marker around last sc worked for
Sleeve placement, skip next 2 dc and next 7 5-dc groups
(armhole), 5 dc in next sc, (skip next 2 dc, sc in next dc, skip
next 2 dc, 5 dc in next sc) 5 times, skip next 2 dc, sc in last dc:
24 5-dc groups.

Row 4: Ch 3, turn; 2 dc in first sc, skip next 2 dc, sc in
next dc, (skip next 2 dc, 5 dc in next sc, skip next 2 dc, sc in
next dc) across to last 3 sts, skip next 2 dc, 3 dc in last sc:
23 5-dc groups.

Row 5: Ch 1, turn; sc in first dc, (skip next 2 dc, 5 dc in next
sc, skip next 2 dc, sc in next dc) across.

Repeat Rows 4 and 5 until Body measures approximately 7½"
from Yoke, ending by working Row 4.

Last Row: Ch 1, turn; sc in each st across; finish off.

RIGHT SLEEVE

Rnd 1: With **right** side facing, join Color A with slip st in sp to
the **right** of marked sc; ch 3, 2 dc in same sp, sc in same dc as
marked sc, (skip next 2 dc, 5 dc in next sc, skip next 2 dc, sc
in next dc) 7 times, skip next 2 dc, 5 dc in base of next
5-dc group, sc around post of next dc; join with slip st to
first dc: 8 5-dc groups.

Rnds 2-15: Turn; slip st in first sc, ch 3, 2 dc in same st, (skip
next 2 dc, sc in next dc, skip next 2 dc, 5 dc in next sc) 8
times, skip next 2 dc, sc in last dc; join with slip st to first dc.

Rnd 16: Ch 1, turn; sc in each st around; join with slip st to first sc: 52 sc.

Rnd 17: Ch 1, turn; sc decrease around; join with slip st to first sc: 26 sc.

Rnds 18-21: Ch 1, turn; sc in each sc around; join with slip st to first sc.
Finish off.

LEFT SLEEVE

Rnd 1: With **right** side facing, join Color A with slip st in marked sc (base of 5-dc group); ch 3, 2 dc in same st, sc around post of next dc, 5 dc at base of next 5-dc group, (skip next 2 dc, sc in next dc, skip next 2 dc, 5 dc in next sc) 7 times, skip next 2 dc, sc in same dc as marked sc; join with slip st to first dc: 8 5-dc groups.

Rnds 2-21: Work same as Right Sleeve.
Finish off.

EDGING

Row 1: With **right** side facing, join MC with slip st in corner of Left Front neck edge; ch 1, sc evenly across end of rows of Neck Edging, sc in each sc across Square changing to Color A in last sc worked *(Fig. 22a, page 138)*, do **not** cut yarn, sc evenly across end of rows to next corner, 3 sc in corner, sc in each sc across to next corner, 3 sc in corner, sc evenly across end of rows to Yoke changing to MC in last sc worked on Body, sc in each sc across Square, sc evenly across end of rows of Neck Edging.

Rows 2 and 3: Ch 1, turn; sc in each sc across working 3 sc in each corner sc and changing colors same as on previous row.
Finish off.

Using photo as a guide for placement, sew buttons to Front Yoke Edging.

BOOTIES

INSTEP

With Color B, ch 4; join with slip st to form a ring.

Rnd 1 (Right side)**:** Work beginning Popcorn in ring, ch 2, (work Popcorn in ring, ch 2) 3 times; join with slip st to top of beginning Popcorn, finish off: 4 Popcorns.

Rnd 2: With **right** side facing and working behind Popcorns, join Color A with slip st in any ch-2 sp; ch 3 **(counts as first dc, now and throughout)**, (2 dc, ch 1, 3 dc) in same sp, ch 1, (3 dc, ch 1) twice in next ch-2 sp and in each ch-2 sp around; join with slip st to first dc, finish off: 24 dc.

Rnd 3: With **right** side facing, join MC with slip st in first ch-1 sp (corner); ch 1, 3 sc in same sp, sc in next 3 dc, sc in next ch-1 sp, sc in next 3 dc, (3 sc in next ch-1 sp, sc in next 3 dc, sc in next ch-1 sp, sc in next 3 dc) 3 times; join with slip st to first sc: 40 sc.

Rnd 4: Slip st in next sc, ch 21 **loosely**; being careful not to twist ch, skip next 9 sc, slip st in next sc, do **not** finish off.

SIDES AND SOLE

Rnd 1: Ch 1, sc in same st and in each sc across 3 sides of Square, sc in each ch across; join with slip st to first sc: 51 sc.

Rnd 2: Ch 1, sc in each sc around; join with slip st to first sc.

Rnd 3: Ch 1, sc in first 9 sc, sc decrease, sc in next 8 sc, sc decrease, sc in each sc around; join with slip st to first sc: 49 sc.

Rnd 4: Ch 1, sc in each sc around; join with slip st to first sc.

Rnd 5: Ch 1, sc in first 8 sc, sc decrease twice, sc in next 4 sc, sc decrease twice, sc in next 14 sc, sc decrease, sc in next 5 sc, sc decrease, sc in last 6 sc; join with slip st to first sc: 43 sc.

Rnd 6: Ch 1, sc in first 8 sc, sc decrease 4 times, sc in next 14 sc, sc decrease, sc in next 3 sc, sc decrease, sc in last 6 sc; join with slip st to first sc: 37 sc.

Rnd 7: Ch 1, sc in first 8 sc, sc decrease twice, sc in next 14 sc, sc decrease, sc in next sc, sc decrease, sc in last 6 sc; join with slip st to first sc: 33 sc.

Rnd 8: Ch 1, sc in first 7 sc, sc decrease twice, sc in next 12 sc, sc decrease, sc in next sc, sc decrease, sc in last 5 sc; join with slip st to first sc: 29 sc.

Rnd 9: Ch 1, sc in each sc around; join with slip st to first sc, finish off.

CUFF

Rnd 1: With **right** side facing, join MC with slip st in first unworked sc on Square; ch 1, sc in same st and in next 8 sc, working in free loops of ch *(Fig. 21b, page 138)*, sc in each ch around; join with slip st to first sc: 30 sc.

Rnd 2: Ch 3, turn; 2 dc in same st, skip next 2 sc, sc in next sc, (skip next 2 sc, 5 dc in next sc, skip next 2 sc, sc in next sc) 4 times, skip last 2 sc, 2 dc in same st as beginning ch-3; join with slip st to first dc: 5 sc.

Rnd 3: Ch 1, turn; sc in same st, skip next 2 dc, 5 dc in next sc, (skip next 2 dc, sc in next dc, skip next 2 dc, 5 dc in next sc) 4 times, skip last 2 dc; join with slip st to first sc.

Rnd 4: Ch 3, turn; 2 dc in same st, skip next 2 dc, sc in next dc, (skip next 2 dc, 5 dc in next sc, skip next 2 dc, sc in next dc) 4 times, skip last 2 dc, 2 dc in same st as beginning ch-3; join with slip st to first dc.

Rnds 5 and 6: Repeat Rows 3 and 4.

Rnd 7: Ch 1, turn; sc in each st around; join with slip st to first sc, finish off.

Sew Sole seam closed working through **both** loops on Rnd 9.

fashion corner

Add pizzazz to your wardrobe with these stylish wearables! Designed with versatility in mind, this collection lets you make the most of your current clothes by dressing them up with colorful new accents. We have a cozy cardigan and a sassy scarf and beret set for chilly days, and a playful beaded ensemble that lends casual chic to everyday wear. The kids will be smitten with our mittens, and you'll enjoy creating all of these fun fashions for your family!

YO-YO CARDIGAN

Round motifs inspired by quilter's yo-yos add fresh appeal to our fall cardigan. Created in a patchwork of rich autumn hues, the jacket front is contrasted with black yo-yos on the back and the three-quarter-length sleeves. A versatile cool-weather cover-up, this roomy top is designed in sizes small, medium, and large.

Size:	Small	Medium	Large
Finished Chest			
Measurement:	40"	44"	48"

Size Note: Yarn amounts are written for size Small with sizes Medium and Large in braces { }.

MATERIALS
Sport Weight Yarn, approximately:
MC (Black) - 11{11-12} ounces,
　[310{310-340} grams, 1,100{1,100-1,200} yards]
Color A (Gold) - 1 ounce, (30 grams, 100 yards)
Color B (Purple) - 1 ounce, (30 grams, 100 yards)
Color C (Green) - 1 ounce, (30 grams, 100 yards)
Color D (Aqua) - 1 ounce, (30 grams, 100 yards)
Color E (Red) - 1 ounce, (30 grams, 100 yards)
Crochet hook, size F (3.75 mm) **or** size needed for gauge
Yarn needle

GAUGE: One Yo-Yo = 2"

BACK
FIRST YO-YO
With MC, ch 3; join with slip st to form a ring.
Rnd 1 (Right side)**:** Ch 6, (dc in ring, ch 3) 11 times; join with slip st to third ch of beginning ch-6: 12 ch-3 sps.
Note: Loop a short piece of yarn around any stitch to mark last round as **right** side.
Rnd 2: Slip st in first ch-3 sp, ch 1, sc in same sp, ch 3, (sc in next ch-3 sp, ch 3) around; join with slip st to first sc, finish off.

ADDITIONAL YO-YOS
Work same as First Yo-Yo through Rnd 1.
Note: Mark last round as **right** side.
Beginning with bottom row of Back, work One-Sided or Two-Sided Joining, following Placement Diagram as a guide, page 105.
Note: Yo-Yos are joined with **wrong** sides together and new Yo-Yo facing throughout.

ONE-SIDED JOINING
Rnd 2: Slip st in first ch-3 sp, ch 1, sc in same sp, (ch 3, sc in next ch-3 sp) 8 times, ★ ch 1, sc in corresponding sp on **adjacent Yo-Yo**, ch 1, sc in next ch-3 sp on **new Yo-Yo**; repeat from ★ 2 times **more**, ch 3; join with slip st to first sc, finish off.

TWO-SIDED JOINING

Rnd 2: Slip st in first ch-3 sp, ch 1, sc in same sp, (ch 3, sc in next ch-3 sp) 5 times, ★ ch 1, sc in corresponding sp on **adjacent Yo-Yo**, ch 1, sc in next ch-3 sp on **new Yo-Yo**; repeat from ★ 5 times **more**, ch 3; join with slip st to first sc, finish off.

LEFT FRONT

Work Additional Yo-Yos in same manner as Back, using color indicated on Placement Diagram. Join Yo-Yos to Back at sides, bottom and top of Sleeves, leaving edge of Yo-Yos along dashed lines unworked for neck opening. For size Medium only, do **not** join Yo-Yos separated by purple dashed lines indicated by arrows on Placement Diagram.

Work Three-Sided Joining when necessary.

THREE-SIDED JOINING

Rnd 2: Slip st in first ch-3 sp, ch 1, sc in same sp, (ch 3, sc in next ch-3 sp) twice, ★ ch 1, sc in corresponding sp on **adjacent Yo-Yo**, ch 1, sc in next ch-3 sp on **new Yo-Yo**; repeat from ★ 8 times **more**, ch 3; join with slip st to first sc, finish off.

RIGHT FRONT

Work same as Left Front.

EDGING

With **right** side facing and working along bottom edge, join MC with slip st around post of any joining sc at center of Back; ch 1, sc in same st, ch 3, (sc in next ch-3 sp, ch 3) 3 times, † sc around post of next joining sc, ch 3, (sc in next ch-3 sp, ch 3) across to next joining sc †, repeat from † to † to Right Front neck edge, (sc around post of next joining sc, ch 3) twice, (sc in next ch-3 sp, ch 3) across to next joining sc, repeat from † to † 7 times, (sc around post of next joining sc, ch 3) twice, (sc in next ch-3 sp, ch 3) across to next joining sc, repeat from † to † around; join with slip st to first sc, finish off.

SLEEVE EDGING

With **right** side facing, join MC with slip st around post of any joining sc; ch 1, sc in same st, ch 3, (sc in next ch-3 sp, ch 3) 3 times, ★ sc around post of next joining sc, ch 3, (sc in next ch-3 sp, ch 3) 3 times; repeat from ★ around; join with slip st to first sc, finish off.

Repeat for second Sleeve.

Sew hole at underarm.

Quick HAIR DRESSINGS

Crafted with cotton thread, these handy hair fashions make dressy accessories for office or evening wear. The barrette features a pretty filet crochet bow, and the ruffled ponytail holder is worked around a braided elastic band.

Finished Size: Hair Bow - approximately 2¼" x 6"
Ponytail Band - approximately 1" wide

MATERIALS

Bedspread Weight Cotton Thread (size 10), approximately:
Hair Bow - 55 yards
Ponytail Band - 50 yards
Steel crochet hook, size 8 (1.50 mm) **or** size needed for gauge
Hair Bow: 15" length of 2½" wide ribbon
4" Barrette
Sewing needle and thread
Tapestry needle
Ponytail Band: Braided elastic hair band

GAUGE: 10 dc and 4 rows = 1"

HAIR BOW

BOW

Ch 26 **loosely**.

Row 1 (Right side): Dc in eighth ch from hook, ch 2, skip next 2 chs, dc in next ch, ch 2, skip next 2 chs, dc in next 4 chs, (ch 2, skip next 2 chs, dc in next ch) 3 times: 6 sps.

Note: Loop a short piece of thread around any stitch to mark last row as **right** side.

Row 2: Ch 5 **(counts as first dc plus ch 2, now and throughout)**, turn; (dc in next dc, ch 2) twice, dc in next 4 dc, (ch 2, dc in next dc) twice, ch 2, skip next 2 chs, dc in next ch: 10 dc.

Rows 3-16: Ch 5, turn; (dc in next dc, ch 2) twice, dc in next 4 dc, (ch 2, dc in next dc) 3 times.

Row 17: Ch 5, turn; dc in next dc, ch 2, dc in next dc, 2 dc in next ch-2 sp, dc in next dc, ch 2, skip next 2 dc, dc in next dc, 2 dc in next ch-2 sp, dc in next dc, (ch 2, dc in next dc) twice: 12 dc.

Row 18: Ch 5, turn; dc in next dc, 2 dc in next ch-2 sp, dc in next dc, ch 4, skip next 3 dc, dc in next ch-2 sp, ch 4, skip next 3 dc, dc in next dc, 2 dc in next ch-2 sp, dc in next dc, ch 2, dc in last dc: 11 dc.

Row 19: Ch 3 **(counts as first dc, now and throughout)**, turn; 2 dc in first ch-2 sp, dc in next dc, ch 6, skip next 3 dc, dc in next ch-4 sp, dc in next dc, dc in next ch-4 sp, ch 6, skip next 3 dc, dc in next dc, 2 dc in next ch-2 sp, dc in last dc.

Row 20: Ch 5, turn; skip next 2 dc, dc in next dc, 3 dc in next loop, ch 3, skip next dc, dc in next dc, ch 3, 3 dc in next loop, dc in next dc, ch 2, skip next 2 dc, dc in last dc: 11 dc.

Row 21: Ch 5, turn; dc in next dc, ch 2, skip next 2 dc, dc in next dc, 3 dc in next ch-3 sp, ch 2, 3 dc in next ch-3 sp, dc in next dc, ch 2, skip next 2 dc, dc in next dc, ch 2, dc in last dc: 12 dc.

Row 22: Ch 5, turn; (dc in next dc, ch 2) twice, skip next 2 dc, dc in next dc, 2 dc in next ch-2 sp, dc in next dc, ch 2, skip next 2 dc, dc in next dc, (ch 2, dc in next dc) twice: 10 dc.

Rows 23-30: Repeat Row 3, 8 times.

Rows 31-36: Repeat Rows 17-22.

Rows 37-51: Repeat Row 3, 15 times; do **not** finish off.

Edging: Ch 3, working in end of rows, (hdc, sc) in first row, (dc, hdc, sc) in next row and in each row across; working in sps and in free loops of beginning ch **(Fig. 21b, page 138)**, sc in each st and in each sp across; (dc, hdc, sc) in end of each row across; sc in each dc and in each ch-2 sp across; join with slip st to first dc, finish off leaving a long end for sewing.

91

BAND

Ch 7 **loosely**.
Row 1: Dc in fourth ch from hook and in each ch across: 5 sts.
Rows 2-11: Ch 3, turn; dc in next dc and in each dc across.
Finish off leaving a long end for sewing.

FINISHING

Sew ends of Bow together to form a loop.
Sew ends of ribbon together to form a loop the same size as Bow.
Slide ribbon loop inside Bow, matching seams.
Fold Bow with seam to center back.
Place Band around center of Bow and sew ends together at back.
Sew Bow to barrette.

PONYTAIL BAND

Rnd 1: Join thread with slip st around band; ch 1, work 72 sc around band; being careful not to twist sts, join with slip st to first sc.
Rnd 2: Ch 1, sc in first 2 sc, ch 7, skip next sc, (sc in next 2 sc, ch 7, skip next sc) around; join with slip st to first sc: 24 loops.
Rnd 3: Ch 1, sc in first 2 sc, (5 dc, ch 2, 5 dc) in next loop, ★ sc in next 2 sc, (5 dc, ch 2, 5 dc) in next loop; repeat from ★ around; join with slip st to first sc.
Rnd 4: Ch 1, sc in first 2 sc, ★ † 2 dc in each of next 5 dc, ch 2, sc in next ch-2 sp, ch 3, slip st in third ch from hook, sc in same ch-2 sp, ch 2, 2 dc in each of next 5 dc †, sc in next 2 sc; repeat from ★ around to last 10 dc, then repeat from † to † once; join with slip st to first sc, finish off.

KIDS' PERKY PULLOVERS

*B*righten *your child's back-to-school wardrobe with these perky pullovers. Created in children's sizes 6-12, the boy's sweater is stitched in brightly colored stripes and the girl's top is adorned with a cross-stitched ladybug.*

Size:	6	8	10	12
Finished Chest				
Measurement:	29"	31"	32"	34"

Size Note: Instructions are written for size 6 with sizes 8, 10, and 12 in braces { }. Instructions will be easier to read if you circle all the numbers pertaining to your size.

MATERIALS

Sport Weight Yarn, approximately:
Ladybug
    Sweater
        10{12-13-15} ounces,
          [280{340-370-430} grams,
            1,000{1,200-1,300-1,500} yards]
    Cross Stitch Design
        Red - 20 yards
        Black - 10 yards
Striped
    MC (Red) - 9{11-12-14} ounces,
      [260{310-340-400} grams,
        900{1,100-1,200-1,400} yards]
    Color A (Black) - 1 ounce, (30 grams, 100 yards)
    Color B (Green) - 1 ounce, (30 grams, 100 yards)
    Color C (White) - 1 ounce, (30 grams, 100 yards)
Crochet hooks, sizes C (2.75 mm) **and** E (3.50 mm) **or** sizes needed for gauge
1½ yards ⅝" wide green ribbon
Yarn needle

GAUGE: With smaller size hook, 11 sc and 11 rows = 2"
        With larger size hook, in pattern,
        22 sts and 22 rows = 4"

STRIPED PULLOVER

Work Sleeves and Back with MC. Work Front Ribbing with MC, then work Body in the following Color Sequence: ★ 4 rows Color A, 4 rows Color B, 4 rows Color C, 10 rows MC; repeat from ★ throughout. Work Front Neck Ribbing in MC.

SLEEVE (Make 2)
RIBBING

With smaller size hook, ch 12{15-15-15} **loosely**.
Row 1: Sc in second ch from hook and in each ch across: 11{14-14-14} sc.
Row 2: Ch 1, turn; sc in Back Loop Only of each sc across *(Fig. 20, page 138)*.
Repeat Row 2 until 17{18-18-18} ribs [34{36-36-36} rows] are complete.

BODY

Change to larger size hook.
Row 1 (Right side)**:** Ch 1, sc in end of each row across increasing 6{8-8-8} sts evenly spaced: 40{44-44-44} sc.
Note: Loop a short piece of yarn around any stitch to mark last row as **right** side.
Row 2: Ch 1, turn; sc in first 2 sc, (ch 1, skip next sc, sc in next sc) across: 40{44-44-44} sts.

Row 3: Ch 1, turn; sc in first sc and in next ch-1 sp, ch 1, (skip next sc, sc in next ch-1 sp, ch 1) across to last 2 sc, skip next sc, sc in last sc.

Row 4 (Increase row)**:** Ch 1, turn; 2 sc in first sc, sc in next ch-1 sp, ch 1, (skip next sc, sc in next ch-1 sp, ch 1) across to last 2 sc, skip next sc, 2 sc in last sc: 42{46-46-46} sts.

Row 5: Ch 1, turn; sc in first sc, ch 1, (skip next sc, sc in next ch-1 sp, ch 1) across to last 3 sc, skip next sc, sc in last 2 sc.

Row 6: Ch 1, turn; sc in first sc, (ch 1, skip next sc, sc in next ch-1 sp) across to last sc, sc in last sc.

Row 7 (Increase row)**:** Ch 1, turn; 2 sc in first sc, (ch 1, skip next sc, sc in next ch-1 sp) across to last sc, 2 sc in last sc: 44{48-48-48} sts.

Row 8: Ch 1, turn; sc in first 2 sc, ch 1, (skip next sc, sc in next ch-1 sp, ch 1) across to last 2 sc, skip next sc, sc in last sc.

Row 9: Ch 1, turn; sc in first sc and in next ch-1 sp, ch 1, (skip next sc, sc in next ch-1 sp, ch 1) across to last 2 sc, skip next sc, sc in last sc.
Repeat Rows 4-9, 6{7-8-9} times, then repeat Rows 4 and 5 once **more**: 70{78-82-86} sts.
Repeat Row 6 until Sleeve measures approximately 11¼{12½-14-15½}" from bottom edge, ending by working a **right** side row.

SLEEVE CAP
Rows 1-6: Turn; slip st in first 8 sts, ch 1, sc in next ch-1 sp, (ch 1, skip next sc, sc in next ch-1 sp) across to last sc, sc in last sc: 22{30-34-38} sts.
Row 7: Turn; slip st in first 4 sts, ch 1, sc in next ch-1 sp, (ch 1, skip next sc, sc in next ch-1 sp) across to last 5 sts, sc in next sc, leave last 4 sts unworked; finish off: 14{22-26-30} sts.

BACK
RIBBING
With smaller size hook, ch 9{12-12-12} **loosely**.
Row 1: Sc in second ch from hook and in each ch across: 8{11-11-11} sc.
Row 2: Ch 1, turn; sc in Back Loop Only of each sc across.
Repeat Row 2 until 40{43-44-47} ribs [80{86-88-94} rows] are complete.

BODY
Change to larger size hook.
Row 1 (Right side)**:** Ch 1, sc in end of each row across: 80{86-88-94} sc.
Note: Mark last row as **right** side.
Row 2: Ch 1, turn; sc in first 2 sc, (ch 1, skip next sc, sc in next sc) across: 80{86-88-94} sts.
Row 3: Ch 1, turn; sc in first sc and in next ch-1 sp, ch 1, (skip next sc, sc in next ch-1 sp, ch 1) across to last 2 sc, skip next sc, sc in last sc.
Repeat Row 3 for pattern until Back measures approximately 17{18½-20-22}" from bottom edge, ending by working a **wrong** side row.

SHOULDER SHAPING
SIZES 6 AND 12 ONLY
Row 1: Turn; slip st in first 14{16} sts, ch 1, sc in next sc, (sc in next ch-1 sp, ch 1, skip next sc) across to last sc, sc in last sc: 66{78} sts.
Row 2: Turn; slip st in first 14{16} sts, sc in next sc, (sc in next ch-1 sp, ch 1, skip next sc) across to last sc, slip st in last sc; finish off: 51{61} sts.

SIZES 8 AND 10 ONLY
Row 1: Turn; slip st in first 15 sts, ch 1, (sc in next ch-1 sp, ch 1, skip next sc) across to last sc, sc in last sc: {71-73} sts.
Row 2: Turn; slip st in first 15 sts, sc in next ch-1 sp, (ch 1, skip next sc, sc in next ch-1 sp) across to last sc, slip st in last sc; finish off: {55-57} sts.

FRONT
Work same as Back until Front measures approximately 14½{16-17-19}" from bottom edge, ending by working a **wrong** side row; do **not** finish off.

LEFT NECK SHAPING
Note: To **decrease**, working in chs and in sc, pull up a loop in next 2 sts, YO and draw through all 3 loops on hook **(counts as one sc)**.
Row 1 (Decrease row)**:** Ch 1, turn; sc in first sc and in next ch-1 sp, (ch 1, skip next sc, sc in next ch-1 sp) 13{14-14-15} times, decrease twice, leave remaining sts unworked: 30{32-32-34} sts.
Row 2: Ch 1, turn; sc in first 2 sc, (ch 1, skip next sc, sc in next ch-1 sp) across to last 2 sc, ch 1, skip next sc, sc in last sc.
Row 3 (Decrease row)**:** Ch 1, turn; sc in first sc, sc in next ch-1 sp, (ch 1, skip next sc, sc in next ch-1 sp) across to last 4 sts, decrease twice: 28{30-30-32} sts.
Row 4: Repeat Row 2.
Row 5: Ch 1, turn; sc in first sc, (sc in next ch-1 sp, ch 1, skip next sc) across to last sc, sc in last sc.
Repeat Row 5 until Front measures approximately 17{18½-20-22}" from bottom edge, ending by working a **wrong** side row.

SHOULDER SHAPING
SIZES 6 AND 12 ONLY
Row 1: Turn; slip st in first 14{16} sts, ch 1, sc in next sc, (sc in next ch-1 sp, ch 1, skip next sc) across to last sc, sc in last sc: 14{16} sts.
Row 2: Ch 1, turn; sc in first sc, (sc in next ch-1 sp, ch 1, skip next sc) across to last sc, slip st in last sc; finish off: 13{15} sts.

SIZES 8 AND 10 ONLY
Row 1: Turn; slip st in first 15 sts, ch 1, (sc in next ch-1 sp, ch 1, skip next sc) across to last sc, sc in last sc: 15 sts.
Row 2: Ch 1, turn; sc in first sc, sc in next ch-1 sp, (ch 1, skip next sc, sc in next ch-1 sp) across to last sc, slip st in last sc; finish off: 14 sts.

RIGHT NECK SHAPING

Row 1 (Decrease row): With **right** side facing, skip 16{18-20-22} sts from Left Neck edge and join yarn with slip st in next sc; ch 1, beginning in same st, decrease twice, ch 1, (skip next sc, sc in next ch-1 sp, ch 1) across to last 2 sc, skip next sc, sc in last sc: 30{32-32-34} sts.

Row 2: Ch 1, turn; sc in first sc, (sc in next ch-1 sp, ch 1, skip next sc) across to last sc, sc in last sc.

Row 3 (Decrease row): Ch 1, turn; decrease twice, ch 1, (skip next sc, sc in next ch-1 sp, ch 1) across to last 2 sc, skip next sc, sc in last sc: 28{30-30-32} sts.

Repeat Row 2 until Right Neck Shaping measures same as Left Neck Shaping, ending by working a **right** side row.

SHOULDER SHAPING

Work same as Left Shoulder Shaping: 13{14-14-15} sts.

FINISHING

With **wrong** sides together and working through **both** loops, whipstitch shoulder seams *(Fig. 25a, page 140)*.

NECK RIBBING

Foundation Rnd: With **right** side facing and smaller size hook, join yarn with slip st at right shoulder seam; ch 1, sc in each st across Back, work 14{14-16-16} sc evenly spaced along Left Front Neck edge, sc in each st across Front, work 14{14-16-16} sc evenly spaced along Right Front Neck edge; join with slip st to first sc: 68{72-80-84} sc.
Ch 5 **loosely**.

Row 1: Sc in second ch from hook and in each ch across, sc in first 2 sc on Foundation Rnd: 6 sc.

Row 2: Turn; skip first 2 sc, sc in Back Loop Only of each sc across: 4 sc.

Row 3: Ch 1, turn; sc in Back Loop Only of each sc across, sc in next 2 sc on Foundation Rnd: 6 sc.

Repeat Rows 2 and 3 around, ending by working Row 2.

Last Row: Ch 1, turn; sc in Back Loop Only of each sc across, slip st in last sc on Foundation Rnd; finish off leaving a long end for sewing.

Whipstitch seam on Neck Ribbing.
Whipstitch Sleeves to pullover, matching center of Sleeve to shoulder seam and beginning 6½{7-7½-8}" down from shoulder seam.
Whipstitch underarm and side in one continuous seam.

LADYBUG - CROSS STITCH

Add cross stitch design to pullover following Chart. Refer to Chart for positioning directions. Pullover should be measured from side to side and from top of shoulder to top of Ribbing to determine center.

Each colored square on the Chart represents one cross stitch. Each cross stitch is worked over a center sc into sc around the center sc. Using yarn needle and long **double** strands of yarn, weave end under several stitches on wrong side of pullover to secure (do not tie knot). With **right** side facing and shoulder seam at top, work cross stitch as follows: bring needle up at 1, down at 2 (half cross made), up at 3, down at 4 **(cross stitch completed, *Fig. 1*)**. All cross stitches should cross in the same direction. Finish off by weaving end under several stitches on the wrong side of pullover; cut close to work.

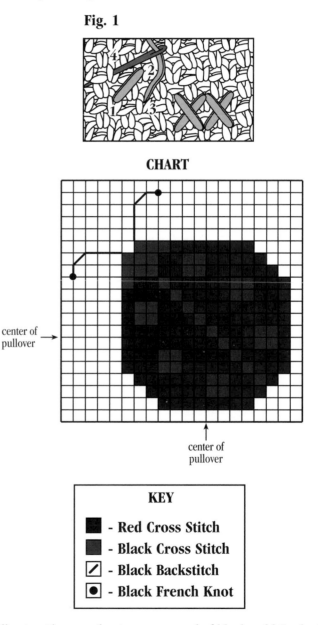

Fig. 1

CHART

center of pullover →

center of pullover

KEY
- ■ - Red Cross Stitch
- ▦ - Black Cross Stitch
- ◪ - Black Backstitch
- ⊙ - Black French Knot

Following Chart, and using one strand of black, add Backstitch *(Figs. 31a & b, page 142)* and French Knots *(Fig. 32, page 142)* for antennae.
Using photo as a guide for placement, use ribbon and add Lazy Daisy Stitch leaves *(Fig. 34, page 142)*.

JAUNTY BERET AND SCARF

A cold-weather must, this cozy scarf and beret set is worked in warming worsted weight yarn. The ample scarf is finished with a generous fringe, and the jaunty beret is gathered with elastic for a snug fit.

Finished Size: Beret - one size fits all
Scarf - 6½" x 46"

MATERIALS

Worsted Weight Yarn, approximately:
Set - 6 ounces, (170 grams, 395 yards)
Beret - 2½ ounces, (70 grams, 165 yards)
Scarf - 4 ounces, (110 grams, 265 yards)
Crochet hook, size I (5.50 mm) **or** size needed for gauge
1 yard tubular elastic

GAUGE: (sc, ch 1) 9 times = 4"

BERET
BAND

Ch 81 **loosely**; being careful not to twist ch, join with slip st to form a ring.

Rnd 1 (Right side): Ch 4, tr in next ch and in each ch around; join with slip st to top of beginning ch-4: 81 sts.

Note: Work in Back Loops Only throughout *(Fig. 20, page 138)*.

Rnd 2: Ch 1, skip beginning ch, (sc in next tr, ch 1, skip next tr) around, sc in first ch-1 worked; do **not** join, place marker.

Note: Markers are used to indicate the beginning of the round should you need to count the number of repeats worked, instead of where the round ends. Place a 2" scrap piece of yarn after each round is complete. Remove when no longer needed.

Rnd 3: ★ (Ch 1, sc in next st) twice, (ch 1, skip next st, sc in next st) 4 times; repeat from ★ 7 times **more**: 97 sts.

Rnd 4: (Ch 1, skip next st, sc in next st) around to last st: 97 sts.

Rnd 5: ★ (Ch 1, sc in next st) twice, (ch 1, skip next st, sc in next st) 3 times; repeat from ★ 11 times **more**: 121 sts.

Rnd 6: (Ch 1, skip next st, sc in next st) around to last st: 121 sts.

Rnd 7: ★ (Ch 1, sc in next st) twice, (ch 1, skip next st, sc in next st) 19 times; repeat from ★ 2 times **more**: 127 sts.

Rnd 8: (Ch 1, skip next st, sc in next st) around to last st: 127 sts.

Rnd 9: ★ (Ch 1, sc in next st) twice, (ch 1, skip next st, sc in next st) 15 times; repeat from ★ 3 times **more**: 135 sts.

Rnd 10: (Ch 1, skip next st, sc in next st) around to last st: 135 sts.

Rnd 11: (Ch 1, skip next st, sc in next st) 8 times, ★ (ch 1, sc in next st) twice, (ch 1, skip next st, sc in next st) 8 times; repeat from ★ 5 times **more**, (ch 1, skip next st, sc in next st) 6 times: 147 sts.

Rnd 12: (Ch 1, skip next st, sc in next st) around to last st, slip st in next 3 sts; finish off: 147 sts.

TOP

Rnd 1: Ch 2, 7 sc in second ch from hook; do **not** join.
Note: Work in Back Loops Only throughout.
Rnd 2: (Ch 1, sc in next st) 8 times, place marker: 15 sts.
Rnd 3: Ch 1, ★ skip next st, (sc in next st, ch 1) 3 times; repeat from ★ 3 times **more**, skip next st, (sc in next st, ch 1) twice, sc in next st: 25 sts.
Rnd 4: Ch 1, ★ skip next st, (sc in next st, ch 1) 3 times; repeat from ★ 4 times **more**, skip next st, (sc in next st, ch 1) twice, sc in next st: 37 sts.
Rnd 5: ★ (Ch 1, skip next st, sc in next st) twice, (ch 1, sc in next st) twice; repeat from ★ 4 times **more**: 47 sts.
Rnd 6: (Ch 1, skip next st, sc in next st) 24 times: 47 sts.
Rnd 7: ★ (Ch 1, skip next st, sc in next st) twice, (ch 1, sc in next st) twice; repeat from ★ 7 times **more**: 63 sts.
Rnd 8: ★ (Ch 1, skip next st, sc in next st) 4 times, (ch 1, sc in next st) twice; repeat from ★ 5 times **more**: 75 sts.
Rnd 9: (Ch 1, skip next st, sc in next st) 35 times: 75 sts.
Rnd 10: ★ (Ch 1, skip next st, sc in next st) 5 times, (ch 1, sc in next st) twice; repeat from ★ 6 times **more**: 89 sts.
Rnd 11: (Ch 1, skip next st, sc in next st) 45 times: 89 sts.
Rnd 12: ★ (Ch 1, skip next st, sc in next st) 3 times, (ch 1, sc in next st) twice; repeat from ★ 10 times **more**: 111 sts.
Rnd 13: (Ch 1, skip next st, sc in next st) 57 times: 111 sts.
Rnd 14: ★ (Ch 1, skip next st, sc in next st) 4 times, (ch 1, sc in next st) twice; repeat from ★ 10 times **more**: 133 sts.
Rnd 15: (Ch 1, skip next st, sc in next st) 66 times: 133 sts.
Rnd 16: ★ (Ch 1, skip next st, sc in next st) 8 times, (ch 1, sc in next st) twice; repeat from ★ 6 times **more**: 147 sts.
Rnd 17: (Ch 1, skip next st, sc in next st) 75 times, slip st in next 3 sts; finish off: 147 sts.

With **wrong** sides together and working through **inside** loops only, whipstitch Band and Top together *(Fig. 25b, page 140)*. Fold Rnd 1 of Band to the wrong side; sew along beginning ch to form a casing inserting elastic before closing.

SCARF

Leaving a 7" end, ch 211.

Row 1: Sc in third ch from hook, (ch 1, skip next ch, sc in next ch) across: 105 sc.

Row 2: Ch 2, turn; working in Front Loops Only *(Fig. 20, page 138)*, sc in next ch, (ch 1, skip next sc, sc in next ch) across: 105 sc.

Repeat Row 2 until Scarf measures approximately $6^1/_2$"; finish off leaving a 7" end.

Add fringe using 2 strands, each 13" long *(Figs. 26a & b, page 140)*; spacing evenly, attach across end of rows on each end of Scarf.

"COOL" VEST SET

The mod fashions of the 1970's are back! And we've captured their youthful appeal in these classic designs. Created with creamy size 3 cotton thread, this "cool" ensemble will dress up your casual wear. Beaded fringe and filet crochet details add interest to the vest and handbag, and the easy-fasten belt cinches with D-rings.

MATERIALS

Crochet Cotton Thread (size 3), approximately:
    Vest - 600{670-800} yards
    Handbag - 200 yards
    Belt - 130 yards (for a Belt measuring 32")
Crochet hook, size D (3.25 mm) **or** size needed for gauge
Assorted beads
Sewing needle and thread
Handbag: 1 - ³/₄" button
    Lining fabric - approximately 12" x 16" piece
Belt: 2 - 2" D-rings

GAUGE: 14 dc and 7 rows = 3"

Note: Each row of Vest and Handbag is worked across height of piece.

BASIC PATTERN

Row 1 (Right side): Dc in fourth ch from hook and in next 3 chs (**3 skipped chs count as first dc, now and throughout**), ch 1, skip next ch, dc in next ch, ch 1, skip next ch, dc in each ch across: 35 dc.

Note: Loop a short piece of thread around any stitch to mark last row as **right** side.

Row 2: Ch 3 (**counts as first dc, now and throughout**), turn; dc in next dc and in each dc across to next ch-1 sp, ch 1, skip next ch, dc in next dc, ch 1, skip next ch, dc in each dc across.

Row 3: Ch 6, turn; dc in fourth ch from hook and in next 2 chs, dc in next dc, (ch 1, skip next dc, dc in next dc) twice, (dc in next ch and in next dc) twice, ch 1, skip next dc, dc in next dc, ch 1, skip next dc, dc in each dc across: 37 dc.

Row 4: Ch 3, turn; dc in next dc and in each dc across to next ch-1 sp, ch 1, skip next ch, dc in next dc, ch 1, skip next ch, dc in next 5 dc, ch 1, skip next ch, dc in next dc, ch 1, skip next ch, dc in each dc across.

Row 5: Ch 6, turn; dc in fourth ch from hook and in next 2 chs, dc in next 5 dc, (dc in next ch and in next dc) twice, (ch 1, skip next dc, dc in next dc) twice, dc in each ch and in each dc across: 43 dc.

Row 6: Ch 3, turn; dc in next dc and in each dc across to next ch-1 sp, ch 1, skip next ch, dc in next dc, ch 1, skip next ch, dc in each dc across.

Row 7: Turn; slip st in first 5 dc, ch 3, dc in next 4 dc, (ch 1, skip next dc, dc in next dc) twice, (dc in next ch and in next dc) twice, ch 1, skip next dc, dc in next dc, ch 1, skip next dc, dc in each dc across: 37 dc.

Row 8: Ch 3, turn; dc in next dc and in each dc across to next ch-1 sp, ch 1, skip next ch, dc in next dc, ch 1, skip next ch, dc in next 5 dc, ch 1, skip next ch, dc in next dc, ch 1, skip next ch, dc in each dc across.

Row 9: Turn; slip st in first 5 dc, ch 3, (dc in next ch and in next dc) twice, (ch 1, skip next dc, dc in next dc) twice, dc in each ch and in each dc across: 35 dc.
Repeat Rows 2-9 for pattern.

VEST

Size:	Small	Medium	Large
Finished Chest			
Measurement:	35"	39"	42"

Size Note: Instructions are written for size Small with sizes Medium and Large in braces { }. Instructions will be easier to read if you circle all the numbers pertaining to your size. If only one number is given, it applies to all sizes.

Ch 39 **loosely.**

Row 1 (Right side): Dc in fourth ch from hook and in each ch across (**3 skipped chs count as first dc, now and throughout**): 37 dc.

Note: Loop a short piece of thread around any stitch to mark last row as **right** side.

Row 2: Ch 6, turn; dc in fourth ch from hook and in next 2 chs, dc in each dc across: 41 dc.

Row 3: Ch 6, turn; dc in fourth ch from hook and in next 2 chs, dc in next dc, ch 1, skip next dc, dc in next dc, ch 1, skip next dc, dc in next 5 dc, ch 1, skip next dc, dc in next dc, ch 1, skip next dc, dc in each dc across.

Row 4: Ch 6, turn; dc in fourth ch from hook and in next 2 chs, dc in each dc across to next ch-1 sp, ch 1, skip next ch, dc in next dc, ch 1, skip next ch, dc in next 5 dc, ch 1, skip next ch, dc in next dc, ch 1, skip next ch, dc in each dc across: 45 dc.

Row 5: Ch 6, turn; dc in fourth ch from hook and in next 2 chs, dc in next 5 dc, (dc in next ch and in next dc) twice, (ch 1, skip next dc, dc in next dc) twice, dc in each ch and in each dc across: 51 dc.

Row 6: Ch 6, turn; dc in fourth ch from hook and in next 2 chs, dc in each dc across to next ch-1 sp, ch 1, skip next ch, dc in next dc, ch 1, skip next ch, dc in each dc across: 55 dc.

Row 7: Turn; slip st in first 5 dc, ch 3 **(counts as first dc, now and throughout)**, dc in next 4 dc, (ch 1, skip next dc, dc in next dc) twice, (dc in next ch and in next dc) twice, ch 1, skip next dc, dc in next dc, ch 1, skip next dc, dc in each dc across: 49 dc.

Row 8: Ch 6, turn; dc in fourth ch from hook and in next 2 chs, dc in each dc across to next ch-1 sp, ch 1, skip next ch,

dc in next dc, ch 1, skip next ch, dc in next 5 dc, ch 1, skip next ch, dc in next dc, ch 1, skip next ch, dc in each dc across: 53 dc.

Row 9: Turn; slip st in first 5 dc, ch 3, (dc in next ch and in next dc) twice, (ch 1, skip next dc, dc in next dc) twice, dc in each ch and in each dc across: 51 dc.

Row 10: Ch 6, turn; dc in fourth ch from hook and in next 2 chs, dc in each dc across to next ch-1 sp, ch 1, skip next ch, dc in next dc, ch 1, skip next ch, dc in each dc across: 55 dc.

Row 11: Ch 6, turn; dc in fourth ch from hook and in next 2 chs, dc in next dc, (ch 1, skip next dc, dc in next dc) twice, (dc in next ch and in next dc) twice, ch 1, skip next dc, dc in next dc, ch 1, skip next dc, dc in each dc across: 57 dc.

Rows 12 and 13: Repeat Rows 4 and 5: 67 dc.

Row 14: Ch 22{22-26} **loosely**, turn; dc in fourth ch from hook and in each ch across, dc in each dc across to next ch-1 sp, ch 1, skip next ch, dc in next dc, ch 1, skip next ch, dc in each dc across: 87{87-91} dc.

Row 15: Repeat Row 7: 81{81-85} dc.

Row 16: Ch 3, turn; dc in next dc and in each dc across to next ch-1 sp, ch 1, skip next ch, dc in next dc, ch 1, skip next ch, dc in next 5 dc, ch 1, skip next ch, dc in next dc, ch 1, skip next ch, dc in each dc across.

Row 17: Repeat Row 9: 79{79-83} dc.

Row 18: Ch 3, turn; dc in next dc and in each dc across to next ch-1 sp, ch 1, skip next ch, dc in next dc, ch 1, skip next ch, dc in each dc across; do **not** finish off.

SIZE SMALL ONLY

Row 19: Ch 6, turn; dc in fourth ch from hook and in next 2 chs, dc in next dc, (ch 1, skip next dc, dc in next dc) twice, (dc in next ch and in next dc) twice, ch 1, skip next dc, dc in next dc, ch 1, skip next dc, dc in next 28 dc, leave remaining dc unworked (armhole): 40 dc.

Rows 20-23: Working same as Basic Pattern, page 98, repeat Rows 4-7.

Row 24: Ch 43 **loosely**, turn; dc in fourth ch from hook and in each ch across, dc in each dc across to next ch-1 sp, ch 1, skip next ch, dc in next dc, ch 1, skip next ch, dc in next 5 dc, ch 1, skip next ch, dc in next dc, ch 1, skip next ch, dc in each dc across: 81 dc.

Rows 25-58: Working same as Basic Pattern, repeat Row 9, then repeat Rows 2-9, 4 times, then repeat Row 2 once **more**.

Row 59: Repeat Row 19.

Rows 60-63: Working same as Basic Pattern, repeat Rows 4-7.

Row 64: Repeat Row 24.

Rows 65-68: Working same as Basic Pattern, repeat Row 9, then repeat Rows 2-4 once.

Row 69: Ch 6, turn; dc in fourth ch from hook and in next 2 chs, dc in next 5 dc, (dc in next ch and in next dc) twice, (ch 1, skip next dc, dc in next dc) twice, dc in each ch and in each dc across to last 20 dc, leave remaining dc unworked: 67 dc.

Rows 70-80: Working same as Basic Pattern, repeat Rows 6-9, then repeat Rows 2-8 once AND AT THE SAME TIME work all **right** side rows to within 4 dc of neck edge leaving remaining dc unworked.

Row 81: Turn; slip st in first 5 dc, ch 3, dc in each ch and in each dc across to last 4 dc, leave remaining dc unworked: 37 dc.

Row 82: Ch 3, turn; dc in next dc and in each dc across; finish off.

Sew shoulder seams.

SIZE MEDIUM ONLY

Rows 19 and 20: Work same as Basic Pattern, page 98, Rows 3 and 4.

Row 21: Ch 6, turn; dc in fourth ch from hook and in next 2 chs, dc in next 5 dc, (dc in next ch and in next dc) twice, (ch 1, skip next dc, dc in next dc) twice, dc in next 31 sts, leave remaining dc unworked (armhole): 46 dc.

Rows 22-25: Working same as Basic Pattern, repeat Rows 6-9.

Row 26: Ch 43 **loosely**, turn; dc in fourth ch from hook and in each ch across, dc in each dc across to next ch-1 sp, ch 1, skip next ch, dc in next dc, ch 1, skip next ch, dc in each dc across: 79 dc.

Rows 27-64: Working same as Basic Pattern, repeat Rows 3-9, then repeat Rows 2-9, 3 times, then repeat Rows 2-8 once **more**.

Row 65: Turn; slip st in first 5 dc, ch 3, (dc in next ch and in next dc) twice, (ch 1, skip next dc, dc in next dc) twice, dc in next 31 sts, leave remaining dc unworked: 38 dc.

Rows 66-69: Working same as Basic Pattern, repeat Rows 2-5.

Row 70: Ch 43 **loosely**, turn; dc in fourth ch from hook and in each ch across, dc in each dc across to next ch-1 sp, ch 1, skip next ch, dc in next dc, ch 1, skip next ch, dc in each dc across: 87 dc.

Rows 71-76: Working same as Basic Pattern, repeat Rows 7-9, then repeat Rows 2-4 once.

Row 77: Ch 6, turn; dc in fourth ch from hook and in next 2 chs, dc in next 5 dc, (dc in next ch and in next dc) twice, (ch 1, skip next dc, dc in next dc) twice, dc in each ch and in each dc across to last 20 dc, leave remaining dc unworked: 67 dc.

Rows 78-88: Working same as Basic Pattern, repeat Rows 6-9, then repeat Rows 2-8 once AND AT THE SAME TIME work all **right** side rows to within 4 dc of neck edge leaving remaining dc unworked.

Row 89: Turn; slip st in first 5 dc, ch 3, dc in each ch and in each dc across to last 4 dc, leave remaining dc unworked: 37 dc.

Row 90: Ch 3, turn; dc in next dc and in each dc across; finish off.

Sew shoulder seams.

SIZE LARGE ONLY

Rows 19 and 20: Work same as Basic Pattern, page 98, Rows 3 and 4.

Row 21: Ch 6, turn; dc in fourth ch from hook and in next 2 chs, dc in next 5 dc, (dc in next ch and in next dc) twice, (ch 1, skip next dc, dc in next dc) twice, dc in next 31 sts, leave remaining dc unworked (armhole): 46 dc.

Rows 22-29: Working same as Basic Pattern, repeat Rows 6-9, then repeat Rows 2-5.

Row 30: Ch 47 **loosely**, turn; dc in fourth ch from hook and in each ch across, dc in each dc across to next ch-1 sp, ch 1, skip next ch, dc in next dc, ch 1, skip next ch, dc in each dc across: 91 dc.

Rows 31-68: Working same as Basic Pattern, repeat Rows 7-9, then repeat Rows 2-9, 4 times, then repeat Rows 2-4 once **more**.

Row 69: Ch 6, turn; dc in fourth ch from hook and in next 2 chs, dc in next 5 dc, (dc in next ch and in next dc) twice, (ch 1, skip next dc, dc in next dc) twice, dc in next 31 sts, leave remaining dc unworked (armhole): 46 dc.

Rows 70-77: Working same as Basic Pattern, repeat Rows 6-9, then repeat Rows 2-5 once.

Row 78: Ch 47 **loosely**, turn; dc in fourth ch from hook and in each ch across, dc in each dc across to next ch-1 sp, ch 1, skip next ch, dc in next dc, ch 1, skip next ch, dc in each dc across: 91 dc.

Rows 79-84: Working same as Basic Pattern, repeat Rows 7-9, then repeat Rows 2-4 once.

Row 85: Ch 6, turn; dc in fourth ch from hook and in next 2 chs, dc in next 5 dc, (dc in next ch and in next dc) twice, (ch 1, skip next dc, dc in next dc) twice, dc in next 31 sts, leave remaining dc unworked: 67 dc.

Rows 86-96: Working same as Basic pattern, repeat Rows 6-9, then repeat Rows 2-8 once AND AT THE SAME TIME work all **right** side rows to within 4 dc of neck edge leaving remaining dc unworked.

Row 97: Turn; slip st in first 5 dc, ch 3, dc in each ch and in each dc across to last 4 dc, leave remaining dc unworked: 37 dc.

Row 98: Ch 3, turn; dc in next dc and in each dc across; finish off.

Sew shoulder seams.

EDGING

With **right** side facing, join thread with sc in any edge st *(see Joining With Sc, page 138)*; sc evenly around entire edge of Vest; join with slip st to first sc, finish off.

TIE (Make 2)

Chain a 18" length **or** chain to desired length; finish off.

FINISHING

Using photo as a guide for placement, use sewing needle and thread to sew clusters of beads around neckline.

For first strand of beaded fringe, string desired number of beads on sewing thread and sew to bottom of Vest. Repeat at even intervals across bottom edge.

Tie knot in end of each Tie. String desired number of beads on sewing thread and stitch to end of each Tie. Sew each Tie to bottom of neck shaping.

HANDBAG

Finished Size: Approximately 7" wide x 9¹⁄₂" long

BODY

Ch 39 **loosely**.

Rows 1-32: Work Basic Pattern, page 98, ending by working Row 8.

Joining Row: Turn; slip st in first 4 dc, with **right** side together and working in each st on Row 32 **and** in free loops of beginning ch *(Fig. 21b, page 138)*, slip st in each st across; do **not** finish off.

TOP EDGING

Turn Body **right** side out.

Ch 1, with **right** side facing, 2 sc in end of each row around; join with slip st to first sc, do **not** finish off: 64 sc.

FLAP

Row 1: Ch 3, dc in next 29 sc, leave remaining sts unworked: 30 dc.

Rows 2 and 3: Ch 3, turn; dc in next dc and in each dc across.

Rows 4-6: Ch 3, turn; skip next dc, dc in next dc and in each dc across to last 2 dc, skip next dc, dc in last dc: 24 dc.

Note: To **decrease**, ★ YO, insert hook in **next** dc, YO and pull up a loop, YO and draw through 2 loops on hook; repeat from ★ once **more**, YO and draw through all 3 loops on hook (**counts as one dc**).

Rows 7-10: Ch 3, turn; skip next dc, decrease, dc in next dc and in each dc across to last 4 dc, decrease, skip next dc, dc in last dc: 8 dc.

Row 11 (Buttonhole row): Ch 3, turn; skip next dc, dc in next dc, skip next 2 dc, dc in next dc, skip next dc, dc in last dc; finish off: 4 dc.

Edging: With **right** side facing, join thread with slip st in second sc to **right** of Flap on Top Edging; ch 1, 2 sc in end of each row across Flap; 3 sc in sp **between** second and third dc on last row; 2 sc in end of each row across, ch 1, skip next sc on Top Edging, slip st in next sc; finish off: 47 sc.

BOTTOM EDGING

Rnd 1: With **right** side and front facing, join thread with slip st in end of Row 2; ch 1, sc in each st and 2 sc in end of each row around entire bottom edge; join with slip st to Back Loop Only of first sc *(Fig. 20, page 138)*.

With **wrong** side together, fold Body flat between Rows 1 and 2 and between Rows 17 and 18.

Joining Row: Ch 1, working through inside loops of **both** thicknesses and matching sts, sc in each sc across; finish off.

STRAP

Row 1: With back facing and bottom toward you, join thread with slip st around post of next to last dc on Row 18; ch 150 **loosely**; being careful not to twist ch, slip st around post of next to last dc on Row 1, turn; 2 sc around post of same st, dc in back ridge of each ch across *(Fig. 2a, page 133)*; sc around post of same st as joining; finish off.

FINISHING

Lining: Using Body as a pattern, cut two pieces of fabric allowing ¼" for seam allowance around entire edge.
With **right** side together, sew seam along both sides and bottom of lining. Make a ¼" hem along opening.
Slip lining into Handbag and sew in place to Top Edging.

Sew button to front.
For first strand of beaded fringe, string desired number of beads on sewing thread and sew to bottom of Handbag. Repeat at even intervals across.

BELT
BODY

Ch 11 **loosely**.
Row 1: Sc in second ch from hook and in each ch across: 10 sc.
Row 2: Ch 1, turn; sc in Back Loop Only of each sc across *(Fig. 20, page 138)*.
Repeat Row 2 until desired length.

TAB

Row 1: Ch 1, turn; skip first sc, sc in next 7 sc, skip next sc, sc in last sc: 8 sc.
Row 2: Ch 1, turn; skip first sc, sc in next 5 sc, skip next sc, sc in last sc: 6 sc.
Row 3: Ch 1, turn; skip first sc, sc in next 3 sc, skip next sc, sc in last sc: 4 sc.
Row 4: Ch 1, turn; skip first sc, sc in next sc, skip next sc, sc in last sc: 2 sc.
Row 5: Ch 1, turn; skip first sc, dc in next sc; finish off.

Insert end of Belt through D-rings, and sew beginning ch to Row 7.

Quick PUPPET MITTENS

*S*ure to amuse, these whimsical mittens double as playful puppet characters and toasty hand-warmers! Little boys will love our friendly floppy-eared puppy, and the cheerful doll will please a young girl. Both projects are created with worsted weight yarn and have instructions for sizes small, medium, and large.

Size:	Small	Medium	Large
Palm Width:	3"	3½"	3½"
Hand Length:	3½"	5"	6¼"

Size Note: Instructions are written for size Small with sizes Medium and Large in braces { }. Instructions will be easier to read if you circle all the numbers pertaining to your size.

MATERIALS
Worsted Weight Yarn, approximately:
  Dog
    1{1½-1¾} ounces, [30{40-50} grams,
      70{105-120} yards]
  Girl
    MC (Blue) - ¾{1¼-1½} ounces,
      [20{35-40} grams, 50{85-105} yards]
    Color A (Yellow) - 15 yards
    Color B (Peach) - 10 yards
Crochet hook size G (4.00 mm) **or** size needed for gauge
Yarn needle
White and red felt
Black embroidery floss

Dog: Pink embroidery floss and black yarn
Girl: Bobbin, fabric glue and ribbon

GAUGE: 8 sc and 8 rows = 2"

Note: Work in back ridge of each chain *(Fig. 2a, page 133)*, and Back Loop Only of each st *(Fig. 20, page 138)* throughout unless otherwise instructed.

DOG
LITTLE FINGER

Ch 44{52-58} **loosely**.
Row 1: Sc in second ch from hook and in next 3{4-4} chs, slip st in next 6 chs, sc in next 10{13-16} chs, slip st in next 3 chs, sc in next 10{13-16} chs, slip st in next 6 chs, sc in last 4{5-5} chs: 43{51-57} sts.
Row 2 (Right side): Ch 1, turn; sc in first 4{5-5} sc, slip st in next 6 slip sts, sc in next 10{13-16} sc, slip st in next 3 slip sts, sc in next 10{13-16} sc, slip st in next 6 slip sts, sc in last 4{5-5} sc.
Note: Loop a short piece of yarn around any stitch to mark last row as **right** side.

BODY

Row 1: Ch 1, turn; sc in first 4{5-5} sc, slip st in next 6 slip sts, sc in next 7{8-9} sc, ch 16{20-24} **loosely**, skip next 9{13-17} sts, sc in next 7{8-9} sc, slip st in next 6 slip sts, sc in last 4{5-5} sc: 50{58-64} sts.

Row 2: Ch 1, turn; sc in first 4{5-5} sc, slip st in next 6 slip sts, sc in next 13{16-19} sts, slip st in next 4 sts, sc in next 13{16-19} sts, slip st in next 6 slip sts, sc in last 4{5-5} sc.

RIGHT MITTEN ONLY

Row 3: Ch 1, turn; sc in first 4{5-5} sc, slip st in next 6 slip sts, sc in next 13(16-19) sts, slip st in next 4 slip sts, sc in **both** loops of next 5{6-6} sc **only** (face), sc in next 8{10-13} sc, slip st in next 6 slip sts, sc in last 4{5-5} sc.

Row 4: Ch 1, turn; sc in first 4{5-5} sc, slip st in next 6 slip sts, sc in next 8(10-13) sc, sc in **both** loops of next 5{6-6} sts **only**, slip st in next 4 slip sts, sc in next 13{16-19} sc, slip st in next 6 slip sts, sc in last 4{5-5} sc.

Repeat Rows 3 and 4, 2{3-4} times, then repeat Row 3 once **more**.

LEFT MITTEN ONLY

Repeat Row 4 of Right Mitten, then repeat Rows 3 and 4, 3{4-5} times.

THUMB

Row 1: Ch 1, turn; sc in first 4{5-5} sc, slip st in next 6 slip sts, sc in next 5{6-7} sc, ch 11{13-15} **loosely**, skip next 20{24-28} sts, sc in next 5{6-7} sc, slip st in next 6 slip sts, sc in last 4{5-5} sc: 41{47-51} sts.

Rows 2-4: Ch 1, turn; sc in first 4{5-5} sc, slip st in next 6 slip sts, sc in next 9{11-13} sts, slip st in next 3 sts, sc in next 9{11-13} sts, slip st in next 6 slip sts, sc in last 4{5-5} sc. Finish off leaving a long end for sewing.

EAR (Make 2)

Ch 8 **loosely**.

Rnd 1: 7 Dc in fourth ch from hook, hdc in next 2 chs, sc in next ch, 4 sc in last ch; working in free loops of beginning ch *(Fig. 21b, page 138)*, sc in next ch, hdc in next 2 chs; join with slip st to top of beginning ch, finish off leaving a long end for sewing.

FINISHING

Using photo as guide for placement, add facial features using pink embroidery floss and French Knot for nose *(Fig. 32, page 142)*. Using black yarn add Straight Stitch for eyes *(Fig. 28, page 141)* and Backstitch for mouth *(Figs. 31a & b, page 142)*. Cut tongue from red felt and spots from white felt using patterns; sew to mittens using black embroidery floss and Straight Stitch.

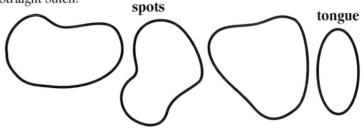

spots   tongue

Cut 6 pieces of matching yarn, each 3" long.
Tie each strand in a knot on top of head and trim to ¾".
With **wrong** sides together and working through **inside** loops only, whipstitch seams closed *(Fig. 25b, page 140)*.
Sew on Ears.

GIRL

Note: Wind a small amount of MC onto bobbin. Work each side of Body with separate yarn. Always keep the bobbin on the wrong side of the mitten.

LITTLE FINGER

With MC, work same as Dog.

BODY - RIGHT MITTEN ONLY

Row 1: Ch 1, turn; sc in first 4{5-5} sc, slip st in next 6 slip sts, sc in next 7{8-9} sc, ch 1{2-4} **loosely**, drop MC, with Color A ch 9{10-10} **loosely**, drop Color A, with Color B, ch 5{6-6} **loosely**, drop Color B, with MC bobbin, ch 1{2-4} **loosely**, skip next 9{13-17} sts, sc in next 7{8-9} sc, slip st in next 6 slip sts, sc in last 4{5-5} sc: 50{58-64} sts.

Row 2: Ch 1, turn; sc in first 4{5-5} sc, slip st in next 6 slip sts, sc in next 8(10-13} sts changing to Color B in last sc worked *(Fig. 22a, page 138)*, sc next 5{6-6} sts changing to Color A in last sc worked, slip st in next 4 sts, sc in next 5{6-6} sts changing to MC in last sc worked, sc in next 8{10-13} sts, slip st in next 6 slip sts, sc in last 4{5-5} sc.

Row 3: Ch 1, turn; sc in first 4{5-5} sc, slip st in next 6 slip sts, sc in next 8(10-13} sc changing to Color A in last sc worked, sc in next 5{6-6} sc, slip st in next 4 slip sts changing to Color B in last slip st worked, sc in **both** loops of next 5{6-6} sc **only** (face) changing to MC in last sc worked, sc in next 8{10-13} sc, slip st in next 6 slip sts, sc in last 4{5-5} sc.

Row 4: Ch 1, turn; sc in first 4{5-5} sc, slip st in next 6 slip sts, sc in next 8{10-13} sc changing to Color B in last sc worked, sc in **both** loops of next 5{6-6} sc **only** changing to Color A in last sc worked, slip st in next 4 slip sts, sc in next 5{6-6} sc changing to MC in last sc worked, sc in next 8{10-13} sc, slip st in next 6 slip sts, sc in last 4{5-5} sc.
Repeat Rows 3 and 4, 2{3-4} times, then repeat Row 3 once **more**.

BODY - LEFT MITTEN ONLY

Row 1: Ch 1, turn; sc in first 4{5-5} sc, slip st in next 6 slip sts, sc in next 7{8-9} sc, ch 1{2-4} **loosely**, drop MC, with Color B ch 5{6-6} **loosely**, drop Color B, with Color A, ch 9{10-10} **loosely**, drop Color A, with MC bobbin, ch 1{2-4} **loosely**, skip next 9{13-17} sts, sc in next 7{8-9} sc, slip st in next 6 slip sts, sc in last 4{5-5} sc: 50{58-64} sts.

Row 2: Ch 1, turn; sc in first 4{5-5} sc, slip st in next 6 slip sts, sc in next 8(10-13} sts changing to Color A in last sc worked, sc in next 5{6-6} sts, slip st in next 4 sts changing to Color B in last slip st worked, sc in next 5{6-6} sts changing to MC in last sc worked, sc in next 8{10-13} sts, slip st in next 6 slip sts, sc in last 4{5-5} sc.

Row 3: Ch 1, turn; sc in first 4{5-5} sc, slip st in next 6 slip sts, sc in next 8(10-13} sc changing to Color B in last sc worked, sc in **both** loops of next 5{6-6} sc **only** (face) changing to Color A in last sc worked, slip st in next 4 slip sts, sc in next 5{6-6} sc changing to MC in last sc worked, sc in next 8{10-13} sc, slip st in next 6 slip sts, sc in last 4{5-5} sc.

Row 4: Ch 1, turn; sc in first 4{5-5} sc, slip st in next 6 slip sts, sc in next 8{10-13} sc changing to Color A in last sc worked, sc in next 5{6-6} sc, slip st in next 4 slip sts changing to Color B in last slip st worked, sc in **both** loops of next 5{6-6} sc **only** changing to MC in last sc worked, sc in next 8{10-13} sc, slip st in next 6 slip sts, sc in last 4{5-5} sc.
Repeat Rows 3 and 4, 2{3-4} times, then repeat Row 3 once **more**.

THUMB

Work same as Dog, page 103.

FINISHING

Using photo as guide for placement, add facial features using black embroidery floss and French Knots for eyes *(Fig. 32, page 142)*.
Cut mouth from red felt and buttons from white felt using patterns.

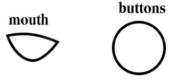

Glue mouth to head. Attach buttons to Body using black embroidery floss and Straight Stitch forming an "x" *(Fig. 28, page 141)*.
Using matching colors, with **wrong** sides together and working in **inside** loops only, whipstitch seams closed *(Fig. 25b, page 140)*.

HAIR

Cut 14 strands of Color A, each 9" long. Holding all strands together, tie a piece of Color A around center and sew to top of head.
For bangs, wind Color A loosely around 2 fingers, 10 times; cut yarn. Insert an 18" length of Color A through center of loops and tie securely around the 10 strands, removing loops from fingers. Sew loops to center of hair.
Tie a strand of Color A around hair on each side of head for pigtails, and sew in place.

YO-YO CARDIGAN

Continued from page 90.

PLACEMENT DIAGRAMS

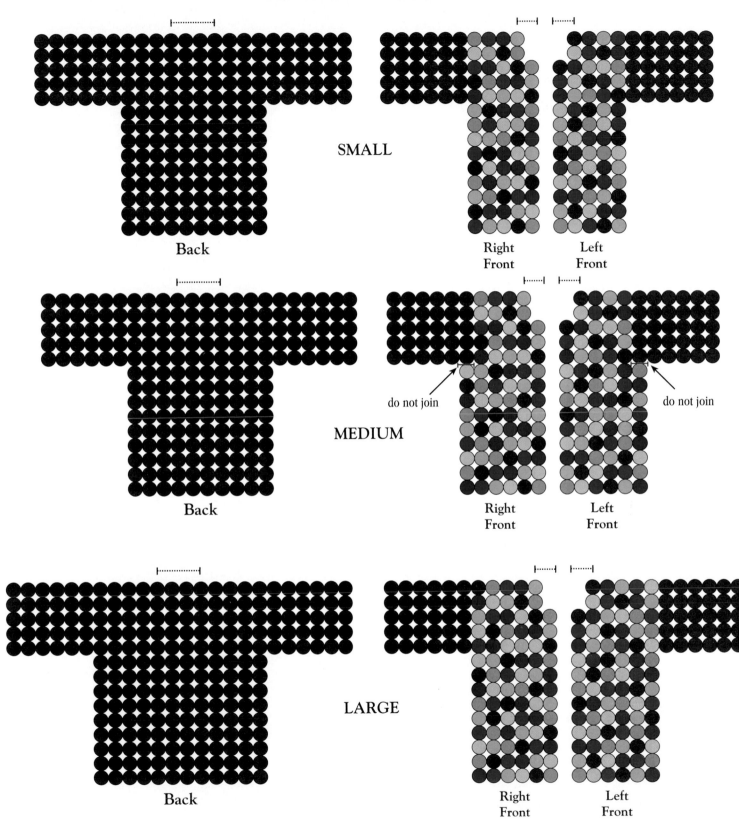

SMALL

Back

Right
Front

Left
Front

MEDIUM

Back

do not join

do not join

Right
Front

Left
Front

LARGE

Back

Right
Front

Left
Front

hooked on holidays

The holidays we celebrate all through the year present endless opportunities to create captivating crocheted accents. Whether you choose to stitch our "beary" sweet couple for Valentine's Day, the quick rag basket for Easter, or the string of cheery Christmas bulbs for a ready-made sweater, you'll love taking these ideas and adding your own personal touches. So go ahead, browse through the following pages, pick a project, and get hooked on holidays!

VALENTINE'S DAY

Sharing a carefree moment on a swing made for two, these sweetheart bears are the perfect pair to dress up our Valentine's Day wreath. The cute couple is created with worsted weight yarn and clad in romantic red for this sentimental occasion.

SWEETHEART BEARS

Finished Size: Approximately 6" high

MATERIALS
Worsted Weight Yarn, approximately:
    Color A (Light Brown) - 1 ounce, (30 grams, 55 yards)
    Color B (Red) - ¹/₂ ounce, (20 grams, 30 yards)
    Color C (White) - 15 yards
    Color D (Brown) - 17 yards
    Color E (Cream) - 7 yards
    Black - small amount
Crochet hook, size G (4.00 mm) **or** size needed for gauge
Yarn needle
Polyester fiberfill
Cardboard - approximately 3" wide x 5" long
Glue gun
Finishing materials: 17" diameter straw wreath, leaves,
    2" wide ribbon, and various sizes of wooden hearts

GAUGE: 16 sc and 16 rows = 4"

BOY BEAR
HEAD AND BODY
Rnd 1 (Right side): With Color A, ch 2, 6 sc in second ch from hook; do **not** join, place marker *(see Markers, page 138)*.
Rnd 2: 2 Sc in each sc around: 12 sc.
Rnd 3: (Sc in next 2 sc, 2 sc in next sc) around: 16 sc.
Rnds 4-6: Sc in each sc around.
Note: To **decrease**, pull up a loop in next 2 sc, YO and draw through all 3 loops on hook **(counts as one sc).**
Rnd 7: Decrease around: 8 sc.
Stuff Head with polyester fiberfill.
Rnd 8: Sc in each sc around.
Rnd 9: 2 Sc in each sc around: 16 sc.
Rnds 10-12: Sc in each sc around changing to Color B in last sc worked on Rnd 12 *(Fig. 22a, page 138)* (center of back).
Rnds 13-15: Sc in each sc around; do **not** finish off.
Stuff Body with polyester fiberfill.

RIGHT LEG

Rnd 1: Sc in next 8 sc, skip next 8 sc: 8 sc.

Rnds 2-7: Sc in each sc around.

Rnd 8 (Cuff): Slip st in Front Loop Only of next sc *(Fig. 20, page 138)*, ch 1, turn; sc in Back Loop Only of each sc around; join with slip st to first sc, finish off.

LEFT LEG

Rnd 1: Join Color B with sc in first skipped sc on Rnd 15 of Body *(see Joining With Sc, page 138)*, sc in next sc and in each sc around; do **not** join, place marker: 8 sc.

Rnds 2-8: Work same as Right Leg.
Stuff both Legs with polyester fiberfill.

FOOT (Make 2)

Rnd 1 (Right side): With Color A, ch 2, 6 sc in second ch from hook; do **not** join, place marker.

Rnd 2: (Sc in next sc, 2 sc in next sc) around: 9 sc.

Rnds 3 and 4: Sc in each sc around.

Rnd 5: (Sc in next sc, decrease) around: 6 sc.
Stuff Foot with polyester fiberfill.

Rnd 6: (Skip next sc, slip st in next sc) around; finish off leaving a long end for sewing: 3 sts.

ARM (Make 2)

Rnd 1 (Right side): With Color A, ch 2, 6 sc in second ch from hook; do **not** join, place marker.

Rnds 2-9: Sc in each sc around; at end of Rnd 9, slip st in next sc, finish off leaving a long end for sewing.
Stuff Arm with polyester fiberfill.

EAR (Make 2)

With Color A, ch 2, 6 sc in second ch from hook; finish off leaving a long end for sewing.

MUZZLE

Rnd 1 (Right side): With Color A, ch 2, 6 sc in second ch from hook; do **not** join, place marker.

Rnd 2: (Sc in next sc, 2 sc in next sc) around; slip st in next sc, finish off leaving a long end for sewing: 9 sc.
Stuff Muzzle with polyester fiberfill.

GIRL BEAR
HEAD AND BODY

Rnds 1-9: Work same as Boy Bear changing to Color C in last sc worked at end of Rnd 9 (center of back): 16 sc.

Rnds 10-12: Sc in each sc around.

Rnd 13: Slip st in Back Loop Only of next sc, sc in Back Loop Only of each sc around.

Rnds 14 and 15: Sc in both loops of each sc around; do **not** finish off.
Stuff Body with polyester fiberfill.

RIGHT LEG

Rnd 1: Sc in next 8 sc, skip next 8 sc: 8 sc.

Rnds 2-6: Sc in each sc around changing to Color A in last sc worked at end of Rnd 6.

Rnd 7: Slip st in Back Loop Only of next sc, sc in Back Loop Only of same st and in each sc around.

Rnds 8 and 9: Sc in both loops of each sc around; at end of Rnd 9, slip st in next sc, finish off.

LEFT LEG

Rnd 1: Join Color C with sc in first skipped sc, sc in next sc and in each sc around; do **not** join, place marker: 8 sc.

Rnds 2-9: Work same as Right Leg.
Stuff both Legs with polyester fiberfill.

FOOT (Make 2)

Rnd 1 (Right side): With Color A, ch 2, 6 sc in second ch from hook; do **not** join, place marker.

Rnd 2: (Sc in next sc, 2 sc in next sc) around: 9 sc.

Rnds 3 and 4: Sc in each sc around.

Rnd 5: (Sc in next sc, decrease) around: 6 sc.
Stuff Foot with polyester fiberfill.

Rnd 6: (Skip next sc, slip st in next sc) around; finish off leaving a long end for sewing: 3 sts.

ARM (Make 2)

Rnd 1 (Right side): With Color A, ch 2, 6 sc in second ch from hook; do **not** join, place marker.

Rnds 2-9: Sc in each sc around; at end of Rnd 9, slip st in next sc, finish off leaving a long end for sewing.
Stuff Arm with polyester fiberfill.

EAR (Make 2)

With Color A, ch 2, 6 sc in second ch from hook; finish off leaving a long end for sewing.

MUZZLE

Rnd 1 (Right side): With Color A, ch 2, 6 sc in second ch from hook; do **not** join, place marker.

Rnd 2: (Sc in next sc, 2 sc in next sc) around; slip st in next sc, finish off leaving a long end for sewing: 9 sc.
Stuff Muzzle with polyester fiberfill.

Continued on page 129.

ST. PATRICK'S DAY

May Irish blessings be yours when you set the table with these shamrock-inspired accents. Stitched with bedspread weight cotton thread, the pretty table runner and coasters feature four lucky shamrocks in the center of each square.

SHAMROCK TABLE RUNNER AND COASTER

Finished Size: Coaster - 4³/₄" square
Table Runner - approximately 11¹/₂" x 26"

MATERIALS
Bedspread Weight Cotton Thread (size 10), approximately:

Coaster
MC (Green) - 18 yards **each**
CC (Ecru) - 12 yards **each**
Table Runner
MC (Green) - 185 yards
CC (Ecru) - 125 yards
Steel crochet hook, size 6 (1.80 mm) **or** size needed for gauge

GAUGE: 4 Clovers = 2" square

PATTERN STITCHES

V-ST
(Dc, ch 3, dc) in st indicated.

CLUSTER
★ YO, insert hook in ch indicated, YO and pull up a loop, YO and draw through 2 loops on hook; repeat from ★ 2 times **more**, YO and draw through all 4 loops on hook *(Figs. 9a & b, page 134)*.

TRIPLE PICOT
(Ch 3, slip st in third ch from hook) 3 times, slip st in hdc just worked.

COASTER

FIRST CLOVER
Foundation Rings: With MC, ch 7; join with slip st to form a ring, (ch 6, slip st in same ch as last slip st) twice: 3 rings.

Rnd 1 (Right side): Ch 1, (sc, hdc, 7 dc, hdc, sc) in each ring around; join with slip st to first sc, ch 9 (Stem), slip st in same st as joining, finish off: 3 Leaves.

Note: Loop a short piece of thread around any stitch to mark last round as **right** side.

NEXT 2 CLOVERS
Foundation Rings: Work same as First Clover.

Rnd 1 (Right side): Ch 1, (sc, hdc, 7 dc, hdc, sc) in first 2 rings, (sc, hdc, 3 dc) in last ring, drop loop from hook, with **right** side facing, insert hook in center dc of first Leaf on **previous Clover**, pull dropped loop through, (4 dc, hdc, sc) in same ring on **new Clover**; join with slip st to first sc, ch 4, slip st in center ch of Stem on **previous Clover**, ch 4, slip st in same st as joining on **new Clover**, finish off.

LAST CLOVER
Foundation Rings: Work same as First Clover.

Rnd 1 (Right side): Ch 1, (sc, hdc, 3 dc) in first ring, drop loop from hook, with **right** side facing, insert hook in center dc of last Leaf on **First Clover**, pull dropped loop through, (4 dc, hdc, sc) in same ring on **Last Clover**, (sc, hdc, 7 dc, hdc, sc) in next ring, (sc, hdc, 3 dc) in last ring, drop loop from hook, with **right** side facing, insert hook in center dc of first Leaf on **previous Clover**, pull dropped loop through, (4 dc, hdc, sc) in same ring on **Last Clover**; join with slip st to first sc, ch 4, slip st in center ch of Stem, ch 4, slip st in same st as joining on **Last Clover**, finish off.

BORDER

Rnd 1: With **right** side facing, join CC with sc in center dc of second Leaf on any Clover *(see Joining With Sc, page 138)*; ch 3, sc in same st, ch 5, hdc in first dc of next Leaf on same Clover, ch 5, hdc in last dc of first Leaf on next Clover, ch 5, ★ (sc, ch 3, sc) in center dc of next Leaf on same Clover, ch 5, hdc in first dc of next Leaf on same Clover, ch 5, hdc in last dc of first Leaf on next Clover, ch 5; repeat from ★ 2 times **more**; join with slip st to first sc.

Rnd 2: Slip st in first ch-3 sp, ch 6, dc in same sp, (ch 3, dc) twice in same sp, ★ † work V-St in center ch of next loop, (dc in next hdc, work V-St in center ch of next loop) twice †, dc in next corner ch-3 sp, (ch 3, dc) 3 times in same sp; repeat from ★ 2 times **more**, then repeat from † to † once; join with slip st to third ch of beginning ch-6: 24 ch-3 sps.

Rnd 3: Slip st in first ch-3 sp, ch 1, sc in same sp, ch 5, work Cluster in center ch of next ch-3 sp, ch 5, ★ sc in next ch-3 sp, ch 5, work Cluster in center ch of next ch-3 sp, ch 5; repeat from ★ around; join with slip st to first sc: 12 Clusters.

Rnd 4: Slip st in first 2 chs, ch 1, sc in next ch, ch 3, ★ † (sc, ch 3) twice in top of next Cluster, [(sc in center ch of next loop, ch 3) twice, sc in top of next Cluster, ch 3] twice †, (sc in center ch of next loop, ch 3) twice; repeat from ★ 2 times **more**, then repeat from † to † **once**, sc in center ch of next loop, ch 3; join with slip st to first sc, finish off.

Rnd 5: With **right** side facing, join MC with sc in first ch-3 sp, ch 3, hdc in next corner ch-3 sp, work Triple Picot, ch 3, ★ sc in next ch-3 sp, ch 3, hdc in next ch-3 sp, work Triple Picot, ch 3; repeat from ★ around; join with slip st to first sc, finish off.

TABLE RUNNER

Work first Motif same as Coaster.

For remaining 9 Motifs, work same as first Motif through Rnd 4 of Border.

Using Placement Diagram as a guide, page 111, join Motifs in indicated order working One-Sided or Two-Sided Joining.

ONE-SIDED JOINING

Rnd 5: With **right** side facing, join MC with sc in first ch-3 sp, ch 3, (hdc in next ch-3 sp, work Triple Picot, ch 3, sc in next ch-3 sp, ch 3) 16 times, ★ † hdc in next ch-3 sp, ch 3, slip st in third ch from hook, ch 1, drop loop from hook, with **right** side facing, insert hook in top loop of corresponding Triple Picot on **previous Motif**, pull dropped loop through, ch 1, slip st in ch-1 before joining, ch 3, slip st in third ch from hook, slip st in hdc just worked, ch 3 †, sc in next ch-3 sp on **new Motif**, ch 3; repeat from ★ 2 times **more**, then repeat from † to † once; join with slip st to first sc, finish off.

TWO-SIDED JOINING

Rnd 5: With **right** side facing, join MC with sc in third ch-3 sp, ch 3, (hdc in next ch-3 sp, work Triple Picot, ch 3, sc in next ch-3 sp, ch 3) 10 times, † hdc in next ch-3 sp, ★ ch 3, slip st in third ch from hook, ch 1, drop loop from hook, with **right** side facing, insert hook in top loop of corresponding Triple Picot on **previous Motif**, pull dropped loop through, ch 1, slip st in ch-1 before joining, ch 3, slip st in third ch from hook, slip st in hdc just worked, ch 3, sc in next ch-3 sp on **new Motif**, ch 3, hdc in next ch-3 sp; repeat from ★ 3 times **more**, work Triple Picot, ch 3 †, sc in next ch-3 sp, ch 3, repeat from † to † once; join with slip st to first sc, finish off.

PLACEMENT DIAGRAM

CENTER FILL-IN MOTIF

With MC, ch 4; join with slip st to form a ring.

Rnd 1: Ch 1, 2 sc in ring, ch 3, slip st in third ch from hook, ch 1, drop loop from hook, with **right** side facing and working in intersection of 4 Motifs, insert hook in top loop of any Triple Picot, ★ † pull dropped loop through, ch 1, slip st in ch-1 before joining, ch 3, slip st in third ch from hook, slip st in sc just worked †, 2 sc in ring, ch 3, slip st in third ch from hook, ch 1, drop loop from hook, insert hook in top loop of Triple Picot on **next Motif**; repeat from ★ 2 times **more**, then repeat from † to † once; join with slip st to first sc, finish off. Repeat for remaining 2 Center Fill-In Motifs.

EDGE FILL-IN MOTIF

With MC, ch 4; join with slip st to form a ring.

Rnd 1: Ch 1, 2 sc in ring, (ch 3, slip st in third ch from hook) 3 times, slip st in sc just worked, 2 sc in ring, ch 3, slip st in third ch from hook, ch 1, drop loop from hook, with **right** side facing and working in intersection of 3 Motifs along edge, insert hook in top loop of corner Triple Picot on first Motif, ★ † pull dropped loop through, ch 1, slip st in ch-1 before joining, ch 3, slip st in third ch from hook, slip st in sc just worked †, 2 sc in ring, ch 3, slip st in third ch from hook, ch 1, drop loop from hook, insert hook in top of Triple Picot on **next Motif**; repeat from ★ once **more**, then repeat from † to † once; join with slip st to first sc, finish off. Repeat for remaining 3 Edge Fill-In Motifs.

See Washing and Blocking, page 140.

EASTER

Spread "hoppy" holiday greetings with these charming Easter offerings! (Below) Sunny flowers bloom on this spring-fresh doily. Crocheted with cotton thread, each motif starts with a three-dimensional daffodil. (Opposite) Crafted using torn-fabric strips and a size Q hook, our delightful Easter basket makes a unique accent when filled with playful bunnies and colorful eggs.

DAFFODIL DOILY

Finished Size: Approximately 10½" in diameter

MATERIALS
Bedspread Weight Cotton Thread (size 10), approximately:
  White - 46 yards
  Yellow - 28 yards
  Green (Variegated) - 28 yards
Steel crochet hooks, sizes 5 (1.90 mm) **and** 7 (1.65 mm)
  or sizes needed for gauge
Tapestry needle

GAUGE: One Daffodil = 1¾"

PATTERN STITCHES
DC CLUSTER
★ YO, insert hook in loop indicated, YO and pull up a loop,
YO and draw through 2 loops on hook; repeat from ★
2 times **more**, YO and draw through all 4 loops on hook
(Figs. 9a & b, page 134).

TR CLUSTER
★ YO twice, insert hook in loop indicated, YO and pull up a
loop, (YO and draw through 2 loops on hook) twice; repeat
from ★ 2 times **more**, YO and draw through all 4 loops on
hook.

DTR CLUSTER
★ YO 3 times, insert hook in loop indicated, YO and pull up
a loop, (YO and draw through 2 loops on hook) 3 times;
repeat from ★ 2 times **more**, YO and draw through all
4 loops on hook.

YO7 CLUSTER
★ YO 7 times, insert hook in **next** ch-4 sp, YO and pull up a
loop, (YO and draw through 2 loops on hook) 7 times;
repeat from ★ 2 times **more**, YO and draw through all
4 loops on hook **(Figs. 10a & b, page 134).**

POINT ST
★ YO 7 times, insert hook in **next** loop, YO and pull up a
loop, (YO and draw through 2 loops on hook) 7 times;
repeat from ★ once **more**, YO and draw through all 3 loops
on hook.

YO5
YO 5 times, insert hook in sp indicated, YO and pull up a
loop, (YO and draw through 2 loops on hook) 6 times.

PICOT
Ch 3, slip st in third ch from hook.

DAFFODIL (Make 6)
With larger size hook and Yellow, ch 4; join with slip st to form
a ring.
Rnd 1 (Right side): Ch 1, 6 sc in ring; do **not** join.

Rnd 2: (Slip st, ch 3, 3 tr, ch 3, slip st) in Back Loop Only of
each sc around **(Fig. 20, page 138)**: 6 petals.
Rnd 3: Bring thread to front; sc in free loop of each sc on Rnd 1
(Fig. 21a, page 138); join with slip st to first sc: 6 sc.
Rnd 4: 2 Sc in each sc around; join with slip st to first sc: 12 sc.
Rnd 5: Ch 1, sc in first 3 sc, 2 sc in next sc, (sc in next 3 sc, 2 sc
in next sc) twice; join with slip st to first sc, finish off: 15 sc.
Top of Petals: With **right** side facing, join Yellow with slip st
in top of beginning ch-3 on Rnd 2; ★ pull up a loop in next 3 tr,
YO and draw through all 4 loops on hook, ch 9; repeat from
★ around; join with slip st to first st, finish off.

FIRST MOTIF
Rnd 1: With **right** side facing and smaller size hook, join
Green with slip st in any loop on last rnd of Daffodil; ch 2, (YO,
insert hook in same loop, YO and pull up a loop, YO and draw
through 2 loops on hook) twice, YO and draw through all
3 loops on hook **(beginning dc Cluster made)**, (ch 2, work
dc Cluster) 4 times in same loop, ★ work dc Cluster in next
loop, (ch 2, work dc Cluster) 4 times in same loop; repeat from
★ around; join with slip st to top of beginning dc Cluster,
finish off: 30 Clusters.
Rnd 2: With **right** side facing and larger size hook, join White
with slip st in same st as joining; ch 1, sc in same st, ch 5,
(sc in next Cluster, ch 5) 3 times, ★ sc in next 2 Clusters, ch 5,
(sc in next Cluster, ch 5) 3 times; repeat from ★ around to last
Cluster, sc in last Cluster; join with slip st to first sc, finish off:
24 loops.

SECOND MOTIF
Rnd 1: Work same as First Motif.
Rnd 2 (Joining rnd): With **right** side facing and larger size
hook, join White with slip st in same st as joining; ch 1, sc in
same st, ch 5, (sc in next Cluster, ch 5) 3 times, ★ sc in next
2 Clusters, ch 5, (sc in next Cluster, ch 5) 3 times; repeat from
★ 2 times **more**, sc in next 2 Clusters, (ch 5, sc in next
Cluster) twice, ch 2, slip st in center ch of any loop on
previous Motif, ch 2, sc in next Cluster on **new Motif**, ch 2,
slip st in center ch of next loop on **previous Motif**, ch 2, sc in
next 2 Clusters on **new Motif**, (ch 2, slip st in center ch of next
loop on **previous Motif**, ch 2, sc in next Cluster on **new
Motif**) twice, (ch 5, sc in next Cluster) twice; join with slip st to
first sc, finish off.

NEXT 3 MOTIFS
Work same as Second Motif, skipping 4 loops from joining on
previous Motif.

LAST MOTIF
Rnd 1: Work same as First Motif.
Rnd 2 (Joining rnd): With **right** side facing and larger size
hook, join White with slip st in same st as joining; ch 1, sc in

same st, † (ch 5, sc in next Cluster) twice, (ch 2, slip st in center ch of corresponding loop on **previous Motif**, ch 2, sc in next Cluster on **new Motif**) twice, sc in next Cluster, (ch 2, slip st in center ch of next loop on **previous Motif**, ch 2, sc in next Cluster on **new Motif**) twice †, ch 5, sc in next Cluster, ch 5, sc in next 2 Clusters, ★ ch 5, (sc in next Cluster, ch 5) 3 times, sc in next 2 Clusters; repeat from ★ once **more**, repeat from † to † once skipping 12 loops from joining on First Motif, (ch 5, sc in next Cluster) twice; join with slip st to first sc, finish off.

CENTER

Rnd 1: With **right** side facing and smaller size hook, join White with slip st in first unworked loop on inside of any Motif; ch 1, sc in same loop, [ch 4, (sc, work Picot, sc) in next loop] twice, ch 4, sc in next loop, work Picot, ★ sc in next loop, [ch 4, (sc, work Picot, sc) in next loop] twice, ch 4, sc in next loop, work Picot; repeat from ★ around; join with slip st to first sc.
Rnd 2: Slip st in first 2 chs, ch 7, ★ YO 7 times, insert hook in **next** ch-4 sp, YO and pull up a loop, (YO and draw through 2 loops on hook) 7 times; repeat from ★ once **more**, YO and draw through all 3 loops on hook, ch 1 **tightly**, (work YO7 Cluster, ch 1) around; join with slip st to top of first st.
Rnd 3: Ch 1, sc in each ch-1 sp around; join with slip st to first sc, finish off: 6 sc.

EDGING

Rnd 1: With **right** side facing and smaller size hook, join White with slip st in eighth unworked loop on any Motif; ch 1, sc in same loop, ★ † ch 3, dc in next loop, ch 3, dtr in next loop, ch 3, work YO5 in next loop, ch 3, work Point St, ch 3, work YO5 in next loop, ch 3, dtr in next loop, ch 3, dc in next loop, ch 3, (sc in next loop, ch 5) 3 times †, sc in next loop; repeat from ★ 4 times **more**, then repeat from † to † once; join with slip st to first sc.
Rnd 2: Slip st in first ch-3 sp, ch 1, (2 sc, work Picot, sc) in same sp and in next 3 ch-3 sps, ★ † ch 7, slip st in seventh ch from hook, (2 sc, work Picot, sc) in next 4 ch-3 sps, ch 2, (work dc Cluster, ch 2) 3 times in next loop, work (tr Cluster, ch 2, dtr Cluster, ch 4, slip st in top of Cluster just worked, ch 2, tr Cluster) in next loop, ch 2, (work dc Cluster, ch 2) 3 times in next loop †, (2 sc, work Picot, sc) in next 4 ch-3 sps; repeat from ★ 4 times **more**, then repeat from † to † once; join with slip st to first sc, finish off.

STAMEN (Make 6)

With Green and larger size hook, ch 5, sc in third ch from hook, slip st in last 2 chs; finish off leaving a long end for sewing.
Sew a Stamen to center of each Daffodil.

See Washing and Blocking, page 140.

Quick RAG BASKET

Finished Size: Approximately 9½" in diameter x 4" high plus handle

MATERIALS

100% Cotton Fabric, 44/45" wide, approximately 3¼ yards
Crochet hook, size Q (15.00 mm) **or** size needed for gauge
1 - 18" length of 22 gauge wire

Prepare fabric and tear into 2" wide strips *(see Preparing Fabric Strips and Joining Fabric Strips, page 139)*.

GAUGE: 6 sc = 5½" and 5 rows = 4"
Rnds 1-4 = 6½"

Rnd 1 (Right side): Ch 2, 6 sc in second ch from hook; do **not** join, place marker *(see Markers, page 138)*.
Rnd 2: 2 Sc in each sc around: 12 sc.
Rnd 3: (Sc in next sc, 2 sc in next sc) around: 18 sc.
Rnd 4: (Sc in next 2 sc, 2 sc in next sc) around; slip st in Back Loop Only of next sc *(Fig. 20, page 138)*: 24 sc.
Rnd 5: Ch 1, sc in Back Loop Only of each sc around; join with slip st to both loops of first sc.
Rnd 6: Ch 1, working in both loops, sc in first 5 sc, 2 sc in next sc, (sc in next 5 sc, 2 sc in next sc) around; join with slip st to first sc: 28 sc.
Rnd 7: Ch 1, sc in each sc around; join with slip st to first sc.
Rnd 8: Ch 1, sc in first 6 sc, 2 sc in next sc, (sc in next 6 sc, 2 sc in next sc) around; join with slip st to first sc: 32 sc.
Rnd 9: Ch 30 **loosely** (handle), skip next 15 sc, slip st in next 16 sc; slip st in front loop only next 30 chs *(Fig. 1)*, slip st in same st as base of handle, **turn**; slip st in free loop of next 30 chs leaving back ridge of ch unworked, slip st in same st as base of handle, slip st in last 15 sc; finish off.

Fig. 1

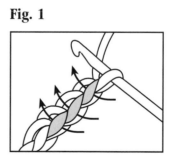

Weave wire through center of handle; fold ½" at each end and form loop to secure.
Shape handle as desired.

HALLOWEEN

There's no trick to these tantalizing treats — just lots of Halloween fun! (Below) Serve ghoulish goodies in this enchanting pumpkin candy keeper. It's fashioned with fabric strips and has a removable lid. (Opposite) You'll be spellbound when these bewitching black kitties cross your path! Waiting for the "purr-fect" moment to pounce, they adorn our snuggly afghan, which is accented with a checkerboard border.

~Quick~ PUMPKIN JAR

Finished Size: Approximately 6" in diameter x 5½" high

MATERIALS
100% Cotton Fabric, 44/45" wide, approximately:
Orange - 1¼ yards
Green - small amount
Crochet hook, size N (9.00 mm) **or** size needed for gauge
Sewing needle and thread

Prepare fabric and tear into 1" wide strips *(see Preparing Fabric Strips and Joining Fabric Strips, page 139)*.

GAUGE: 4 sc = 2" and Rnds 1-3 = 3"

BASKET
Rnd 1: With Orange, ch 2, 6 sc in second ch from hook; join with slip st to first sc.
Rnd 2: Ch 1, 2 sc in each sc around; join with slip st to first sc: 12 sc.
Rnd 3: Ch 1, sc in first sc, 2 sc in next sc, (sc in next sc, 2 sc in next sc) around; join with slip st to Back Loop Only of first sc *(Fig. 20, page 138)*: 18 sc.
Rnd 4: Ch 1, working in Back Loops Only, sc in first sc, 2 sc in next sc, (sc in next sc, 2 sc in next sc) around; join with slip st to both loops of first sc: 27 sc.
Rnd 5: Ch 1, working in both loops, sc in first 2 sc, 2 sc in next sc, (sc in next 2 sc, 2 sc in next sc) around; join with slip st to first sc: 36 sc.
Rnds 6-8: Ch 1, sc in each sc around; join with slip st to first sc.
Note: To **decrease**, pull up a loop in next 2 sc, YO and draw through all 3 loops on hook **(counts as one sc)**.
Rnd 9: Ch 1, sc in first 7 sc, decrease, (sc in next 7 sc, decrease) around; join with slip st to first sc: 32 sc.
Rnd 10: Ch 1, sc in each sc around; join with slip st to first sc.
Rnd 11: Ch 1, sc in first 6 sc, decrease, (sc in next 6 sc, decrease) around; join with slip st to first sc, finish off: 28 sc.

LID
Rnd 1: With Orange, ch 2, 6 sc in second ch from hook; join with slip st to first sc.
Rnds 2 and 3: Ch 1, 2 sc in each sc around; join with slip st to first sc: 24 sc.
Rnd 4: Ch 1, sc in first 5 sc, 2 sc in next sc, (sc in next 5 sc, 2 sc in next sc) around; join with slip st to first sc, finish off: 28 sc.

STEM
With Green, ch 5 **loosely**.
Row 1: Sc in second ch from hook and in each ch across; finish off leaving a long end for attaching.

Weave end of Stem through center of Lid and sew to secure.

BEWITCHING KITTIES COVER-UP

Finished Size: Approximately 48" x 73"

MATERIALS
Worsted Weight Yarn, approximately:
Color A (Gold) - 15 ounces, (430 grams, 945 yards)
Color B (Black) - 26 ounces, (740 grams, 1,635 yards)
Color C (Cream) - 10 ounces, (280 grams, 630 yards)
Crochet hook, size J (6.00 mm) **or** size needed for gauge
Yarn needle

GAUGE: One Square = 2½"

ONE COLOR SQUARE
(Make 47 with Color A, 204 with Color B, and 114 with Color C)
Ch 4; join with slip st to form a ring.
Rnd 1 (Right side): Ch 3, 15 dc in ring; join with slip st to top of beginning ch: 16 sts.
Note: Loop a short piece of yarn around any stitch to mark last round as **right** side.
Rnd 2: Ch 5 **(counts as first tr plus ch 1, now and throughout)**, dc in same st, ★ dc in next 3 dc, (dc, ch 1, tr, ch 1, dc) in next dc; repeat from ★ 2 times **more**, dc in last 3 dc and in same st as joining, ch 1; join with slip st to first tr, finish off: 5 dc **each** side.

TWO COLOR SQUARE (Make 18)
Note: Colors are changed at opposite corners so that the Square is divided diagonally *(Figs. 22a & b, page 138)*.
Do **not** cut yarn; work **over** first color, held **behind** work with normal tension *(Fig. 1)*, so that it will be in position to work the next round.

Fig. 1

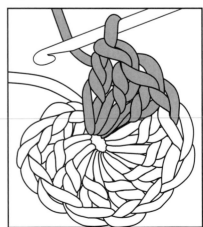

With Color C, ch 4; join with slip st to form a ring.

Rnd 1 (Right side): Ch 3, 7 dc in ring changing to Color B in last dc worked, 8 dc in ring; join with slip st to top of beginning ch changing to Color C: 16 sts.

Note: Mark last round as **right** side.

Rnd 2: Ch 5, dc in same st, dc in next 3 dc, (dc, ch 1, tr, ch 1, dc) in next dc, dc in next 4 dc, cut Color C, with Color B, ch 1, (tr, ch 1, dc) in same st, dc in next 3 dc, (dc, ch 1, tr, ch 1, dc) in next dc, dc in last 3 dc and in same st as joining, ch 1; join with slip st to first tr, finish off: 5 dc **each** side.

ASSEMBLY

With **wrong** sides together, using appropriate color, and working through **inside** loops only, whipstitch 23 Squares into 13 vertical strips following Placement Diagram A *(Fig. 25b, page 140)*; then whipstitch strips together.

PLACEMENT DIAGRAM A

BORDER

Rnd 1: With **right** side facing and working in Back Loops Only *(Fig. 20, page 138)*, join Color A with slip st in any corner tr; ch 5, dc in same st, ★ † dc in next ch-1 sp, dc in next 5 dc, dc in next ch-1 sp, (dc in next joining and in next ch-1 sp, dc in next 5 dc, dc in next ch-1 sp) across to next corner tr †, (dc, ch 1, tr, ch 1, dc) in corner tr; repeat from ★ 2 times **more**, then repeat from † to † once, dc in same st as joining, ch 1; join with slip st to first tr: 580 dc.

Rnds 2-4: Ch 5, working in both loops, dc in same st, dc in next ch-1 sp and in each dc across to next ch-1 sp, dc in next ch-1 sp, ★ (dc, ch 1, tr, ch 1, dc) in corner tr, dc in next ch-1 sp and in each dc across to next ch-1 sp, dc in next ch-1 sp; repeat from ★ around, dc in same st as joining, ch 1; join with slip st to first tr: 628 dc.

Finish off.

Following Placement Diagram B, whipstitch remaining Squares together.

Whipstitch Squares to Border.

EDGING

Work same as Border.

PLACEMENT DIAGRAM B

Celebrate the joyous spirit of the Yuletide season with the festive projects in this collection! Shown here, our stuffed Santa doll will be a merry addition to your holiday decor. The posable figure is stitched with sport and worsted weight yarns and features a fluffy beard created with loop stitches. His familiar red jacket and hat are removable.

SOFT SANTA

Finished Size: Approximately 12" tall

MATERIALS
Worsted Weight Yarn, approximately:
 Ecru - 2 ounces, (60 grams, 130 yards)
Worsted Weight Brushed Acrylic Yarn, approximately:
 White - 1/4 ounce, (10 grams, 20 yards)
Crochet hook, size F (3.75 mm) **or** size needed for gauge
Polyester fiberfill
Yarn needle
Soft sculpture needle
Black embroidery floss
Pink crayon for cheeks
For Clothes and Bag, see materials on page 126.

GAUGE: 5 sc = 1"

HEAD

Rnd 1 (Right side): With Ecru, ch 2, 8 sc in second ch from hook; join with slip st to first sc.

Rnd 2: Ch 1, 2 sc in each sc around; join with slip st to first sc: 16 sc.

Rnd 3: Ch 1, sc in first sc, 2 sc in next sc, (sc in next sc, 2 sc in next sc) around; join with slip st to first sc: 24 sc.

Rnd 4: Ch 1, sc in first 2 sc, 2 sc in next sc, (sc in next 2 sc, 2 sc in next sc) around; join with slip st to first sc: 32 sc.

Rnds 5-14: Ch 1, sc in each sc around; join with slip st to first sc.

Rnd 15: Ch 1, skip first sc, sc in next sc, (skip next sc, sc in next sc) around; join with slip st to first sc: 16 sc.

Rnds 16 and 17: Ch 1, sc in each sc around; join with slip st to first sc.
Finish off.
Stuff Head **firmly** with polyester fiberfill.

BODY

Rnd 1 (Right side): With Ecru, ch 2, 10 sc in second ch from hook; join with slip st to first sc.

Rnd 2: Ch 1, sc in first sc, 2 sc in next sc, (sc in next sc, 2 sc in next sc) around; join with slip st to first sc: 15 sc.

Rnd 3: Ch 1, sc in first sc, (2 sc in next sc, sc in next sc) around; join with slip st to first sc: 22 sc.

Rnd 4: Ch 1, sc in each sc around; join with slip st to first sc.

Rnd 5: Ch 1, sc in first sc, 2 sc in next sc, (sc in next sc, 2 in next sc) around; join with slip st to first sc: 33 sc.

Rnds 6-11: Ch 1, sc in each sc around; join with slip st to first sc.

Rnd 12: Ch 1, sc in first 10 sc, 2 sc in next sc, (sc in next sc, 2 sc in next sc) 6 times, sc in last 10 sc; join with slip st to first sc: 40 sc.

Rnds 13-17: Ch 1, sc in each sc around; join with slip st to first sc.

Rnd 18: Ch 1, sc in first 10 sc, (skip next sc, sc in next 2 sc) 6 times, skip next sc, sc in last 11 sc; join with slip st to first sc: 33 sc.

Rnds 19-21: Ch 1, sc in each sc around; join with slip st to first sc.

Rnd 22: Ch 1, sc in each sc around to last 4 sc, skip next sc, sc in last 3 sc; join with slip st to first sc: 32 sc.

Rnd 23: Ch 1, sc in first 3 sc, skip next sc, (sc in next 3 sc, skip next sc) around; join with slip st to first sc: 24 sc.

Rnd 24: Ch 1, sc in first 2 sc, skip next sc, (sc in next 2 sc, skip next sc) around; join with slip st to first sc: 16 sc.

Rnds 25-27: Ch 1, sc in each sc around; join with slip st to first sc.
Finish off leaving a long end for sewing.
Stuff Body **firmly** with polyester fiberfill.
Sew Head to Body, matching joinings and sts on opening.

ARM (Make 2)

Rnd 1 (Right side): With Ecru, ch 2, 9 sc in second ch from hook; join with slip st to first sc.

Rnd 2: Ch 1, sc in first 2 sc, 2 sc in next sc, (sc in next 2 sc, 2 sc in next sc) twice; join with slip st to first sc: 12 sc.

Rnds 3-11: Ch 1, sc in each sc around; join with slip st to first sc.

Rnd 12: Ch 1, sc in first 4 sc, skip next sc, sc in last 7 sc; join with slip st to first sc: 11 sc.

Rnd 13: Ch 1, sc in first 9 sc, skip next sc, sc in last sc; join with slip st to first sc: 10 sc.

Rnds 14-20: Ch 1, sc in each sc around; join with slip st to first sc; at end of Rnd 20, do **not** finish off.
Stuff Arm **firmly** with polyester fiberfill.

HAND AND FINGERS

Row 1: Ch 1, flatten Arm across Rnd 20 having ch-1 at fold; working through **both** thicknesses, sc in each sc across: 5 sc.

Row 2: Ch 3, turn; slip st in first sc (thumb), sc in next 4 sc.

Row 3: Ch 2, turn; slip st in second ch from hook and in first sc (little finger), slip st in next sc, ch 3, slip st in second ch from hook and in next ch (finger), ★ sc in next sc, ch 3, slip st in second ch from hook and in next ch (finger); repeat from ★ once **more**, slip st in same st as last sc worked; finish off.

LEG (Make 2)

Rnd 1 (Right side): With Ecru, ch 2, 10 sc in second ch from hook; join with slip st to first sc.

Rnd 2: Ch 1, sc in first sc, 2 sc in next sc, (sc in next sc, 2 sc in next sc) around; join with slip st to first sc: 15 sc.

Rnds 3-12: Ch 1, sc in each sc around; join with slip st to first sc.

Rnd 13: Ch 1, sc in first 4 sc, skip next sc, sc in last 10 sc; join with slip st to first sc: 14 sc.

Rnd 14: Ch 1, sc in each sc around; join with slip st to first sc.

Rnd 15: Ch 1, sc in first 7 sc, skip next sc, sc in last 6 sc; join with slip st to first sc: 13 sc.

Rnd 16: Ch 1, sc in each sc around; join with slip st to first sc.

Rnd 17: Ch 1, sc in first 10 sc, skip next sc, sc in last 2 sc; join with slip st to first sc: 12 sc.

Rnds 18-28: Ch 1, sc in each sc around; join with slip st to first sc.

Rnd 29: Ch 1, sc in first 4 sc, skip next sc, sc in next 4 sc, skip next sc, sc in last 2 sc; join with slip st to first sc: 10 sc.

Rnd 30: Ch 1, sc in each sc around; join with slip st to first sc. Stuff Leg **firmly** with polyester fiberfill.

Ankle: Ch 1, flatten Leg across Rnd 30 having ch-1 at fold; working through **both** thicknesses, sc in each sc across; do **not** finish off: 5 sc.

FOOT

Rnd 1: Ch 1, **turn**; sc in Front Loop Only of each sc across **(Fig. 20, page 138)**, **turn**; sc in free loop of same 5 sc **(Fig. 21a, page 138)**; join with slip st to first sc to begin working in rnds: 10 sc.

Rnds 2-5: Ch 1, sc in each sc around; join with slip st to first sc; at end of Rnd 5, do **not** finish off. Stuff Foot **lightly** with polyester fiberfill.

TOES

Row 1: Ch 1, flatten Foot across Rnd 5 having ch-1 at fold; working through **both** thicknesses, sc in each sc across: 5 sc.

Left Leg Only - Row 2: Turn; (slip st, ch 3, slip st) in first sc (big toe), (slip st, ch 2, slip st) in each of last 4 sc; finish off.

Right Leg Only - Row 2: Turn; (slip st, ch 2, slip st) in each of first 4 sc, (slip st, ch 3, slip st) in last sc (big toe); finish off.

ASSEMBLY

Position Arms on Body, placing joining to the back and Arms with thumbs facing to the front. Thread a soft sculpture needle with a doubled 24" length of Ecru. Insert needle through Arm **(Fig. 1)** between Rnds 3 and 4 (at 1), then back into Arm one stitch over (at 2) and through Arm again (at 1). Insert needle completely through Body between Rnds 20 and 21 and out second side (at 3), through second Arm between Rnds 3 and 4, then back into Arm one stitch over (at 4), through Arm again (at 3) and back through Body (at 5).

Pull both ends of yarn so that Arms fit tightly against the Body, but are still able to move freely at sides.

Knot the strands **tightly**, weave the ends under several stitches, and cut close to work.

Fig. 1

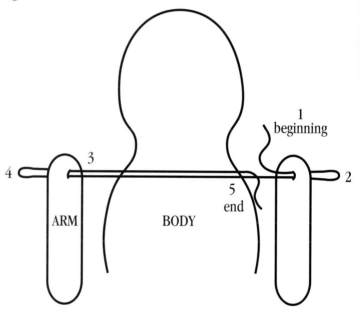

Attach Legs in same manner, inserting needle between Rnds 4 and 5 on Leg and between Rnds 5 and 6 on Body. Bend Foot at Ankle and tack Rnd 1 to Rnd 30 of Leg.

FINISHING

EYES

With black embroidery floss and a soft sculpture needle, add French Knots for eyes **(Fig. 32, page 142)**, allowing needle to pass between Rnds 9 and 10, and leaving 4 sts between eyes.

HAIR (Make 2)

With White, ch 17 **loosely**.

Row 1: Work Loop St in second ch from hook and in each ch across, wrapping yarn around finger 2 times for each st and pulling each loop to measure 1" **(Figs. 11a-c, page 135)**; finish off.

Continued on page 126.

Let these tiny snowflakes drift down upon your tree to bring the spirit of a white Christmas indoors. Fashioned with bedspread weight cotton thread, the stiffened designs can also be used to dress up a wreath or gifts.

Quick TINY SNOWFLAKES

Finished Size: Snowflake #1 - approximately 2"
Snowflake #2 - approximately 2¼"

MATERIALS

Bedspread Weight Cotton Thread (size 10), approximately:
  Snowflake #1 (White) - 4 yards **each**
  Snowflake #2 (White) - 5 yards **each**
Steel crochet hook, size 7 (1.65 mm)
Translucent nylon thread
Starching materials: Commercial fabric stiffener, blocking board, plastic wrap, resealable plastic bag, terry towel, paper towels, and stainless steel pins

Note: Gauge is not important. Snowflakes can be smaller or larger without changing the overall effect.

SNOWFLAKE #1

Ch 6; join with slip st to form a ring.
Rnd 1 (Right side)**:** Ch 1, (sc in ring, ch 5) 6 times; join with slip st to first sc: 6 loops.
Rnd 2: Slip st in first loop, ch 1, 3 sc in same loop, ch 5, slip st in third ch from hook, (ch 3, slip st in third ch from hook) 4 times, slip st in last 2 chs of previous ch-5, 3 sc in same loop, ★ 3 sc in next loop, ch 5, slip st in third ch from hook, (ch 3, slip st in third ch from hook) 4 times, slip st in last 2 chs of previous ch-5, 3 sc in same loop; repeat from ★ around; join with slip st to first sc, finish off.

123

Light up your holidays with this merry sweater embellished with a string of colorful crocheted bulbs!

SNOWFLAKE #2

Ch 6; join with slip st to form a ring.

Rnd 1 (Right side): Ch 1, (sc in ring, ch 4) 6 times; join with slip st to first sc: 6 ch-4 sps.

Rnd 2: Slip st in first ch-4 sp, ch 1, sc in same sp, (ch 3, sc) twice in same sp, ★ sc in next ch-4 sp, (ch 3, sc) twice in same sp; repeat from ★ around; join with slip st to first sc: 12 ch-3 sps.

Rnd 3: Slip st in first 2 chs, ch 1, sc in same sp, ch 2, sc in next ch-3 sp, ch 5, slip st in third ch from hook, ch 3, slip st in third ch from hook, ch 5, slip st in fifth ch from hook, (ch 3, slip st in third ch from hook) twice, slip st in next ch of previous ch-5, ch 2, ★ sc in next ch-3 sp, ch 2, sc in next ch-3 sp, ch 5, slip st in third ch from hook, ch 3, slip st in third ch from hook, ch 5, slip st in fifth ch from hook, (ch 3, slip st in third ch from hook) twice, slip st in next ch of previous ch-5, ch 2; repeat from ★ around; join with slip st to first sc, finish off.

FINISHING

See Starching and Blocking, page 143.
Using nylon thread, add hanger.

Quick HOLIDAY LIGHTS

Finished Size: Approximately 1¼" x 1¾"

MATERIALS

Bedspread Weight Cotton Thread (size 10), approximately:
  MC (Various Colors) - 3½ yards for **each** bulb
  CC (Black) - ½ yard for **each** bulb
Steel crochet hook, size 7 (1.65 mm)
Black silk cording
Sewing needle and thread
Purchased sweater

Note: Gauge is not important. Light Bulbs can be smaller or larger without changing the overall effect.

LIGHT BULB

With CC, ch 4 **loosely**.

Row 1 (Right side): Sc in second ch from hook and in each ch across: 3 sc.

Note: Loop a short piece of thread around any stitch to mark last row as **right** side.

Row 2: Ch 1, turn; 2 sc in first sc, sc in next sc, 2 sc in last sc: 5 sc.

Row 3: Ch 1, turn; sc in each sc across changing to MC in last sc *(Fig. 22a page 138)*.

Rows 4-6: Ch 1, turn; 2 sc in first sc, sc in each sc across to last sc, 2 sc in last sc: 11 sc.

Rows 7-11: Ch 1, turn; sc in each sc across.

Note: To **decrease**, pull up a loop in next 2 sc, YO and draw through all 3 loops on hook **(counts as one sc)**.

Rows 12-15: Ch 1, turn; decrease, sc in each sc across to last 2 sc, decrease: 3 sc.

Row 16: Ch 1, turn; pull up a loop in each sc, YO and draw through all 4 loops on hook; finish off.

Repeat for desired number of Light Bulbs.

FINISHING

Using photo as a guide for suggested placement, sew cording to sweater.

With **right** sides facing, sew Light Bulbs to cording and sweater as desired.

SOFT SANTA

Continued from page 122.

BEARD

With White, ch 19 **loosely**.

Row 1: Work Loop St in second ch from hook and each ch across, wrapping yarn around finger 3 times for each st and pulling each loop to measure 1"; finish off.

MUSTACHE

With White, ch 10; finish off.
Tie knot close to each end and trim.

Using photo as a guide for placement, sew Mustache and Beard in place. Sew Hair to back of Head forming 2 rows.

Eyebrows: Cut six, 3" strands of White. Using one strand, add fringe working around 3 sts 2 rounds above each eye *(Figs. 26a & b, page 140)*. Unravel plies and trim just above knot.

Use crayon to blush Santa's cheeks.

SANTA'S CLOTHES AND BAG

MATERIALS

Sport Weight Yarn, approximately:
    MC (Red) - 2 ounces, (60 grams, 175 yards)
    Color A (Black) - 1½ ounces, (40 grams, 130 yards)
    Color B (White) - 1¼ ounces, (35 grams, 110 yards)
Crochet hooks, sizes D (3.25 mm) **and** F (3.75 mm) **or** sizes needed for gauge
Yarn needle
Polyester fiberfill
Sewing needle and thread
2 - ³/₈" pearl buttons
Small buckle
Size 3/0 snap

GAUGE: With larger size hook, 5 dc = 1"
              With smaller size hook, 6 dc = 1"

PATTERN STITCHES

DC DECREASE

★ YO, insert hook in **next** st, YO and pull up a loop, YO and draw through 2 loops on hook; repeat from ★ once **more**, YO and draw through all 3 loops on hook **(counts as one dc)**.

SC DECREASE

Pull up a loop in next 2 sts, YO and draw through all 3 loops on hook **(counts as one sc)**.

FRONT POST SINGLE CROCHET *(abbreviated FPsc)*

Insert hook from **front** to **back** around post of st indicated *(Fig. 15, page 136)*, YO and pull up a loop, YO and draw through both loops on hook.

BACK POST SINGLE CROCHET *(abbreviated BPsc)*

Insert hook from **back** to **front** around post of st indicated, YO and pull up a loop, YO and draw through both loops on hook.

PUFF ST

★ YO, insert hook in st indicated, YO and pull up a loop even with loop on hook; repeat from ★ 2 times **more**, YO and draw through all 7 loops on hook *(Fig. 12, page 135)*.

UNDERSHIRT

With larger size hook and Color B, ch 50 **loosely**; being careful not to twist ch, join with slip st to form a ring.

Rnd 1 (Right side)**:** Ch 3 **(counts as first dc, now and throughout)**, dc in next ch and in each ch around; join with slip st to first dc: 50 dc.

Note: Loop a short piece of yarn around any stitch to mark last round as **right** side.

Rnd 2: Ch 3, dc in next 6 dc, ch 5 **loosely** (armhole), skip next 10 dc, dc in next 16 dc, ch 5 **loosely** (armhole), skip next 10 dc, dc in last 7 dc; join with slip st to first dc: 30 dc.

Rnd 3: Ch 3, dc in next 5 dc, 2 dc in next dc, dc in next 5 chs, 2 dc in next dc, dc in next 14 dc, 2 dc in next dc, dc in next 5 chs, 2 dc in next dc, dc in last 6 dc; join with slip st to first dc: 44 dc.

Rnds 4-8: Ch 3, dc in next dc and in each dc around; join with slip st to first dc.
Finish off.

PANTS

With smaller size hook and MC, ch 55 **loosely**.

Row 1 (Right side)**:** Sc in second ch from hook and in each ch across: 54 sc.

Note: Mark last row as **right** side.

Row 2: Ch 3, turn; dc in next 2 sc, 2 dc in next sc, (dc in next 3 sc, 2 dc in next sc) 12 times, dc in last 2 sc: 67 dc.

Note: Begin working in rounds.

Rnd 1: Ch 3, turn; dc in next dc and in each dc across; join with slip st to first dc.

Rnds 2-5: Ch 3, do **not** turn; dc in next dc and in each dc around; join with slip st to first dc; at end of Rnd 5, do **not** finish off.

LEFT LEG

Rnd 1: Ch 4, skip next 33 dc, slip st in next dc, ch 2, dc in same st, dc in next 32 dc, dc in next 4 chs; skip beginning ch-2 and join with slip st to first dc: 37 dc.

Rnds 2-4: Ch 2, dc in same st and in each dc around; skip beginning ch-2 and join with slip st to first dc.

Rnd 5: Ch 2, dc in next dc, dc decrease around to last dc, dc in last dc; skip beginning ch-2 and join with slip st to first dc: 19 dc.

Rnd 6: Ch 1, sc in each dc around; join with slip st to first sc.

Rnds 7-9: Ch 1, sc in same st, (work FPsc around next st, work BPsc around next st) around; join with slip st to first sc. Finish off.

RIGHT LEG

Rnd 1: With **right** side of back facing, join MC with slip st in first unworked dc on Rnd 5; ch 2, dc in same st, dc in next 32 dc, dc in free loops of next 4 chs *(Fig. 21b, page 138)*; skip beginning ch-2 and join with slip st to first dc: 37 dc.

Rnds 2-9: Work same as Left Leg.
Finish off.

LEFT SUSPENDER

Row 1: With **right** side facing, smaller size hook and working in free loops of beginning ch, skip 5 chs to **left** of opening at back of Pants and join Color A with sc in next ch *(see Joining With Sc, page 138)*, sc in next 2 chs: 3 sc.

Row 2: Ch 1, turn; sc in each sc across.

Repeat Row 2 until Suspender measures approximately 6".

Last Row: Ch 4, turn; skip first 2 sc, slip st in last sc (buttonhole); finish off.

RIGHT SUSPENDER

Work same as Left Suspender, beginning in eighth ch to **right** of opening.

JACKET

With smaller size hook and MC, ch 31 **loosely**.

Row 1: Sc in second ch from hook and in each ch across: 30 sc.

Row 2 (Right side): Ch 3, turn; 2 dc in next sc, (dc in next sc, 2 dc in next sc) across: 45 dc.

Note: Mark last row as **right** side.

Row 3: Ch 1, turn; sc in each dc across.

Row 4: Ch 3, turn; dc in next sc, 2 dc in next sc, (dc in next 2 sc, 2 dc in next sc) across: 60 dc.

Row 5: Ch 1, turn; sc in first 11 dc, ch 8 **loosely** (armhole), skip next 10 dc, sc in next 18 dc, ch 8 **loosely** (armhole), skip next 10 dc, sc in last 11 dc: 40 sc.

Row 6: Ch 3, turn; dc in next 9 sc, 2 dc in next sc, dc in next 8 chs, 2 dc in next sc, dc in next 16 sc, 2 dc in next sc, dc in next 8 chs, 2 dc in next sc, dc in last 10 sc: 60 dc.

Row 7: Ch 1, turn; sc in each dc across.

Row 8: Ch 3, turn; dc in next 21 sc, 2 dc in next sc, (dc in next 4 sc, 2 dc in next sc) 3 times, dc in last 22 sc: 64 dc.

Row 9: Ch 1, turn; sc in each dc across.

Row 10: Ch 3, turn; dc in next sc and in each sc across.

Rows 11-16: Repeat Rows 9 and 10, 3 times.
Finish off.

SLEEVE

Rnd 1: With **right** side facing and working in free loops of ch-8 and in unworked dc of armhole, join MC with slip st in first ch; ch 2, sc in next 6 chs, hdc in last ch, dc in side of next sc, dc in next 10 dc, dc in side of next sc; join with slip st to top of beginning ch-2: 20 sts.

Rnds 2 and 3: Ch 2, sc in next 6 sc, hdc in next hdc, dc in last 12 dc; join with slip st to top of beginning ch-2.

Rnds 4-6: Ch 3, dc in next st and in each st around; join with slip st to first dc.

Rnd 7: Ch 1, sc in each dc around; join with slip st to first sc changing to Color B.

Rnd 8: Ch 1, sc in each sc around; join with slip st to first sc.

Rnd 9: Ch 2, work Puff St in same st and in each sc around; skip beginning ch-2 and join with slip st to top of first Puff St: 20 Puff Sts.

Rnd 10: Ch 1, sc in each st around; join with slip st to first sc, finish off: 20 sc.

Repeat for second Sleeve.

EDGING

Rnd 1: With **right** side facing and working in free loops of beginning ch, join Color B with slip st in first ch; ch 1, 3 sc in same st, sc in each ch across to last ch, 3 sc in last ch; work 24 sc evenly spaced across end of rows; 3 sc in first dc, sc in each dc across to last dc, 3 sc in last dc; work 24 sc evenly spaced across end of rows; join with slip st to first sc: 150 sc.

Rnd 2: Ch 2, work Puff St in same st and in each sc around; skip beginning ch-2 and join with slip st to top of first Puff St: 150 Puff Sts.

Rnd 3: Ch 1, sc in first st, ch 1, (sc in next st, ch 1) 33 times, sc in next 24 sts, ch 1, (sc in next st, ch 1) 3 times, sc in next 62 sts, ch 1, (sc in next st, ch 1) 3 times, sc in next 24 sts, ch 1; join with slip st to first sc, finish off.

BOOT (Make 2)

SOLE

With smaller size hook and Color A, ch 11 **loosely**.

Rnd 1 (Right side): 2 Sc in second ch from hook, sc in next 8 chs, 4 sc in last ch; working in free loops of beginning ch, sc in next 8 chs, 2 sc in next ch; join with slip st to first sc: 24 sc.

Note: Mark last round as **right** side.

Rnd 2: Ch 1, 2 sc in same st, sc in next 10 sc, 2 sc in each of next 2 sc, sc in next 10 sc, 2 sc in last sc; join with slip st to first sc: 28 sc.

Rnd 3: Ch 1, sc in each sc around; join with slip st to Back Loop Only of first sc, do **not** finish off.

SIDES

Rnd 1: Ch 1, working in Back Loops Only, 2 sc in same st, sc in next 26 sc, 2 sc in last sc; join with slip st to both loops of first sc: 30 sc.

Rnds 2-4: Ch 1, sc in both loops of each sc around; join with slip st to first sc.

Rnd 5: Ch 1, sc in first 7 sc, dc decrease 8 times, sc in last 7 sc; join with slip st to first sc: 22 sts.

Rnd 6: Ch 1, sc in each st around; join with slip st to first sc.

Rnd 7: Ch 1, sc in first 3 sc, sc decrease, sc in next 12 sc, sc decrease, sc in last 3 sc; join with slip st to first sc: 20 sc.

Rnd 8: Ch 3, dc in same st, dc in next sc and in each sc around; join with slip st to first dc: 21 dc.

Rnds 9 and 10: Ch 3, dc in next dc and in each dc around; join with slip st to first dc changing to Color B at end of Rnd 10 *(Fig. 22b, page 138)*.

Rnd 11: Ch 1, 2 sc in same st, sc in next dc and in each dc around; join with slip st to first sc: 22 sc.

Rnd 12: Ch 2, work Puff St in first sc and in each sc around; skip beginning ch-2 and join with slip st to top of first Puff St: 22 Puff Sts.

Rnd 13: Ch 1, sc in each st around; join with slip st to first sc, finish off.

SOLE EDGING

With Sole toward you, join Color A with sc in first free loop on Rnd 3, sc in next sc and in each sc around; join with slip st to first sc, finish off.

CAP

With smaller size hook and Color B, ch 49 **loosely**; being careful not to twist ch, join with slip st to form a ring.

Rnd 1 (Right side)**:** Ch 1, sc in each ch around; join with slip st to first sc: 49 sc.

Note: Mark last round as **right** side.

Rnd 2: Ch 2, work Puff St in first sc and in each sc around; skip beginning ch-2 and join with slip st to top of first Puff St: 49 Puff Sts.

Rnd 3: Ch 1, sc in each st around; join with slip st to first sc changing to MC: 49 sc.

Rnd 4: Ch 3, dc in next sc and in each sc around; join with slip st to first dc.

Rnd 5: Ch 3, dc in next 4 dc, dc decrease, (dc in next 5 dc, dc decrease) around; join with slip st to first dc: 42 dc.

Rnd 6: Ch 3, dc in next 3 dc, dc decrease, (dc in next 4 dc, dc decrease) around; join with slip st to first dc: 35 dc.

Rnd 7: Ch 3, dc in next dc and in each dc around; join with slip st to first dc.

Rnd 8: Ch 3, dc in next 2 dc, dc decrease, (dc in next 3 dc, dc decrease) around; join with slip st to first dc: 28 dc.

Rnd 9: Ch 3, dc in next dc, dc decrease, (dc in next 2 dc, dc decrease) around; join with slip st to first dc: 21 dc.

Rnd 10: Ch 3, dc in next dc and in each dc around; join with slip st to first dc.

Rnd 11: Ch 3, dc decrease, (dc in next dc, dc decrease) around; join with slip st to first dc: 14 dc.

Rnd 12: Ch 2, dc in next dc, dc decrease around; skip beginning ch-2 and join with slip st to first dc: 7 dc.

Rnd 13: Ch 3, dc in next dc and in each dc around; join with slip st to first dc.

Rnd 14: (Skip next dc, slip st in next dc) around working last st in first dc; finish off.

BELT

Row 1: With smaller size hook, join Color A with sc around loop of buckle, sc twice in same loop: 3 sc.

Row 2: Ch 1, turn; sc in each sc across.
Repeat Row 2 until Belt measures approximately 12".
Finish off.

Belt Loop: Join Color A with slip st in end of row approximately 1" from buckle; ch 4; slip st in opposite end of same row; finish off.

BAG

Rnd 1 (Right side)**:** With larger size hook and Color A, ch 4, 14 dc in fourth ch from hook; join with slip st to top of beginning ch: 15 sts.

Rnd 2: Ch 3, dc in same st, 2 dc in next dc and in each dc around; join with slip st to first dc: 30 dc.

Rnd 3: Ch 3, 2 dc in next dc, (dc in next dc, 2 dc in next dc) around; join with slip st to first dc: 45 dc.

Rnd 4: Ch 3, dc in next dc, 2 dc in next dc, (dc in next 2 dc, 2 dc in next dc) around; join with slip st to first dc: 60 dc.

Rnds 5-13: Ch 3, dc in next dc and in each dc around; join with slip st to first dc.

Rnd 14: Ch 4, skip next dc, (dc in next dc, ch 1, skip next dc) around; join with slip st to third ch of beginning ch-4: 30 ch-1 sps.

Rnd 15: Slip st in first ch-1 sp, ch 3, dc in same sp, 2 dc in next ch-1 sp and in each ch-1 sp around; join with slip st to first dc, finish off.

Tie: With Color A, chain a 16" length; finish off.

FINISHING

Sew buttons to front of Pants.
Sew snap to back opening of Pants.
Place Undershirt and Pants on Santa.
Crossing Suspenders in back, button to front.
Place Jacket, Boots, and Belt on Santa.

TASSEL

Using Color B, make a 2" long tassel *(Figs. 27a & b, page 141)*. Pull ends through top of Cap, and tie securely.

Sew Cap to Head if desired.
Weave Tie through Rnd 14 of Bag.
Stuff Bag with polyester fiberfill.

SWEETHEART BEARS

Continued from page 108.

SKIRT

Rnd 1 (Right side): With Head toward you and working in free loops of Rnd 12 on Body *(Fig. 21a, page 138)*, join Color B with slip st in sc at center of back; ch 3 **(counts as first dc, now and throughout)**, dc in same st, 2 dc in next sc and in each sc around; join with slip st to first dc: 32 dc.

Rnd 2: Ch 3, 2 dc in next dc, (dc in next dc, 2 dc in next dc) around; join with slip st to first dc: 48 dc.

Rnd 3: (Ch 3, skip next dc, slip st in next dc) around working last st in first st; finish off.

STRAP (Make 2)

With Color B, ch 15 **loosely**.

Row 1: Sc in second ch from hook and in each ch across; finish off leaving a long end for sewing: 14 sc.

SWING

SEAT

With Color D, ch 21 **loosely**.

Row 1 (Right side): Sc in second ch from hook and in each ch across: 20 sc.

Note: Loop a short piece of yarn around any stitch to mark last row as **right** side.

Rows 2-12: Ch 1, turn; sc in Back Loop Only of each sc across. Finish off leaving a long end for sewing.

FINISHING

Both Bears: Using photo as a guide for placement, center Muzzle on front of Head and sew in place.

With black yarn, add French Knots for eyes *(Fig. 32, page 142)* and Satin St for nose *(Fig. 29, page 141)*.

Sew Ears to top of Head.

Flatten last rnd of Arms and sew to each side of Body.

Sew opening closed between Legs.

Boy Bear Only: Turn up Rnd 8 of Right Leg (Cuff) and sew Foot (toe pointing forward) to free loop of Rnd 7. Repeat for Left Leg.

Girl Bear Only: Sew Foot (toe pointing forward) to end of Right Leg. Repeat for Left Leg.

Sew each Strap to back of Skirt at top. Cross Straps in back and sew second end to front of Skirt at top, leaving last st of each Strap free.

Swing Seat: With **wrong** sides together, fold Seat in half between Rows 6 and 7. Using Seat as a pattern, cut cardboard to size and place inside folded Seat. Working through **both** loops, whipstitch around three open sides of Seat *(Fig. 25a, page 140)*.

Swing Rope: With Color E, chain an 8" length **or** chain to desired length; finish off.

Tie knot at beginning end of chain. Thread yarn needle with other end of chain. Insert needle through Seat, approximately 1/2" from end and centered across the width. Draw length through, pulling knot up tight to underside of Seat.

Repeat on opposite end of Seat.

Glue Bears to Swing and attach to decorated wreath.

general instructions

basic information

HISTORY OF CROCHET

The origins of crochet date back to 16th century France, where nuns used hooks for making beautiful lace. In fact, the word "crochet" comes from the French term for hook. The art of crochet was carried by the nuns to Ireland. Here, Irish girls skillfully copied many rare old patterns and crochet became a refined accomplishment required of well-bred young ladies. Although modern crochet dates back to the 16th century, various crude forms of the art have been found in many earlier societies as far back as 2000 BC. One of these forms was accomplished with a needle similar to a fisherman's needle. Another form was developed from an early mariner's technique of looping without tying a knot. It is thought that weavers combined these methods in an attempt to find a simpler method of weaving using sticks. These crude "hand weaving" tools eventually became crochet hooks.

Crochet was refined into a craft during the 16th century in French convents, but it was not until the 19th century that crochet was recognized as one of the "womanly arts" on a level of popularity with knitting and embroidery. Women fleeing France brought the technique and the French name "crochet" to England around 1820. A quarter of a century later, crochet was introduced in Ireland as a cottage industry with which people could make a meager living. The beautiful rose designs of Irish crochet were used in edgings, tablecloths, and delicate blouses sold all over the world. Unfortunately, the modern machine copies have lost much of the delicacy and beauty of the original handmade crochet.

Traditionally, crochet has been worked in cotton threads for purely utilitarian items such as tablecloths, napkins, and bedspreads. Today, crocheting employs many types of threads and yarns for an endless variety of garments, afghans, and decorations for around the house.

YARN

Yarn weight (type or size) is divided into four basic categories: **Fingering** (baby clothes), **Sport** (light-weight sweaters and afghans), **Worsted** (sweaters, afghans, toys), and **Bulky** (heavy sweaters, pot holders, and afghans).

Baby yarn may either be classified as Fingering or Sport - check the label for the recommended gauge.

These weights have absolutely nothing to do with the number of plies. Ply refers to the number of strands that have been twisted together to make the yarn. There are fingering weight yarns consisting of four plies - and there are bulky weight yarns made of a single ply.

SUBSTITUTING YARN

Once you know the **weight** of the yarn specified for a particular pattern, **any** brand of the **same** weight may be used for that pattern.

You may wish to purchase a single skein first, and crochet a gauge swatch. Compare your gauge to the gauge specified in the pattern and make sure it matches. Then compare the way the new yarn looks to the photographed item to be sure that you'll be satisfied with the finished results.

The number of skeins to buy depends on the **yardage**.

Compare the labels and don't hesitate to ask the shop owner for assistance. Ounces and grams can vary from one brand of the same weight yarn to another, but the yardage required to make a garment or item, in the size and pattern you've chosen, will always remain the same provided gauge is met and maintained.

DYE LOTS

Yarn is dyed in large batches. Each batch is referred to as a "dye lot" and is assigned a number which will be listed on the yarn label. See below for a sample yarn label. The color will vary slightly in shade from one dye lot to another. This color variance may be noticeable if skeins of yarn from different dye lots are used together in the same project.

So, when purchasing more than one skein of yarn for a particular color in your project, be sure to select skeins of yarn labeled with **identical** dye lot numbers. It is a good practice to purchase an extra skein to be sure that you have enough to complete your project.

READING A YARN LABEL

Yarn labels provide you with important information that is helpful in selecting the type of yarn needed and the number of skeins necessary for your project. Labels from different yarn companies may vary, so be sure to read them carefully. See below for a sample yarn label.

1. Color number and name
2. Dye lot number
3. Yarn brand name
4. Ply and weight
5. Type of yarn - wool, cotton, etc.
6. Grams or ounces per ball or skein
7. Yards per ball or skein
8. Suggested knitting or crochet gauge
9. Washing instructions (sometimes this will be listed on the inside of the label)

TIPS FOR PURCHASING YARN AND THREAD

1. Always purchase the same **weight** yarn or thread as specified in your project instructions.
2. It is best to refer to the yardage to determine how many skeins to purchase, since the number of yards per ounce may vary from one brand to another.
3. For each color in your project, purchase skeins in the same dye lot at one time, or you may risk being unable to find the same dye lot again.
4. If you are unsure if you will have enough yarn or thread, buy an extra skein. Some stores will allow you to return unused skeins. Ask your local yarn shop about their return policy.

HOOKS

Crochet hooks used for working with **yarn** are made from aluminum, plastic, bone, or wood. They are lettered in sizes ranging from size B (2.25 mm) to the largest size Q (15.00 mm) - **the higher the letter, the larger the hook size**. Crochet hooks used for **thread** work are most commonly made of steel. They are numbered in sizes ranging from size 00 (3.50 mm) to a very small size 14 (.75 mm) and, unlike aluminum hooks, **the higher the number, the smaller the hook size**.

ABBREVIATIONS

Crochet instructions are written in a special language consisting of abbreviations, punctuation marks, and other terms and symbols. This method of writing saves time and space, and is actually easy to read once you understand the crochet shorthand.

BLO	Back Loop(s) Only
BPdc	Back Post double crochet(s)
BPsc	Back Post single crochet(s)
CC	Contrasting Color
ch(s)	chain(s)
dc	double crochet(s)
dtr	double treble crochet(s)
Ex sc	Extended single crochet(s)
FLO	Front Loop(s) Only
FPdc	Front Post double crochet(s)
FPsc	Front Post single crochet(s)
hdc	half double crochet(s)
MC	Main Color
mm	millimeters
Rnd(s)	Round(s)
sc	single crochet(s)
sp(s)	space(s)
st(s)	stitch(es)
tr	treble crochet(s)
YO	yarn over

SYMBOLS

★ — work instructions following ★ as many **more** times as indicated in addition to the first time.

† to † — work all instructions from first † to second † **as many** times as specified.

( ) or [ ] — work enclosed instructions **as many** times as specified by the number immediately following **or** work all enclosed instructions in the stitch or space indicated **or** contains explanatory remarks.

TERMS

chain loosely — work the chain **only** loose enough for the hook to pass through the chain easily when working the next row or round into the chain.

multiple — the number of stitches required to complete one repeat of a pattern.

post — the vertical shaft of a stitch.

right vs. left — the side of the garment as if you were wearing it.

right side vs. wrong side — the **right** side of your work is the side that will show when the piece is finished.

work across or around — continue working in the established pattern.

GAUGE

Gauge is the number of stitches and rows or rounds per inch and is used to determine the finished size. All crochet patterns will specify the gauge that you must match to ensure proper size and to be sure you have enough yarn to complete the project. Hook sizes given in instructions are merely guides. Because everyone crochets differently - loosely, tightly, or somewhere in between - the finished size can vary even when crocheters use the very same pattern, yarn, and hook.

Before beginning any crocheted item, it is absolutely necessary for you to crochet a gauge swatch in the pattern stitch indicated with the weight of yarn or thread and hook size suggested. Your swatch must be large enough to measure your gauge. Lay your swatch on a hard, smooth, flat surface. Then measure it, counting your stitches and rows or rounds carefully. If your swatch is smaller than specified or you have too many stitches per inch, try again with a larger size hook; if your swatch is larger or you don't have enough stitches per inch, try again with a smaller size hook. Keep trying until you find the size that will give you the specified gauge. DO NOT HESITATE TO CHANGE HOOK SIZE TO OBTAIN CORRECT GAUGE. On garments and afghans, once proper gauge is obtained, measure width of piece approximately every 3" to be sure gauge remains consistent.

basic stitch guide

CHAIN

When beginning a first row of crochet in a chain, always skip the first chain from the hook, and work into the second chain from hook (for single crochet), third chain from hook (for half double crochet), or fourth chain from hook (for double crochet), etc. *(Fig. 1)*.

Fig. 1

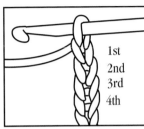

WORKING INTO THE CHAIN

Method 1: Insert hook into back ridge of each chain indicated *(Fig. 2a)*.
Method 2: Insert hook under top two strands of each chain *(Fig. 2b)*.

Fig. 2a   **Fig. 2b**

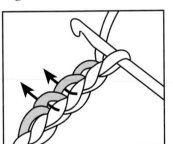
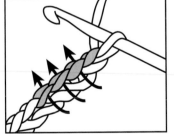

SLIP STITCH *(abbreviated slip st)*

This stitch is used to attach new yarn, to join work, or to move the yarn across a group of stitches without adding height. Insert hook in stitch or space indicated, YO and draw through stitch **and** loop on hook.

MAKING A BEGINNING RING

Chain amount indicated in instructions. Being careful not to twist chain, slip stitch in first chain to form a ring *(Fig. 3)*.

Fig. 3

SINGLE CROCHET *(abbreviated sc)*

Insert hook in stitch or space indicated, YO and pull up a loop, YO and draw through both loops on hook *(Fig. 4)*.

Fig. 4

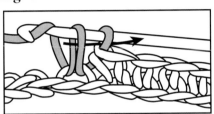

LONG SINGLE CROCHET
(abbreviated Long sc)

Insert hook in stitch indicated *(Fig. 5)*, YO and pull up a loop **even** with loop on hook, YO and draw through both loops on hook **(counts as one sc)**.

Fig. 5

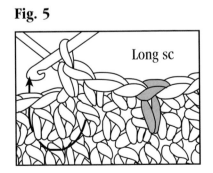

Long sc

133

HALF DOUBLE CROCHET
(abbreviated hdc)
YO, insert hook in stitch or space indicated, YO and pull up a loop, YO and draw through all 3 loops on hook *(Fig. 6)*.

Fig. 6

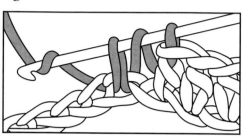

DOUBLE CROCHET *(abbreviated dc)*
YO, insert hook in stitch or space indicated, YO and pull up a loop, YO and draw through 2 loops on hook *(Fig. 7a)*, YO and draw through remaining 2 loops on hook *(Fig. 7b)*.

Fig. 7a

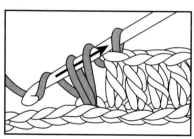

Fig. 7b

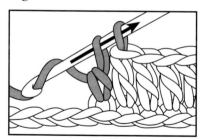

TREBLE CROCHET *(abbreviated tr)*
YO twice, insert hook in stitch or space indicated, YO and pull up a loop *(Fig. 8a)*, (YO and draw through 2 loops on hook) 3 times *(Fig. 8b)*.

Fig. 8a

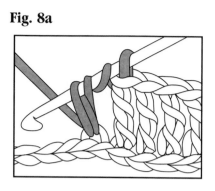

Fig. 8b

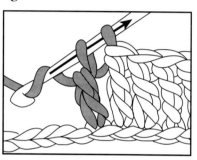

CLUSTER
A Cluster can be worked all in the same stitch or space *(Figs. 9a & b)*, **or** across several stitches *(Figs. 10a & b)*.

Fig. 9a

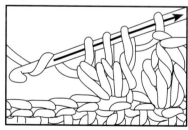

Fig. 9b

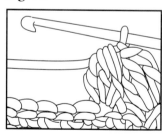

Fig. 10a

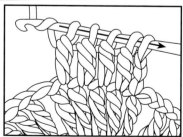

Fig. 10b

LOOP STITCH

Insert hook in stitch indicated, wrap yarn around index finger of left hand as many times as instructed, insert hook through loops on finger following direction indicated by arrow *(Fig. 11a)*, being careful to hook all loops *(Fig. 11b)*, draw through stitch pulling each loop as specified in instructions, remove finger from loop, YO and draw through all loops on hook **(Loop St made, Fig. 11c)**.

Fig. 11a

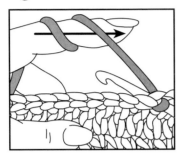

Fig. 11b

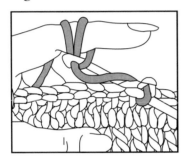

Fig. 11c

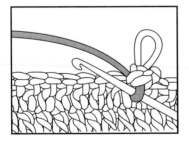

PUFF STITCH

Work as instructed for each design *(Fig. 12)*.

Fig. 12

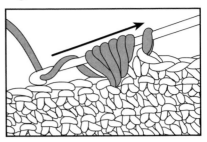

POPCORN

5 Dc in st indicated, drop loop from hook, insert hook in first dc of 5-dc group, hook dropped loop and draw through *(Fig. 13)*.

Fig. 13

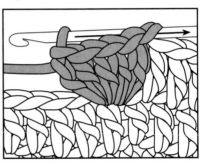

CROSS STITCH

Work as instructed for each design *(Figs. 14a & b)*.

Fig. 14a

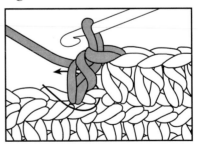

Fig. 14b

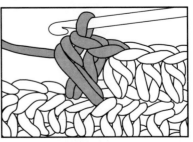

135

POST STITCH

Work around post of stitch indicated, inserting hook in direction of arrow *(Fig. 15)*.

Fig. 15

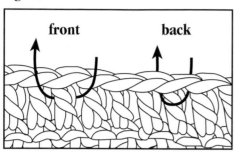

FRONT POST DOUBLE CROCHET
(abbreviated FPdc)

YO, insert hook from **front** to **back** around post of stitch indicated *(Fig. 15)*, YO and pull up a loop *(Fig. 16)*, (YO and draw through 2 loops on hook) twice.

Fig. 16

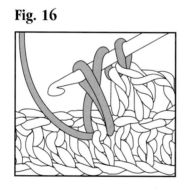

BACK POST DOUBLE CROCHET
(abbreviated BPdc)

YO, insert hook from **back** to **front** around post of stitch indicated *(Fig. 15)*, YO and pull up a loop *(Fig. 17)*, (YO and draw through 2 loops on hook) twice.

Fig. 17

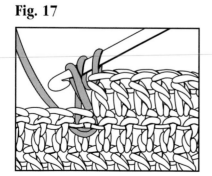

REVERSE SINGLE CROCHET
(abbreviated Reverse sc)

Working from **left** to **right**, insert hook in stitch to right of hook *(Fig. 18a)*, YO and draw through, under and to left of loop on hook (2 loops on hook) *(Fig. 18b)*, YO and draw through both loops on hook *(Fig. 18c)* (**Reverse sc made, Fig. 18d**).

Fig. 18a

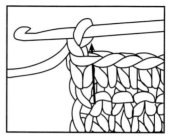

Fig. 18b

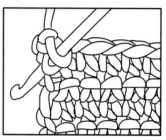

Fig. 18c

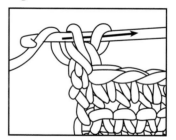

Fig. 18d

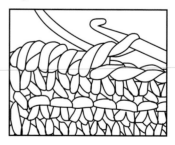

stitching tips

DECIDING WHICH SIZE TO CROCHET

Most garment patterns are written for at least three different sizes. Instructions usually include an actual chest measurement or generic size (small, medium, large) and the finished measurement of the garment, which usually allows several inches for ease.

Measure around the fullest part of the chest of the person the garment is being made for, keeping tape under their arms. Compare this measurement to the chest and finished measurements given in the instructions, allowing for the desired amount of ease.

You may want to measure a favorite sweater with similar styling, and crochet the size that has the nearest finished measurement.

WEAVING IN YARN ENDS

Good finishing techniques make a big difference in the quality of any crocheted piece. Make a habit of taking care of loose ends as you work. **Never** tie a knot in your yarn. They may poke through to the right side and will sometimes come untied and unravel. Weaving in the ends gives a much better result. Thread a yarn needle with the yarn end. With **wrong** side facing, weave the needle through several stitches, then reverse the direction and weave it back through several more stitches. When the end is secure, clip the yarn off close to your work. You may also hide your ends as you work by crocheting over them for several inches to secure, then weave in opposite direction; clip the remaining lengths off close to your work. Always check your work to be sure the yarn ends do not show on the right side.

HOW TO DETERMINE THE RIGHT SIDE

Many designs are made with the **front** of the stitch as the **right** side. Notice that the **fronts** of the stitches are smooth *(Fig. 19a)* and the **backs** of the stitches are bumpy *(Fig. 19b)*. For easy identification, it may be helpful to loop a short piece of yarn, thread, or fabric around any stitch to mark **right** side.

Fig. 19a 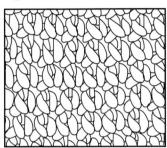   **Fig. 19b**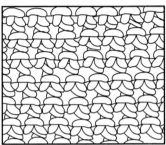

EDGING
SINGLE CROCHET EVENLY ACROSS OR AROUND

When instructed to single crochet evenly across or around, the single crochets should be spaced to keep the piece lying flat. Work a few single crochets at a time, checking periodically to be sure your edge is not distorted. If the edge is puckering, you need to add a few more single crochets; if the edge is ruffling, you need to remove some single crochets. Keep trying until the edge lies smooth and flat.

BACK OR FRONT LOOP ONLY

Work only in loop(s) indicated by arrow *(Fig. 20)*.

Fig. 20

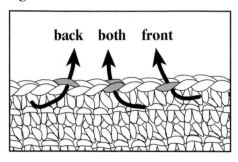

FREE LOOP

After working in Back or Front Loops Only on a row or round, there will be a ridge of unused loops. These are called the free loops. Later, when instructed to work in the free loops of the same row or round, work in these loops *(Fig. 21a)*. When instructed to work in a free loop of a beginning chain, work in loop indicated by arrow *(Fig. 21b)*.

Fig. 21a

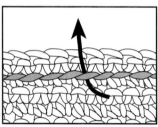

Fig. 21b

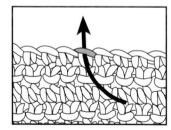

JOINING WITH SC

When instructed to join with sc, begin with a slip knot on hook. Insert hook in stitch or space indicated, YO and pull up a loop, yarn over and draw through both loops on hook.

MARKERS

Markers are used to help distinguish the beginning of each round being worked. Place a 2" scrap piece of yarn or fabric before the first stitch of each round, moving marker after each round is complete. Remove when no longer needed.

CHANGING COLORS

Work the last stitch to within one step of completion, hook new yarn *(Fig. 22a)* and draw through loops on hook. Cut old yarn and work over both ends unless otherwise specified.

When working in rounds, drop old yarn or fabric and join with slip stitch to first stitch using new yarn or fabric *(Fig. 22b)*.

Fig. 22a

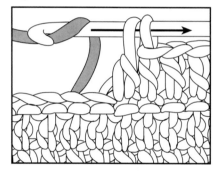

Fig. 22b

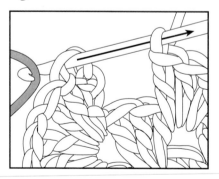

PREPARING FABRIC STRIPS

Fabric selected should be high quality, even weave 100% cotton, such as those sold for piecing quilts. Yardages given are based on fabrics 44/45" wide.

If the fabric is not pre-shrunk, it should be gently machine washed and dried. Straighten your fabric by pulling it across the bias. It may be necessary to lightly press the fabric.

To avoid joining strips often, we recommend that your strips be two yards or longer.

TEARING STRIPS

Tear off selvages, then tear into strips as instructed.

CUTTING STRIPS

1. Fold the fabric in half, short end to short end, as many times as possible, while still being able to cut through all thicknesses *(Fig. 23a)*.

Fig. 23a

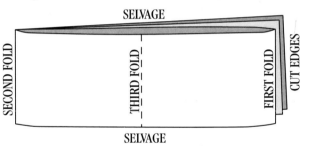

2. Cut off selvages, then cut fabric into 1" wide strips *(Fig. 23b)*. For quick results, a rotary cutter and mat may be used to cut several layers of fabric at one time.

Fig. 23b

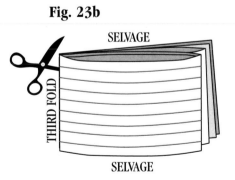

JOINING FABRIC STRIPS

The following is a technique for joining fabric strips without sewing strips together, and eliminates knots or ends to weave in later.

1. To join a new strip of fabric to working strip, cut a ½" slit, about ½" from ends of both fabric strips *(Fig. 24a)*.

Fig. 24a

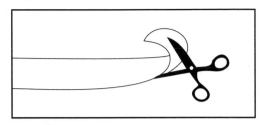

2. With **right** sides up, place end of new strip over end of working strip and match slits *(Fig. 24b)*.

Fig. 24b

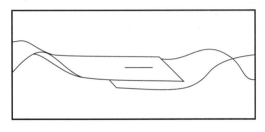

3. Pull free end of new strip through both slits from bottom to top *(Fig. 24c)*.

Fig. 24c

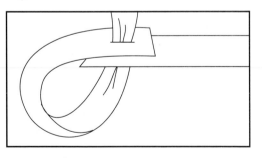

4. Pull new strip firmly to form a small knot *(Fig. 24d)*. Right sides of both strips should be facing up. Continue working with new strip.

Fig. 24d

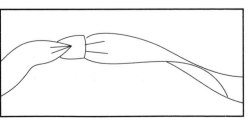

finishing

WASHING AND BLOCKING

Blocking "sets" a crocheted item and smoothes the stitches to give your work a professional appearance. Before blocking, check the yarn label for any special instructions because many acrylics and some blends may be damaged during blocking. *Note:* Always use stainless steel pins.

Thread projects should be washed before blocking. Using a mild detergent and warm water, gently squeeze suds through the piece, being careful not to rub, twist, or wring. Rinse several times in cool, clear water. Roll piece in a clean terry towel and gently press out the excess moisture. Lay piece on a flat surface and shape to proper size; where needed, pin in place. Allow to dry **completely**. Doilies can be spray starched for extra crispness.

On fragile **acrylics** that can be blocked, pin the item to the correct size on a towel-covered board, and cover the item with dampened bath towels. When the towels are dry, the item is blocked.

If the item is **hand washable**, carefully launder it using a mild soap or detergent. Rinse it without wringing or twisting. Remove any excess moisture by rolling it in a succession of dry towels. If you prefer, you may put it in the final spin cycle of your washer - but do not use water. Lay the item on a large towel on a flat surface out of direct sunlight. Gently smooth and pat it to the desired size and shape, comparing the measurements to the pattern instructions as necessary. When the item is completely dry, it is blocked.

Steaming is an excellent method of blocking crochet items, especially those made with **wool or wool blends**. Turn the item wrong side out and pin it to the correct size on a board covered with towels. Hold a steam iron or steamer just above the item and steam it thoroughly. Never let the weight of the iron touch your item because it will flatten the stitches. Leave the garment pinned until it is completely dry.

SEAMS

A tapestry or yarn needle is best to use for sewing seams because the blunt point will not split the yarn as easily. Use the same yarn the item was made with to sew the seams. However, if the yarn is textured or bulky, it may be easier to sew the seam with a small, smooth yarn of the same color, such as tapestry yarn or an acrylic needlepoint yarn. If a different yarn is used for the seams, be sure the care instructions for both yarns are the same. If the yarn used to crochet the item is machine washable, the seam yarn must also be machine washable.

WHIPSTITCH

With **wrong** sides together, and beginning in corner stitch, sew through both pieces once to secure the beginning of the seam, leaving an ample yarn end to weave in later. Insert needle from **front** to **back** through **both** loops of **each** piece *(Fig. 25a)* **or** through **inside** loops *(Fig. 25b)*. Bring needle around and insert it from **front** to **back** through the next loops of **both** pieces. Continue in this manner across to corner, keeping the sewing yarn fairly loose.

Fig. 25a   **Fig. 25b**

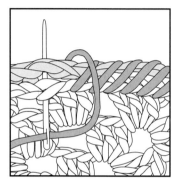

FRINGE

Cut a piece of cardboard 8" wide and half as long as specified in instructions for finished strands. Wind the yarn **loosely** and **evenly** around the length of the cardboard until the card is filled, then cut across one end; repeat as needed. Align the number of strands specified and fold in half.

With **wrong** side facing and using a crochet hook, draw the folded end up through a row or stitch and pull the loose ends through the folded end *(Fig. 26a)*; draw the knot up **tightly** *(Fig. 26b)*. Repeat, spacing as specified. Lay flat on a hard surface and trim the ends.

Fig. 26a   **Fig. 26b**

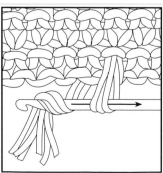

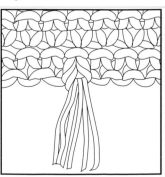

TASSEL

Cut a piece of cardboard 3" wide by the desired length of finished tassel. Wind a double strand of yarn or thread around the length of the cardboard approximately 20 times for yarn and 12 times for thread. Cut a long length of yarn or thread and insert it under all of the strands at the top of the cardboard; pull up **tightly** and tie securely. Leave the ends long enough to attach the tassel. Cut the strands at the opposite end of the cardboard *(Fig. 27a)* and then remove them. Cut a long length of yarn or thread and wrap it **tightly** around the tassel twice, leaving a space below the top *(Fig. 27b)*; tie securely. Trim the ends.

Fig. 27a

Fig. 27b

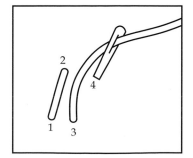

STRAIGHT STITCH

Straight Stitch is just what the name implies, a single, straight stitch. Bring needle up at 1 and go down at 2 *(Fig. 28)*. Continue in same manner.

Fig. 28

SATIN STITCH

Satin Stitch is a series of straight stitches worked side by side so they touch but do not overlap as shown in **Fig. 29a**, or entering and exiting the same hole as in **Fig. 29b**. Bring needle up at odd numbers and go down at even numbers.

Fig. 29   **Fig. 29b**

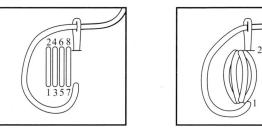

BLANKET STITCH

To join 2 pieces together, hold wrong sides together and bring needle up from wrong side through first stitch on front piece only, leaving an end to be woven in later. Insert needle from **back** to **front** through **both** loops of first stitch on **each** piece keeping yarn below point of needle *(Fig. 30a)*. Bring needle around and insert it from **back** to **front** through the next loops of **both** pieces keeping yarn below point of needle. Continue in this manner across to corner *(Fig. 30b)*.

Fig. 30a

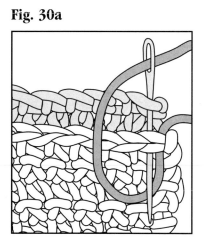

Fig. 30b

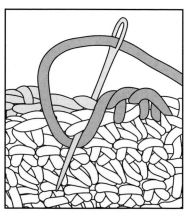

BACKSTITCH

Working from right to left, bring needle up at 1 leaving an end to be woven in later, go down at 2 and come up at 3 (*Fig. 31a*). The second stitch is made by going down at 1 and coming up at 4 (*Fig. 31b*). Continue in same manner.

Fig. 31a

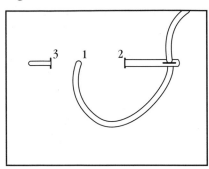

Fig. 31b

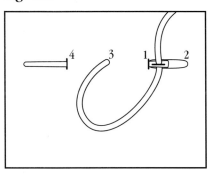

FRENCH KNOT

Bring needle up at 1. Wrap yarn desired number of times around needle and go down at 2, holding end of yarn with non-stitching fingers (*Fig. 32*). Tighten knot; then pull needle through, holding yarn until it must be released.

Fig. 32

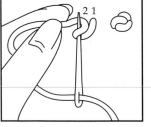

CROSS STITCH

Each square on the Chart represents one sc and each colored square represents one cross stitch. Thread a yarn needle with a long strand of color indicated. With **right** side facing and bottom edge toward you, bring needle up at 1 leaving a 3" end on back. Work over this end to secure. Insert needle down at 2 (half Cross made), bring needle up at 3 and go down at 4 (**Cross Stitch completed,** *Fig. 33*). You can work across an area in half crosses and then work back, crossing them as you go. Just be sure that the top half of every cross stitch is worked in the same direction. After each row is worked, weave yarn through stitches on back to point where next cross is worked (long strands of yarn should not show on back). Straighten yarn every few crosses by dropping the needle and allowing the yarn to hang free. Finish off by weaving under several stitches on back; cut yarn.

Fig. 33

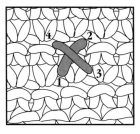

LAZY DAISY STITCH

Come up at 1 and make a counterclockwise loop with the ribbon. Go down at 1 and come up at 2, keeping the ribbon below the point of the needle (*Fig. 34*). Secure the loop by bringing the ribbon over the loop and down at 3. Repeat for the desired number of leaves.

Fig. 34

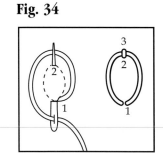

STARCHING & BLOCKING

TIPS

1. If using the same fabric stiffener for both white and colored items, starch the white items first, in case thread dye should bleed into the solution.

2. A good blocking board can make pinning easier. You can use heavy cardboard, an ironing board, ceiling board, etc.

3. Stainless steel pins with balls on the end will be easier to use and will help keep fingers from hurting. Fabric stiffener will permanently damage pins used for sewing. These can be set aside for all starching projects.

4. Fabric stiffener can be returned to the bottle after starching if it has not been contaminated with particles and dye. Clip one corner of the bag, then squeeze the bag, forcing the solution to flow into the bottle.

5. An acrylic spray can be used after starching to protect the piece from heat and humidity.

STARCHING

Read the following instructions before beginning.

1. Using a mild detergent and warm water gently squeeze suds through the piece, being careful not to rub, twist, or wring. Rinse several times in cool, clear water. Roll each piece in a clean terry towel and gently press out the excess moisture. Lay piece flat and allow to dry **completely**.

2. Pour fabric stiffener in a resealable plastic bag. Do not dilute stiffener. *Note:* This method is permanent and will not wash out.

3. Immerse dry piece in fabric stiffener, remove air, and seal the bag. Work solution thoroughly into each piece. Let soak for several hours or overnight.

BLOCKING

1. The blocking pattern given is designed to make accurate blocking of Snowflakes easier. Photocopy or trace the blocking pattern as many times as necessary to obtain the number of patterns needed for the quantity of Snowflakes you will be blocking at one time. Cut patterns apart. Place patterns on blocking board or ironing board and cover with plastic wrap.

2. Remove Snowflake(s) from solution and squeeze gently to remove as much excess stiffener as possible. Blot with a paper towel several times to remove excess from holes.

3. With **right** side facing, spread a Snowflake over a blocking pattern, lining up the points on the Snowflake with the lines on the pattern. Pin in place, being careful not to split the thread when inserting pins between the stitches.

4. Allow to dry **completely**.

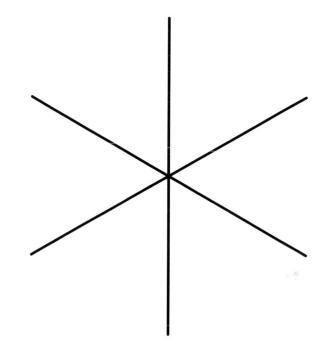

credits

We extend a warm *thank you* to the generous people who allowed us to photograph some of our projects at their homes: *Wrapped Up in Afghans* — Mr. and Mrs. James Adams, Nancy Gunn Porter, and Dr. Dudley and Cathy Rodgers. *All Through the House* — Bill and Nancy Appleton and Dr. Dan and Sandra Cook. *Gifts for All* — Bill and Nancy Appleton. *Just for Fun* — Shawn and Rhonda Fitz and Susan Wildung. *Fashion Corner* — Bill and Nancy Appleton. *Hooked on Holidays* — Nancy Gunn Porter.

We also thank Ethan Allen Home Interiors, Little Rock, Arkansas, for allowing us to photograph our *Hearts and Flowers* afghan at their place of business. We appreciate Linda Westergarde of Pinnacle Vista Lodge, 7510 Hwy. 300, Little Rock, Arkansas 72212, for allowing us to photograph our *Bandanna Afghan* on the property and for the use of her wagon.

To Magna IV Color Imaging of Little Rock, Arkansas, we say thank you for the superb color reproduction and excellent pre-press preparation. We want to especially thank photographers Larry Pennington, Ken West, Karen Shirey, and Mark Mathews of Peerless Photography, Little Rock, Arkansas, and Jerry R. Davis of Jerry Davis Photography, Little Rock, Arkansas, for their time, patience, and excellent work.

A special word of thanks goes to the talented designers who created the lovely projects in this book:

Mary Lamb Becker: *Crossed Trebles*, page 16, and *Handsome Ripples*, page 20
Carolyn Christmas: *Granny Circles*, page 18
Madeline Cooper: *Romantic Doily*, page 52
Lana Corey: *Granny Square Layette*, page 74
Maureen Egan Emlet: *Billowy Broomstick Lace*, page 22
Nancy Fuller: *Jaunty Beret and Scarf*, page 96
Sue Galucki: *Dishcloth #2*, page 42
Shobha Govindan: *Bloomer Magnets*, page 68, and *Thumbless Mittens*, page 77
Anne Halliday: *Bandanna Afghan*, page 65
Sheila Hardy: *Hearts and Flowers*, page 6
Cindy Harris: *Colorful Clown*, page 58; *Crib Caterpillar*, page 81; and *Sweetheart Bears*, page 106
Jan Hatfield: *Delightful Mile-A-Minute*, page 24
Carol L. Jensen: *Puppet Mittens*, page 102
Terry Kimbrough: *Basket Frills #3*, page 46; *Rosy Coaster*, page 55; *Victorian Charmers*, page 62; *Summer-Fresh Broom*, page 70; and *Receiving Blanket Edging*, page 80
Ann Kirtley: *Ruffled Peacock Shawl*, page 48
Jennine Korejko: *Reversible Wrap*, page 12, and *Cuddly Wraps*, page 78
Tammy Kreimeyer: *Soft and Roomy Tote*, page 56, and *Rag Basket*, page 115

Patricia Kristoffersen: *Daffodil Doily*, page 114
Cynthia Lark: *Garden Plot Quilt*, page 14
Linda Luder: *Basket Frills #1*, page 44
Helen Milinkovich Milton: *Tiny Snowflakes*, page 123
Linda Mershon: *Shamrock Table Runner and Coaster*, page 109
Cindy Peecher: *Pretty Bookmarks*, page 50
Lois Phillips: *Dishcloth #1*, page 42, and *Holiday Lights*, page 125
Carole Prior: *Rock-A-Bye Ripples*, page 84
Katherine Satterfield Robert: *Square in a Square Pot Holder*, page 40; *Pinwheel Block Pot Holder*, page 40; and *Rainbow Rivers Rug*, page 72
C. Strohmeyer: *Mantel Skirt*, page 29; *Basket Frills #2*, page 46; and *Gumdrop Bottle Cover*, page 82
Carole Rutter Tippett: *Golden Treasure*, page 10
Joyce Winfield Vanderslice: *Hair Dressings*, page 90
Beth Ann Webber: *Soft Santa*, page 120
Maggie Weldon: *Victorian Lace Afghan*, page 36; *Sheet and Pillowcase Edging*, page 37; and *Friendship Cup*, page 54
Margie Wicker: *"Cool" Vest Set*, page 98
Emma L. Willey: *Starflower Tablecloth*, page 30

We extend a sincere *thank you* to the people who assisted in making and testing the projects for this book: Anitta Armstrong, Jennie Black, JoAnn Bowling, Mike Cates, Lee Ellis, Linda Galloway, Linda Graves, Naomi Greening, Raymelle Greening, Jean Hall, Kathleen Hardy, Lisa Hightower, Maedean Johnson, Cheryl Knepper, Carol McElroy, Margie Norris, Dale Potter, Hilda Rivero, Donna Soellner, and Sherry Williams.